STATEMENT CONCERNING PUBLICATIONS OF
RUSSELL SAGE FOUNDATION

Russell Sage Foundation was established in 1907 by Mrs. Russell Sage "for the improvement of social and living conditions in the United States of America." In carrying out its purpose the Foundation maintains a staff which, among other duties, conducts studies of social conditions, authorized by the General Director, where new information, its analysis and interpretation seem necessary in order to formulate and advance practicable measures aimed at improvement. From time to time the Foundation publishes the results of these studies in book or pamphlet form.

In formulating the problem for study, in mapping out a plan of work on it, in collecting facts, in drawing conclusions, and in the presentation of findings, authors of Foundation studies, who are always either members of the staff or specially commissioned research workers, have the benefit of the criticism and advice of their colleagues in the organization. Full freedom is given research workers for the final decision on all of these steps, and in presenting and interpreting both factual material and conclusions in their own way. While the general responsibility for management of the Foundation is vested in the board of trustees, the responsibility for facts, conclusions, and interpretations rests with the research workers alone and not upon the Foundation, its trustees, or other members of the staff. Publication under the imprint of the Foundation does not imply agreement by the organization or its members with opinions or interpretations of authors. It does imply that care has been taken that the research on which a book is based has been thoroughly done.

YOUR COMMUNITY

ITS PROVISION FOR HEALTH, EDUCATION,
SAFETY, AND WELFARE

BY

JOANNA C. COLCORD

Revised by DONALD S. HOWARD
Director of the Department
of Social Work Administration
Russell Sage Foundation

NEW YORK
RUSSELL SAGE FOUNDATION
1947

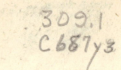
E. L. HILDRETH AND COMPANY
printers at Brattleboro, Vermont

TABLE OF CONTENTS

CHAPTER 7

HOUSING, PLANNING, AND ZONING .

CHAPTER 8

HEALTH CONDITIONS AND RESOURCES

CHAPTER 12

OPPORTUNITIES FOR RECREATION

CHAPTER 13

RELIGIOUS AGENCIES

CHAPTER 14

PUBLIC ASSISTANCE . . 182

FOREWORD

YOUR COMMUNITY was first published in 1939 and was revised in 1941. These editions were both written by Joanna C. Colcord, then director of the Charity Organization Department of Russell Sage Foundation, who has since retired.

Immediately upon publication, Your Community was warmly received. The book has been widely used in schools. Many community and civic organizations have also used the book, often as the basis for community self-surveys. One of the most extensive of these was that conducted in Portland, Maine, in 1941, under the auspices of the Community Chest. In 1939 the Delaware State Conference of Social Work adopted Your Community as the basic guide in informing citizens of the state regarding their home communities. In 1945 the Smith College Club of St. Petersburg, Florida, sponsored a series of 20 broadcasts based upon Your Community. The resultant program "Know Your Community" was rated, by Billboard Magazine's nationwide poll of radio editors, among the top local radio programs.

With the necessity for another reprinting, made apparent by a dwindling stock early in 1946, it was decided again to revise the text to bring the book abreast of the changing times. Since 1941, when the book was last revised, America has passed through World War II and has embarked upon an era of postwar reconstruction. Consequently the community emphases with respect to social problems have changed; new programs have been established and old ones modified. Particularly in the fields of housing, medical care, consumer protection, and public assistance, have recent developments necessitated extensive textual revisions. However, other sections too have been amended to give increased or lessened emphasis, depending upon conditions now prevailing. References to literature in the various fields discussed have been reviewed and, where indicated, additions or substitutions made.

In bringing up to date Miss Colcord's earlier work, invaluable assistance has been rendered by a wide variety of voluntary and governmental agencies. To these as to the many individual experts who graciously gave much valued assistance, the Foundation is deeply grateful. To Dr. Franz Goldmann, clinical professor of public health, Yale University School of Medicine, special acknowledgment is made for extensive aid in the revision of sections dealing with health problems and services, particularly Chapter 9, which deals with a field in which vast change has occurred since this volume was last revised. Within the Foundation staff itself particular credit goes to Sigrid Holt, research assistant, who has throughout carried large responsibilities for the revision.

As pointed out in the Foreword to the previous edition, Your Community is successor to an earlier work, What Social Workers Should Know About Their Own Communities, by Margaret F. Byington. This pamphlet, begun by Miss Byington at the request of the Foundation in 1911, eventually passed through four editions, each revised as changing times and needs made necessary.

While the text and arrangement of the material in the several editions of Your Community have been quite different from those of Miss Byington's pamphlet, the device of listing questions to be answered has been borrowed from her. Most grateful acknowledgment is made again to Miss Byington for the pioneer work she did in this field and for the many suggestions it has offered for the subsequent work.

The Foundation is also grateful to Arthur Dunham who gave much help in working out the original scope and arrangement of Your Community.

The present edition, while embodying modifications required by rapidly changing events, leans heavily upon Miss Colcord's work and, it is hoped, preserves the general tone which she established. In fact, the work of revision has evoked a new appreciation of and respect for the breadth and soundness of Miss Colcord's original approach, and has vividly recalled that between the post-depression period during which Miss Colcord wrote, and the present postwar period, many of our nation's health, welfare, and related services experienced monumental gains.

Spurred by jet planes and rockets, the people of the world are rapidly becoming aware of their constantly increasing community of interest. In the largest sense one's community is coextensive with the world. Still, despite the extensive ramifications of modern life (with which some other publications of the Foundation are concerned), the present volume focuses primarily upon the local community, which even in a day of world-shrinking miracles continues powerfully to affect health and social well-being.

DONALD S. HOWARD, *Director*
Department of Social Work Administration

1. YOUR COMMUNITY: How To Study Its Health, Education, Safety, and Welfare

THIS OUTLINE contains suggestions for groups of persons desirous of securing a rounded picture of their own community, especially as to the provision which that community makes to conserve the health and safety and to promote the education and general welfare of its inhabitants. The outline is not intended as a guide to technically equipped surveyors engaged in making social evaluations of a professional thoroughness. It suggests rather the type of information that might be assembled and studied by intelligent citizens and citizens-to-be, in order to have a background from which to attack the problem of supplying community lacks and improving existing services.

Members of civic clubs, forums, women's associations, parent-teacher associations, or high school and college classes and graduate students preparing for definite careers in the areas it describes, were the persons kept principally in mind as the text was being prepared. It may also have some value for newcomers to a community, who want to understand it better.

I. HOW TO USE THE BOOK

It is proper to ask first, what is meant by "community"? This outline was prepared in the expectation that the area to be studied would coincide with some political subdivision of government—township, borough, city, or county. While it is possible to use it for the study of smaller units— neighborhoods, census enumeration tracts, suburban developments within a metropolitan area, wards of a city and the like—in such cases modifications will have to be made especially in respect to the collection and tabulation of factual data which may not be separately available for the precise area selected for study. However, the first step will be to lay out the geographical boundaries of that area which for practical purposes includes or defines the community to which the outline is to be applied.

The second point to be determined is what aspects of a community are to be studied. The entire area explored in this outline may be more than a study group wishes to undertake. The material has been set up by chapters, with many cross references, so that even a single chapter can be used by itself as a guide when it is desired to restrict the inquiry to a single phase of community life.

The questions asked in the text have been designed to cover what services are found in the best-equipped communities, both urban and rural. Not all the topics treated will have equal importance for all students; for instance, in studying a large town or city, its agriculture might be passed over without remark, although the outskirts of most cities do contain truck gardens and small farms. Similarly, if the unit to be studied were the town or village center of an agricultural region, the section on Urban Dwellings would probably be largely inapplicable to it. Within the separate chapters many of the questions will doubtless not apply to the conditions to be found in a given community, and may thus be disregarded. Neither is it expected that every suggestion be adopted literally. For instance, if it is found that the age groupings suggested for tabulation do not precisely correspond with the classifications already available in public records and agency reports, the sensible thing to do would be to modify table headings to agree with what is easily available.

Thus it remains for the student to select, out of the possible suggestions to be found here, those which will be of use in the study of a particular community. To help in this choice, certain things common to all communities have been placed first in our list of subjects—the community setting (location, population, and relation to its immediate region); the founding and development of the community, covering a brief statement of the salient points in its history; the system of local government, including relationship to superior units of government; the chief economic and industrial factors which condition the lives of those who dwell in the community.

Much of the material for such a study as is here outlined may be available at one of the central agencies in a community, such as a council of social agencies, community chest, city planning commission, or institute of municipal research. Some of the material may be secured at the public library, the chamber of commerce, or even the office of a leading newspaper. The first step in collecting information is, therefore, to consult these organizations. If they do not have the specific information desired, they can at least give information as to whether it is obtainable and where it may be found.

Information not obtainable within a community sometimes may be had from outside sources such as departments of federal and state governments,[1]

---

[1] A group of users of this book have reported, for example, that they were able to secure a far more complete picture of juvenile delinquency in their community from the State Probation Department than from their local juvenile court.

or by correspondence with national functional agencies of different types to which reference is made in the text.

It will also prove helpful, as questions here and there in this book will indicate, to consult the people who are responsible for administering governmental or community services, and to get their opinions as well as the objective facts concerning their work. These are all valuable supplements to materials obtained in other ways and may point out avenues of further study which would otherwise be overlooked. The personal observations of the student are important also.

Reference should also be made to directories, gazetteers, laws, reports, and to other material gathered in previous surveys. An especially helpful adjunct for use in connection with such a study would be the latest issue of the World Almanac.[1] One of the most useful handbooks for studying community health, welfare, and social programs undertaken by public and private agencies is the Social Work Year Book. Issued biennially by the Russell Sage Foundation, the Year Book is a compendium of information. In it will be found a complete directory of national voluntary and governmental agencies which operate in these areas. It will need to be consulted at many points in such a study as is here projected. In fact, the study of many aspects of community life would be greatly aided if students, before embarking upon their work, were to read the relevant article or articles in the Social Work Year Book.

Interesting suggestions as to methods of study may be gleaned from several pamphlets to which general reference is here made: Let's Make a Study;[2] Action for Cities: A Guide for Community Planning;[3] Planning for the Future in Your Community;[4] Know Your Town's Future;[5] Social Welfare: A Guide for Studying the Welfare Facilities of the Local Community, by Elizabeth S. May;[6] and Your City, by Edward L. Thorndike.[7]

The names of all agencies mentioned are given, together with their addresses as of 1946, in the List of Agencies on page 251.

II. RECORDING AND REPORTING

The project will mean much more to the individual or to the study group if an effort is made to record systematically answers to questions as they are gathered. A loose-leaf book or a group of such books would serve the purpose. Both questions and answers could be written or typed, and clippings

[1] New York World-Telegram, New York (annual).
[2] Community Chests and Councils, Inc., Bulletins 114-A and 114-B, New York, 1942.
[3] Public Administration Service, Chicago, 1943.
[4] United Service Organizations, Inc., New York, 1945.
[5] National League of Women Voters, Washington, 1945.
[6] American Association of University Women, Washington, 1940.
[7] Harcourt, Brace and Co., New York, 1939.

pasted on the loose leaves.   Maps and charts could be folded in.   Pages from reports could be inserted, or references given to full reports accompanying the loose-leaf volumes.

Extensive knowledge of the use of statistics and graphs is not presupposed on the part of those undertaking such a study as is here outlined. Only simple tabulations are called for, in answer to a few of the questions that follow.   Two graphic devices will, however, be found useful by groups which undertake a thorough study of their community.

The first of these is an *organization chart*.[1]   For complicated structures, such as a city government, with departments, subdepartments and semi-independent commissions and bureaus, interlocking and related in different ways to the central authority, it is useful to be able to draw a picture on paper, so that one can visually trace the lines of authority, responsibility, and relationship.   A good organization chart will show at a glance information which would take many pages to record in writing.

Do not try to include too much detail on an organization chart.   Attempts to show financial data or volume of work in connection with the units shown on the chart usually give it a congested appearance and interfere with its main purpose of showing structure and relationships.

The other device is a *map of social resources*.   For this it is necessary to secure a map of the region to be studied.   Ordinary road maps are not well adapted, being too detailed and crowded with printing.   It may be possible to secure maps suitable to the purpose at local stationery shops; if not, the council of social agencies or some of the city departments such as those of taxation, health, or engineering, may be able to furnish copies.[2]

The map should be mounted either upon heavy cardboard or stout cloth, when it will be ready to have affixed to it symbols indicating the type and location of different social, health, or educational resources.   These may be painted on it in colors, or the Social Map Symbols designed by the Department of Statistics of the Russell Sage Foundation may be used as shown on page 21.[3]   If the map is to be rigidly mounted, pins or thumbtacks with

---

[1] On p. 17 is shown a sample organization chart of departmental relationships in a medium-sized city.

[2] If no other maps are available for rural sections, the maps prepared by the Geological Survey, United States Department of the Interior, will be helpful.   Different areas have been mapped on different scales, the common ones being two miles, one mile, or one-half mile to the inch.   The maps are sold by the Geological Survey for 10 cents each.   A circular showing the areas mapped in a particular state may be had free on application to the Director, Geological Survey, Washington 25, D.C.

[3] A sample sheet containing the 102 symbols pictured on pp. 18–19, with duplicates of those most frequently used, will be furnished free upon application to the Publication Department, Russell Sage Foundation.   The symbols are ⅜ of an inch in diameter and suitable for cutting out and pasting.   If more than one sheet is desired a charge of 5 cents a sheet is made.

(Reproduced by permission of American Municipal Association.)

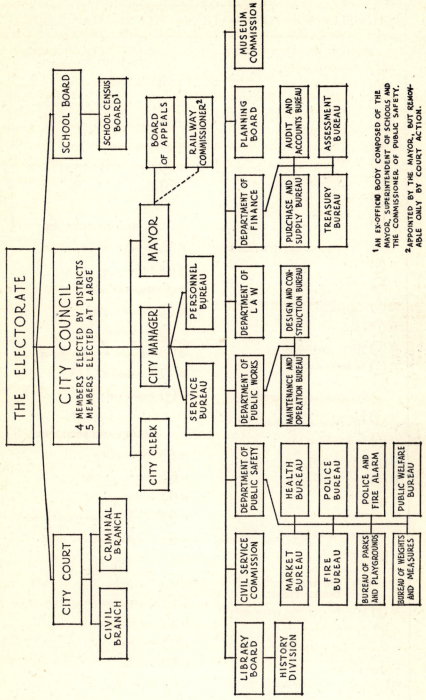

RUSSELL SAGE FOUNDATION   SOCIAL MAP SYMBOLS

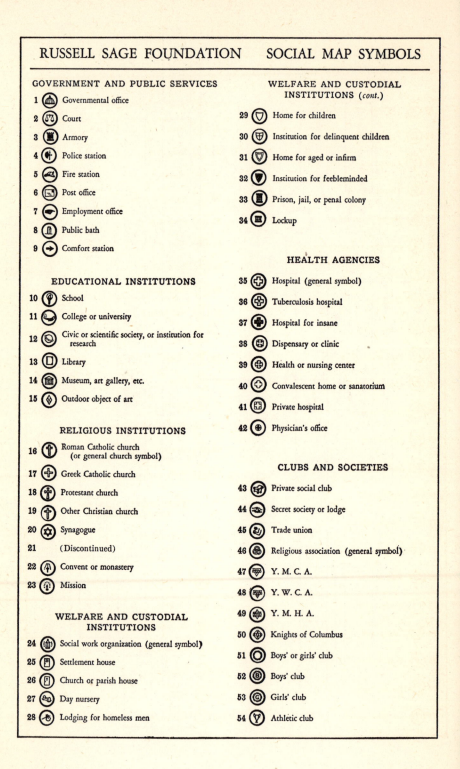

GOVERNMENT AND PUBLIC SERVICES

1 Governmental office
2 Court
3 Armory
4 Police station
5 Fire station
6 Post office
7 Employment office
8 Public bath
9 Comfort station

EDUCATIONAL INSTITUTIONS

10 School
11 College or university
12 Civic or scientific society, or institution for research
13 Library
14 Museum, art gallery, etc.
15 Outdoor object of art

RELIGIOUS INSTITUTIONS

16 Roman Catholic church (or general church symbol)
17 Greek Catholic church
18 Protestant church
19 Other Christian church
20 Synagogue
21 (Discontinued)
22 Convent or monastery
23 Mission

WELFARE AND CUSTODIAL INSTITUTIONS

24 Social work organization (general symbol)
25 Settlement house
26 Church or parish house
27 Day nursery
28 Lodging for homeless men

WELFARE AND CUSTODIAL INSTITUTIONS (cont.)

29 Home for children
30 Institution for delinquent children
31 Home for aged or infirm
32 Institution for feebleminded
33 Prison, jail, or penal colony
34 Lockup

HEALTH AGENCIES

35 Hospital (general symbol)
36 Tuberculosis hospital
37 Hospital for insane
38 Dispensary or clinic
39 Health or nursing center
40 Convalescent home or sanatorium
41 Private hospital
42 Physician's office

CLUBS AND SOCIETIES

43 Private social club
44 Secret society or lodge
45 Trade union
46 Religious association (general symbol)
47 Y. M. C. A.
48 Y. W. C. A.
49 Y. M. H. A.
50 Knights of Columbus
51 Boys' or girls' club
52 Boys' club
53 Girls' club
54 Athletic club

RUSSELL SAGE FOUNDATION   SOCIAL MAP SYMBOLS

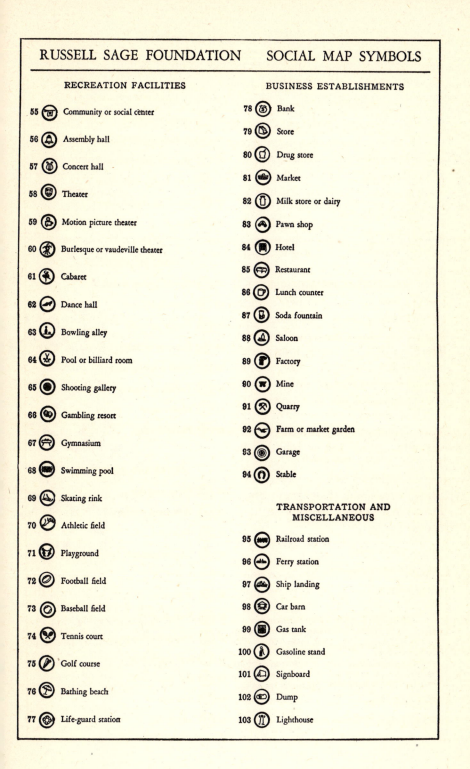

RECREATION FACILITIES

55 Community or social center

56 Assembly hall

57 Concert hall

58 Theater

59 Motion picture theater

60 Burlesque or vaudeville theater

61 Cabaret

62 Dance hall

63 Bowling alley

64 Pool or billiard room

65 Shooting gallery

66 Gambling resort

67 Gymnasium

68 Swimming pool

69 Skating rink

70 Athletic field

71 Playground

72 Football field

73 Baseball field

74 Tennis court

75 Golf course

76 Bathing beach

77 Life-guard station

BUSINESS ESTABLISHMENTS

78 Bank

79 Store

80 Drug store

81 Market

82 Milk store or dairy

83 Pawn shop

84 Hotel

85 Restaurant

86 Lunch counter

87 Soda fountain

88 Saloon

89 Factory

80 Mine

91 Quarry

92 Farm or market garden

83 Garage

94 Stable

TRANSPORTATION AND MISCELLANEOUS

95 Railroad station

96 Ferry station

97 Ship landing

98 Car barn

99 Gas tank

100 Gasoline stand

101 Signboard

102 Dump

103 Lighthouse

heads of different colors and patterns may be used. There are advantages, however, in the cloth-mounted map which can be easily rolled or folded and carried about for display.

III. USES OF STUDY MATERIAL

When the material has been recorded and organized in charts, graphs, and loose-leaf books, consideration may be given to its further use. If nothing more is planned, at least the report volumes could be placed in such centers as club headquarters, in a school library, or in a public library.[1]

An important factor in deciding how to use the data will be the confidence which the study group has reason to feel in the accuracy and objectivity of its work; obviously, material should not be given out to the public in any form, which cannot be substantiated either as to its facts or its implications.

Possible uses of the data would be: (a) preparation of a series of papers or talks for presentation before meetings or on the radio, (b) preparation of newspaper articles, or making the information available to newspaper writers, (c) preparation of study outlines for various groups who may be given access to the material, (d) exhibits of selected material at a fair, a civic exposition, in an empty store, or other convenient place,[2] or (e) publication in a civic bulletin.[3] Inexpensive film strips could be prepared, if the group wished to reach many audiences.

The "pictograph" method of presenting the findings of a study, originally devised by Dr. Otto Neurath, has come to be widely accepted. On pages 22 and 23 examples will be found of how this method was used by the Social Planning Council of St. Louis several years ago to present facts about its community. Pictograph Corporation[4] has numerous ready-made pictograph symbols for use in chart, graph, and map production, which may be secured at nominal prices. In addition, it makes charts and graphs for clients on special order.

While the number of questions between these covers may seem formidable, they are in fact only suggestions from among which choices are to be selected by the student. No attempt has been made at such comprehensive treatment of any phase of community life and activity, as, for instance, that

---

[1] The survey members of the Cincinnati League of Women Voters, for example, in 1943 published their findings in an attractive pamphlet, Know Your City.

[2] See Exhibits—How to Plan and Make Them, National Publicity Council for Health and Welfare Services, New York, 1943.

[3] For example, "Sixty-three Boston Neighborhoods—A Comparison in Favorability," in The Bulletin, Greater Boston Community Council, January-February, 1946, pp. 2–3.

[4] For address see List of Agencies, p. 251.

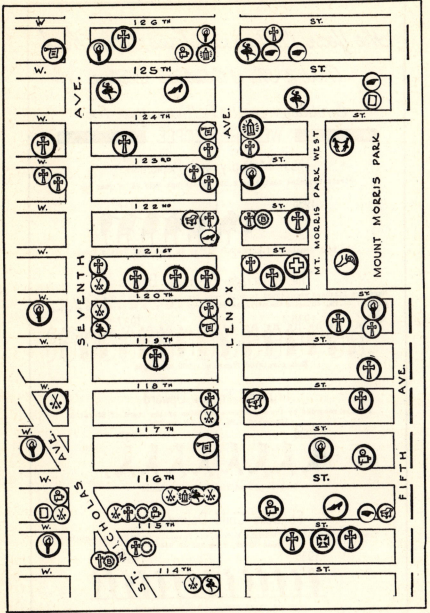

SOCIAL BASE MAP OF PART OF CENTRAL HARLEM, NEW YORK CITY

The Year 1937 in St. Louis Social Work

Part 2. The Statistical Picture

Conditions in 1937 – And a Year Ago

WE, THE PEOPLE

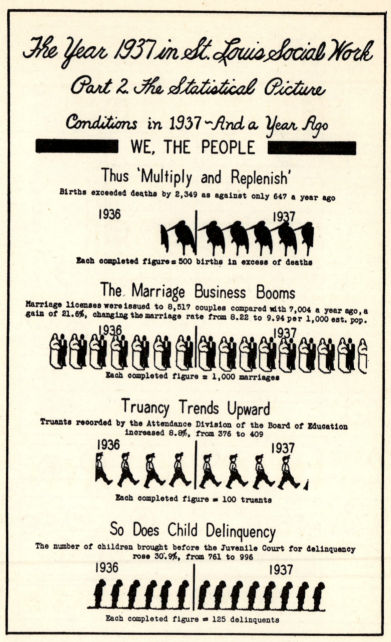

Thus 'Multiply and Replenish'

Births exceeded deaths by 2,349 as against only 647 a year ago

1936   1937

Each completed figure = 500 births in excess of deaths

The Marriage Business Booms

Marriage licenses were issued to 8,517 couples compared with 7,004 a year ago, a gain of 21.6%, changing the marriage rate from 8.22 to 9.94 per 1,000 est. pop.

1936   1937

Each completed figure = 1,000 marriages

Truancy Trends Upward

Truants recorded by the Attendance Division of the Board of Education increased 8.8%, from 376 to 409

1936   1937

Each completed figure = 100 truants

So Does Child Delinquency

The number of children brought before the Juvenile Court for delinquency rose 30.9%, from 761 to 996

1936   1937

Each completed figure = 125 delinquents

This is the form in which the Social Planning Council of St. Louis presented its statistics. Do you find this graphic method interesting and effective?

Cost of Relief Falls Off

Relief agencies expended 17.8% less or $3,392,696 compared with $4,127,596 a year ago

1936   1937

Each completed figure = $500,000

Attendance at Museums Increases

Combined attendance at three museums gained 0.8%, from 3,410,494 to 3,438,507: Art Museum,-5.6%; Shaw's Garden,+13.6%; Zoo, no change

1936   1937

Each completed figure = 1,000,000 attendances

So Does Attendance at Playgrounds

School and city playgrounds gained 3.3% in attendance, from 1,313,969 to 1,357,499 during respective fiscal years

1936   1937

Each completed figure = 200,000 attendances

More Mothers Receive Aid

Mothers' Aid was given to a monthly average of 212 families as against 172 families previously, a gain of 23.3%

1936   1937

Each completed figure = 25 families

Old Age Pensions Zoom High

Average monthly number of old people receiving grants increased 119.4%, from 3752 to 8231; amount of grants 148.9%, from $463,661 to $1,154,002

1936   1937

Each completed figure = 1,000 pensions

Would comparisons between the two years be easier if the figures were beneath each other rather than side by side? What other suggestions have you?

which the Lynds gave Middletown,[1] or as that given a number of cities by general social surveys, of which Philip Klein's study of Pittsburgh is outstanding.[2]

While it is realized that intelligent people must inevitably form judgments about what they see and learn, definite questions about adequacy or efficiency of operation have been omitted from the present volume. The book outlines a descriptive and not an evaluative study. In order to appraise performance, it would be necessary to have comprehensive knowledge, first, of the various standards of excellence that have been developed in any given field, and second, of how far those standards have been found practicable and applicable in other communities of the same or similar size. When standards are available in published form, reference has been made to them so that the inquirer who wishes to take the initial steps in evaluation can have some base lines from which to proceed. Evaluations ought not to be undertaken, however, without the close direction of persons trained and competent to make such appraisals in their respective specialized fields.

From a good descriptive study, however, it should be possible to list problems calling for further attention. Do answers to questions suggest that in certain fields there are gaps and uncovered areas in a community's equipment? Are there health and welfare needs of a community with which no existing agency, either state or local, seems prepared to deal? Or are two or more agencies attempting to provide a specific service without, so far as can be ascertained, clear delimitation of the functions of each?

In the earnest hope that the suggestions herein contained may be found of use to inquiring citizens of this commonwealth of states, the writer wishes the readers "good hunting" in their search for facts.

---

[1] Lynd, Robert S., and Helen M., Middletown: A Study in Contemporary American Culture. Harcourt, Brace and Co., New York, 1929. *Idem,* Middletown in Transition: A Study in Cultural Conflicts. Harcourt, Brace and Co., 1937.
[2] A Social Study of Pittsburgh: Community Problems and Social Services of Allegheny County. Columbia University Press, New York, 1938.

2. COMMUNITY SETTING, FOUNDING, AND DEVELOPMENT

THE SIZE of a community and its location with relation to natural and man-made resources is an important part of the background of any study. An industrial city of the Middle West, an important seaport on the Pacific Coast, a resort town on the Atlantic seaboard, a trading city which is a gateway for migratory labor in the Northwest, an oil city in the Southwest, would each have different problems to meet and different ways of meeting them. From a governmental point of view, a state capital may have more resources but less political and financial power than its rival, a large industrial city. A county seat in a flourishing agricultural region is an entirely different sort of place from one in a depressed mining area.

The subsidiary units of government themselves mean very different things. The state of Connecticut, for instance, where the county is of no political significance whatever, has been described as a "federation of independent townships," while farther west the township may be scarcely more than a surveyor's unit on a map and the county by far the more important unit of local government. The city may be coterminous with the county, or it may enjoy independent status within the county. The municipality may carry out some governmental functions, and the county others, within the same area.

I. RELATION TO THE SURROUNDING REGION

1. What is the name of your community?
2. In what state and county is your community located? What is its area in square miles?
3. What is its governmental status—city, county, township, unincorporated town or village? Is it a *subdivision* of any of these units?
4. How does your community rank in size of population with other communities in your state? In the nation?
5. What are the geographical characteristics of the region? Of your community? Is it located on or near any navigable body of water?
6. What transportation facilities are available into and out of your community?
7. What are visitors to your community told about or taken to see as the chief objects of interest? Are there any features of your community which are not willingly exhibited to visitors?

II. POPULATION

For population figures, the volumes of the United States Bureau of the Census should be consulted. The census is taken at ten-year intervals; but the Statistical Abstract, published annually, contains estimates (but only by states) of population changes during intervening years. Recent estimates for cities may, however, be obtained from current Census Bureau releases, issued periodically. It may be that some local university or governmental research bureau has broken down the census data by the smaller "enumeration tracts" set up within your community, and that the subarea you wish to study can be chosen so as to coincide with such boundaries.[1]

8. What is the total population, by census periods, as far back as available?[2]

Population changes from decade to decade can be related to only two sets of factors: (1) the preponderance of births over deaths or vice versa; and (2) migration into and out of the community. If, therefore, to the total population reported at the next to the last census, one adds the births and subtracts the deaths reported for each of the ensuing ten years, the difference between the figure thus arrived at and total population reported at the most recent census will represent roughly the net gain or loss due to two-way migration.

9. During the last census decade, what was the estimated net increase or decrease due to births and deaths? To migration?

10. For each of the last two census enumerations, what was the population in detail: males and females by (a) age groups, (b) marital status, (c) race, (d) citizenship, (e) nativity and mother tongue? (Among European-born people, the last item is of greater significance than country of birth, since persons of many different ethnic stocks may inhabit a single country.)

11. In which of these groupings have significant changes taken place?

Density of population, that is, the number of people per square mile living within a given area, is reported by the Census Bureau for each state and county in the United States and for each metropolitan area.

12. What is the density of population in your community? How does it compare with that of similar communities in your state, in other states?

If the community you are studying does not happen to coincide with the geographical areas of the census, or if you seek to discover density of popu-

[1] Rochester, New York, is an example of a city where the Council of Social Agencies has translated the statistical data of the Census Bureau into graphic forms that are readily usable.

[2] It should be noted that changes in procedure may make the earlier census figures not strictly comparable with the later. Study the footnotes to the tables, and discard or make allowance for variation in any population figures which were obviously collected on a different basis.

lation in different portions of your community, and cannot find that a density map is already available from governmental or private sources in your community, you will probably have to do some figuring of your own.

In most communities no attempts are made to estimate population between census years, but in many others such estimates are made from time to time by the department of health, bureau of vital statistics, or some comparable agency.

As has been said, a few communities subdivide their area into "census enumeration tracts" as the basic unit in collecting and computing census data, and data regarding these tracts can be combined in all sorts of ways to yield desired information for larger areas.

Cautions to be kept in mind are (1) that only land area in square miles is used in computing density of population, and (2) that great care should be taken that the divisor (square miles) and the dividend (population) both relate to exactly the same territory.

13. Find the areas of densest population in your community, and indicate on an outline map by a system of crosslines or different colors where the population is (a) densest, (b) moderate, (c) sparse.

(If in assembling information later about sickness, bad housing, delinquency, and dependency, you find that maps are available showing areas where there is high incidence of these ills in your community, compare them with your density map. While not necessarily related as cause and effect, these evils are frequently found associated with crowding of population.)

III. INDUSTRIES

The economic conditions of a community would be material for a very detailed and expert study in itself. The nature of a community's industrial and economic life has an important bearing upon its culture and social well-being. Interesting suggestions as to how communities may be differently affected by a preponderance of large as opposed to small industries are presented in a recent Senate committee report.[1] Answers to the questions that follow will require, however, only setting down items of common knowledge among persons informed on business conditions in your community. The chamber of commerce, research divisions of local banks, and the industrial division of your community fund can all be called upon for in-

[1] U.S. Senate Document no. 135, Small Business and Civic Welfare: Report of the Smaller War Plants Corporation to the Special Committee to Study Problems of American Small Business. 79th Congress, 2d Session. Government Printing Office, Washington, 1946.

formation.[1] (For material relating to workers and conditions of their employment, see Chapter 6.)

14. What do your informants say are the important industries of your community?[2]

15. Rank in their importance in your community in terms of the value or quantity of their output the following types of industry:

Production of raw materials (e.g., agriculture, forestry, fishing, mining)
Processing or production of manufactured goods
Trade, transportation, and finance
Service industries (e.g., hotels, restaurants, amusements)

16. Of goods produced, manufactured, or processed in your community, what proportion, roughly, are consumed within the community or the immediate area?

17. In what proportion of the industrial plants is the stock mostly owned locally, with responsible management in your community? What proportion are "branches," with ownership and responsible management outside your community?

18. Which industries are seasonal; i.e., have a regularly recurring slack season each year? What are the slack months in each of your principal industries? Which industries are accustomed to import labor from other regions in rush seasons? (See pages 57–58.)

19. Of agencies engaged in trade, transportation, and finance (banks, brokerage houses, insurance companies, railroads, wholesale and retail stores, and so on) what proportion have their head offices in your community? What proportion are under outside management?

20. What reflection of your community's business growth and the savings of its citizens is to be found in the statements of its banks during the past ten years?

21. Is your community a center for retail buying by people from other communities? Do the inhabitants of your community do retail buying to any important extent in other nearby communities?

22. Does your community contain resort or amusement features which attract people from a distance?

23. Are conventions frequently held in your community? Has it a convention bureau? If so, list conventions held within the past five years, with estimated attendance.

24. What proportion of the circulation of your leading newspaper goes outside the limits of your community?

25. Does your post office serve contiguous areas outside the limits of your community?

---

[1] Consult also the economic classification of cities having over 10,000 population in Municipal Yearbook, 1945, International City Managers' Association, Chicago, 1945, pp. 30–68.
[2] Certain volumes issued by the U.S. Bureau of the Census may be used to check information gathered from local sources. There is, for example, the biennial census of Manufactures. Volume 3 of the 1940 census is a state report containing statistics for cities. A Census of Business, 1939, in several volumes, was issued in 1941–1943. Similar reports may be expected to result from later censuses.

IV. HISTORY

What the original settlers brought to a town often influences its traditions for many generations. The civic patterns of a Pennsylvania town may long be shaped, for instance, by whether its early inhabitants were predominantly Scotch-Irish miners or German agriculturists. A Minnesota community may differ in its institutions and ways of looking at things according as its first settlers were individualists from New England or co-operators from Finland. A community in the Rocky Mountain area may be profoundly affected in its later development by whether it was settled by Mormon families in search of a home, or single miners in search of silver.

If a published history of your community is available, it should be read before the study is begun. Histories of your state may contain references to your community. When no history is obtainable in print, local libraries or the state library or state historical association, if one exists, may have material in manuscript that can be placed at your disposal. Sometimes published genealogies of leading settlers' families contain data regarding the early history of a locality. Few regions are without some person or persons with whom its local history is a hobby, and such people will almost invariably be delighted to be called upon for information. Most local newspapers run contributed historical articles from time to time, and their files may be consulted. It may be possible to read the minutes of proceedings of local governing bodies; but this is a time-consuming process, and recourse should be had to all the short cuts available. When this part of the study is completed, information should be in hand to answer questions such as the following:

26. When was your community first settled? Whence did the first settlers come, and what was the predominant religious, national, and racial stock? Was your community settled by permanent home seekers, or by migratory wealth seekers?

27. When was your community incorporated as a local governmental unit? Have there been significant governmental changes since? What and when (e.g., change of nationality as in the Southwest; change of state boundaries; change from territorial to state status; change from town to city)?

28. Was your community ever affected by actual warfare within its limits, or by a major disaster? When, and with what effects upon it?

29. When were the important industries established? Discontinued? Due to what causes?

30. When was the period of most rapid growth of population? Due to what causes?

31. Does the present population represent largely the descendants of original settlers? What other groups have come in, and when?

32. What groups now hold control over local industry and government?

There are several sources from which to check the degree to which your community contains or has produced men and women who have achieved national prominence.

33. How many persons now living in your community are listed in the latest edition of Who's Who in America?[1]

34. If you know of other eminent living persons living elsewhere but born in your community, how many of them do you find listed in Who's Who in America?

For distinguished people no longer living, the best source is the Index of the Dictionary of American Biography.[2]   Check the list of persons born in your state for names of those born in your community.

---

[1] Who's Who in America: A Biographical Dictionary of Notable Living Men and Women of the United States.   Revised and reissued biennially by the A. N. Marquis Co., Chicago.

[2] Dictionary of American Biography.   Index to vols. 1–20.   Charles Scribner's Sons, New York, 1937.   Contains a list of birthplaces by states, pp. 246–309.

3. LOCAL GOVERNMENT

IN STUDYING a community in relation to its health, education, safety, and welfare, it will not be necessary to study all functions of government in great detail. Close attention will need to be paid, of course, to the departments or bureaus of government which concern most intimately the people's welfare; and procedure to this end will be outlined in the chapters that follow. In this chapter we shall take, so to speak, a bird's-eye view of government in the large.

The form of government, the powers assigned to it, and its methods of securing, appropriating, and disbursing funds are important factors to be ascertained. Local government impinges at every point upon the health, education, and welfare of its citizens; its activities in these areas have been for a number of years past markedly on the increase. Whether or not this enlarged responsibility results in better service to citizens depends in the main upon a community's political set-up, upon quality and competence of elected and appointed personnel engaged in administration, and upon availability of funds sufficient to carry out the responsibilities vested in the local government. These statements apply equally to a township, governed perhaps by selectmen chosen at a town meeting; to a county, with an elected board of county commissioners; and to a municipality, governed by a mayor and board of aldermen or by a commission which appoints a city manager.

In most American communities three, four, or five governments are in operation: municipal, possibly township or town, county, state, federal. Sometimes school districts or other special districts will need to be considered. We need a picture of all these governmental units as they affect this community. Particularly do we need an integrated picture of the local units of government, which most directly affect the lives of its citizens. No real insight into many of the phases of community life can be gained except through such an integrated picture.

In studying the public functions assumed by government in your community, and the machinery set up for exercising them, the first step should be to read that portion of the state constitution which defines the powers and duties of local subdivisions of government, and the charter or organic act which establishes the government of your community. Reference will need to be made also in the course of your study to ordinances passed by the local council. It is probable that in large and complicated city administrations, an organization chart (see page 17) can be secured from the mayor's or city manager's office, showing in graphic form the interrelations and administrative dependence of the various departments and bureaus of the city government. If the county or municipality issues a consolidated annual report, a file of these reports should be available for study and reference. Sometimes individual departments, such as those of health, welfare, and education, issue separate reports. Find out how complete a collection of such material is available in your public library. In any case, the existence, whereabouts, and availability of these documentary sources should be listed and used as a guide for later reference.

A good general text for reading at this point and in connection with chapters to follow is Municipal Administration, by John M. Pfiffner.[1] Valuable also for reference at this and later stages of considering the efficiency of the work done by government will be Municipal Management, by Thomas H. Reed.[2] The September, 1938, issue of The Annals of the American Academy of Political and Social Science consists of articles on "Better City Government," of which those on "Testing the Functions of Municipal Government" (pages 106–170) may furnish valuable help in this portion of a community study. Planning for Postwar Municipal Services[3] is a study analyzing some of the current and probable future problems and trends of municipal activity.

The National Municipal League[4] is prepared to answer inquiries from student groups about problems of local municipal government.

The Bureau of the Census publishes annually a report on City Finances, applicable to cities having populations over 25,000, which will be valuable to consult for checking and comparison of your unit of government with others of similar size.

The most valuable local source of information on government will be a municipal research bureau, if one exists in your community. In some states there is a state league of municipalities which should be able to furnish valuable information, especially concerning comparisons between communities in the state.

[1] The Ronald Press, New York, 1940.
[2] McGraw-Hill Book Co., New York, 1941.
[3] International City Managers' Association, Chicago, 1945.
[4] For address see List of Agencies, p. 251.

1. What functions of government are exercised in your community by (a) state authorities, (b) federal authorities? (For example, the state police may control some of the highways. Certain cities have joint authorities to control the waters of a harbor common to both. Federal authorities such as the Tennessee Valley Authority may take over some of the functions which would otherwise be exercised by local government in the region.)

2. Below the state level, what governmental unit or units operate in your community? Is the area you are studying made up of (a) a single township, (b) a single city, (c) several townships, (d) a combination of city and township units?

3. Does it comprise part or the whole of a single county? Part or the whole of several counties?

4. Is it, for special purposes, part of a "district" (e.g., school district; health district, as in Massachusetts; welfare district, as in some parts of the Middle West)?

5. Distinguish between township, city, and county units as to (a) general governmental responsibilities assumed by each, (b) type of central governing body administering each (e.g., selectmen, trustees, for townships; mayor-council or city manager-commission, for cities; county supervisors, commissioners, freeholders, burgesses, judges, or whatever the title may be, for county governing boards).

6. Have any proposals been recently made, debated, in your community, state, for doing away with some of these superimposed layers of government by consolidation? Has legislation been introduced to bring this about? Describe it.

I. ELECTIONS AND LOCAL POLITICAL SITUATION

7. When are local elections held? At the same time as state or national elections? If so, are the tickets separate so that voters are not encouraged to carry their partisan political views into local elections?

8. Are local candidates nominated exclusively through party primaries? What is the method of securing independent or nonpartisan nominations?

9. What have been the important local issues in recent elections?

10. What political parties have central committees in your community? Ward committees?

11. What political parties have dominated local elections during the past ten years?

12. What was the number of registered voters at the last primary election? What percentage was this of the population?[1] What was the number of votes cast, by parties, for (a) presidential electors, (b) governor, (c) chief municipal official or officials?

[1] A study of the elections in 33 Colorado municipalities in 1937 showed average percentage of population voting, 33.2; average cost of elections per vote cast, 47.2 cents. There was little correlation between size of community and effectiveness in getting out the vote, or cost per vote cast.

For the three largest cities the percentage of population voting ranged from 40.6 to 16.3; cost per vote cast from 26 to 48 cents. In the smaller communities, percentage of population voting ranged from 87.5 to 2.4; cost per vote cast from 9 cents to $1.32—both in towns of under 5,000 inhabitants. (A Survey of Civic Conditions in Colorado: A Study of Municipal Government Among Thirty-three of Colorado's Largest Cities . . ., by William H. Slaton. Colorado Municipal League, Boulder, 1939, p. 17.)

13. Are voting machines or ballots used? Is the system of proportional representation employed?

14. Does your state employ initiative, referendum, or recall? If used in your community during the past ten years, give for each, use, purpose, vote, result.

15. Does your state law require publication of amounts spent in political campaigns? What amount was reported as having been spent by each party in each of the past five elections? What was the cost per capita of the population? Per vote cast?

16. Is there general recognition of the existence of a political "boss" in your community? What are his party affiliations? How long has his political power been apparent?

17. Have there been within the past five years (a) any investigations by state or local authorities of alleged corrupt election practices or malfeasance in public office, (b) any prosecutions? With what results?

18. What are the political affiliations of the leading newspapers published in your community?

19. Is there any citizens' committee or nonpartisan organization (city club, good government league, league of women voters, etc.) which scrutinizes actions of local government, analyzes the budget, and keeps watch over fulfillment of election promises? How many members? Has it a paid staff? Do its reports receive serious attention in the newspapers, and from citizens generally?

II. ADMINISTRATIVE POWERS AND DUTIES

20. Has your community a special charter, or is there a general charter covering the class of localities to which it belongs? How may the charter be amended? How often has it been amended, and in what respects, during the past ten years?[1]

21. What is the title of the chief administrative official of your community? Is he elected or appointed? When and by whom? For what term? What did he promise to do for the community when elected? What progress has he made toward carrying out his campaign promises?

22. List for the past ten years, mayors, giving name, dates of office, occupation, and political party. For city managers, list name, dates of office, previous experience, and cause of termination of service.

23. What appointments are made by the chief executive officer? Has he power to remove his appointees from office, and for what causes?

24. What body is responsible for passing local legislation (city or town ordinances)? How many members? How chosen? What important legislation has it passed within the past five years, directly affecting the health, education, safety, and welfare of the people? Are its deliberations open to the public? Are they reported regularly in the local newspapers? Are local ordinances obtainable in published form?

25. What body is responsible for appropriating and allocating funds to local divisions of government? How many members? How chosen? Does it hold open hearings?

26. What public utilities are operated by government in your community (e.g.,

[1] See Model City Charter: Committee Report, National Municipal League, New York, 1941.

water supply, gas and electricity, street car or bus systems)? If these are operated by private companies, what department of government is responsible for supervising the quality and cost of service given?

27. What separate departments of local government exist in your community? List duties and powers of each. How many of them have been created within the past ten years?

III. PERSONNEL

Important factors to be considered here are methods of selection and appointment of municipal employes, and personnel practices, including in-service training, wage scales, promotion, demotion, retirement, dismissal, sick leave, vacation, and such matters. Selection may be based upon the results of competitive examinations; in this case it is said to be made on a merit basis. Merit systems may be informal, and may exist within a single department, or they may be formally set up under a civil service law. Two references useful at this point are Public Personnel Administration, by William E. Mosher and John D. Kingsley,[1] and Civil Service in Public Welfare, by Alice C. Klein.[2]

28. Is there a local civil service commission? How appointed? Does it employ a full-time, technically trained staff? Whose duty is it to (a) set up eligibility qualifications, (b) draw up examination questions, (c) conduct oral examinations, (d) score and grade the results of examinations, (e) set up eligible lists? To what extent are experts not on the paid staff of the commission drawn in to perform these duties?

29. Is there a state civil service commission? Does it select any local appointees, set up general eligibility lists from which local appointees may be drawn? Does the state commission exercise any supervision over the local?

30. Do other state departments specify that local appointment must be made on a merit basis, as a condition of state aid? Describe.[3]

31. Which heads of departments are elected officials? Which are appointed (a) under a merit system; (b) under exemption from a merit system (who appoints them, and for what terms)?

32. Which subordinate positions are under a civil service or other merit system? Which are exempted? What statements are made by responsible public officials as to methods of selection to fill exempted positions?

33. Has the *proportion* of municipal employes under civil service or other merit system increased or decreased during the past five years?

34. Are there restrictions, prohibitions, relating to political activity on the part of civil service appointees? Other public employes?

[1] Harper and Bros., New York, 1941.
[2] Russell Sage Foundation, New York, 1940. Although it deals specifically with one field of public service, its conclusions may be applied to other fields.
[3] Note that a condition of approval of any state plan submitted to the Social Security Administration is "the establishment and maintenance of personnel standards on a merit basis." This affects local as well as state personnel engaged in administering any of the features of the Social Security Act.

35. Do civil service examinations held in your community give preference to veterans? Veterans' dependents? How much?

36. Do qualifications include residence in the state? The locality? For what periods? Have any posts demanding professional training been filled under civil service by nonresidents? How recently?

37. Is a rating system in effect by which the performance of employes is appraised at regular intervals? Describe. Are promotions made on the basis of seniority? Performance? Are promotion examinations given by the civil service commission?

38. What provision exists for removal or demotion of civil service appointees? Are there hearings? Is the appointee allowed counsel?

39. Are different qualifications set up, different salary scales in effect, for positions in different departments involving the same or similar duties? Is any plan in effect for co-ordinating qualifications and salaries throughout?

40. Can you learn of any examples of courses given in public departments as "in-service training"? Are leaves of absence with pay given to take training away from the job?

41. What is the local government's stated policy in regard to (a) sick leave, (b) vacations with pay, (c) retirement on pension? Have agreements been carried out in practice?

42. Are any groups of municipal employes unionized? If so, what effect has this had on their terms of employment?

IV. TAXATION AND FINANCE

The extent to which health, education, safety, and welfare can be served by the government of a community depends largely upon the sources from which funds can be raised and the manner in which they are allocated and expended.

The tax rate and budget must be matters of immediate concern in such a study as this, since many desirable governmental activities will have to go by default if money raised through taxation is inadequate or is wasted. Study carefully the sources of the community's revenues, and still more carefully the distribution of its expenditures.

Governmental Income

43. What was the total revenue of your community for each of the past five years, listing separately and indicating percentage of each to total revenue:

    Proceeds of taxes on real estate
    Proceeds of other taxes
    Grants for specified purposes from superior units of government
    Other sources (specify)

44. What was the governmental revenue of your community per capita of the population in each of the past five years?

45. Does your state, your community, levy a sales tax? Does it apply to luxuries, necessities, or all purchases? What taxes in your community are "ear-

marked" for special purposes (so-called "mill taxes")? Do officials responsible for financial policy consider these sound forms of taxation?

46. What different taxes are collected in your community? By what units of government? How are their several levies co-ordinated? Of taxes collected jointly, what proportion is retained for local expenditure?

47. What was the tax rate on (a) farms and residence property, (b) business property, (c) unimproved property in each of the past five years?

48. Are real estate taxes based on assessment at full value? If not, on what fractions of assessed value? What governmental agency assesses the value of property? How frequently are reassessments made? Are land and improvements assessed separately? What methods are used to assess property?

49. What is the assessed value of real property exempt from taxation (a) industrial, (b) religious, educational, and philanthropic? What ratio does this bear to the total taxable real property in the community?

50. Is there a legal tax-rate limit in your community? What is it? Is it fixed by charter, by state legislation, or by the state constitution?

51. What has been the percentage of delinquent taxes for each of the past five years? How does this rate compare with that of similar communities in your state? Has legislation been passed reducing the penalties for delinquency? Are taxpayers permitted to pay taxes on the installment plan? What efforts are being made to collect delinquent taxes?

52. Does your community follow the pay-as-you-go policy? Is there a legal limit of bonded indebtedness? What limit? What is your community's outstanding debt per capita?

53. During each of the past five years, how much, if any, of its revenues has your local government placed in sinking funds? How much spent to retire the principal of obligations owed? How much spent for interest on its obligations?

54. What important public improvements have been financed by the sale of bonds during the past five years? Has it been possible to sell all the bonds offered? Have they sold at a discount, or at a premium? What attitude has been taken by local banks toward flotation of new issues? Has the community defaulted on any of its bonds? If so, what effect has this had on its credit?

55. If short-term loans have been resorted to, has this been (a) because expenditures exceeded estimates or income, (b) because of inability to collect taxes, (c) to bridge gaps between tax year and budget year? Have any steps been taken to avoid or reduce the necessity of short-term borrowing?

Governmental Expenditures

56. What was the total cost of local government (township, city, county) in your community for each of the past five years? The per capita cost? Can you secure information from any source as to how this figure compares with that of similar communities in your state?

57. What was the total cost in your community for each of the past five years of each of the separate departments of local government? If these are very numerous, select those with which this study is especially concerned; e.g., sanitation and health, education (including museums and libraries), parks and recreation, public assistance (institutional and noninstitutional), police and fire protection, courts. Make a table showing (a) the per capita cost of each service, (b) the

percentage of total expenditures spent on each service. (This table will be found useful in connection with later sections of your study.[1])

58. What changes are noticeable over the five-year period? Can you secure corresponding information about other similar communities in your state? How do the expenditures compare? Can you secure explanations of the differences from the finance office of your community?

59. Does your community have a capital budget for permanent improvements? How frequently is it revised? What agency drafts it? What relation has the planning commission (see page 88) to the capital budget?

60. What separate steps are gone through in setting up the annual budget for your community? Are the citizens given opportunity to study it before it is approved? Is it published in full? Interpreted in the newspapers? Presented before clubs and organizations? Are public hearings held before it is approved?

61. What methods of fiscal control are employed? Are monthly or quarterly allotments made to departments? What is done if allotments are exceeded? If income is less than was estimated? If unanticipated needs suddenly require expenditures in excess of budget estimates?

62. How often are the accounts audited? By public officials, or by an outside agency? Is publicity given to the audit?

63. Have any special studies of the community's accounts been made within the past five years? With what results?

64. Is there central purchasing of supplies, or does each department buy separately? Is it mandatory to solicit competitive bids?

Efforts made by governmental bodies to effect economies may be salutary and desirable, or they may result in political favoritism, injustice to certain groups of municipal employes, deprivation of dependent citizens, and crippling effective administration of certain departments.

65. Have investigations resulted in dismissal of employes alleged to be superfluous? From what departments? Do informed citizens believe that efficiency of operation has been improved thereby?

66. Has it been necessary to reduce expenditures severely below approved budgets? In what departments? Have economies taken the form of curtailment of staff, salary cuts, or failure to pay salaries over long periods? Of reduction in amounts available for public assistance?

67. Have needed public improvements been postponed? With what results? Has public property been allowed to depreciate?

---

[1] If your community is one of those included in the following study, you may be able to check your table for the services it covers: Expenditures for Community Health and Welfare, Community Chests and Councils, Inc., New York, 1946.

4. PROVISION FOR DEALING WITH CRIME

DURING RECENT years there has been a nationwide wave of interest in the detection and punishment of crime. Not nearly so much public interest is aroused in the *prevention* of crime. Concern with prevention leads to self-examination and self-criticism which only alert and progressive communities are willing to face. A useful reference for this part of your study is Crime in the United States, a symposium in the September, 1941, issue of The Annals of the American Academy of Political and Social Sciences.

A comprehensive examination of crime and punishment in the United States was made by the National Commission on Law Observance and Enforcement (NCLOE)—the so-called "Wickersham Commission." While this report was issued in 1931, it still is the most comprehensive and useful study available. It is therefore frequently referred to in the text of this chapter. Modern concepts of child care exclude children altogether from the ranks of criminals. Therefore this section, which treats of the community's machinery for dealing with crime, makes no reference to juvenile delinquency. The juvenile court, juvenile probation, and institutions for the commitment of juvenile delinquents will be treated in Chapter 16. There is, however, a no-man's land between childhood and full adulthood where post-juvenile delinquency plays a sad, and some believe a growing, part in our pattern of community living.

I. THE LAWBREAKERS

A first approach to the subject should be to the persons involved in breaches of law. If any studies have been made in your community of the incidence of crime, copies should be secured and read. Reports and records of police departments should be available to give the number of complaints and arrests, and court records and reports to give the number of convictions. To save repeated references to the same source material, it will probably be best to set up a simple table and secure all the data at once.

You will find the accepted penological classification of crimes in the Uniform Crime Reports for the United States, published semiannually by the

Federal Bureau of Investigation.[1] For your purposes, however, it might be desirable to use the following headings for the vertical columns in your table:

1. Petty Offenses
   Simple assault, petit larceny, trespass, vagrancy, breach of the peace and disorderly conduct (including prostitution), drunkenness, cruelty to animals, maintaining a nuisance, and violating liquor, traffic, gambling laws, or other local ordinances.
2. Serious Offenses
   (a) Offenses against the person (such as murder in its several degrees, conspiracy to kill or maim, robbery with violence, burglary, kidnaping, traffic in drugs and women, sex offenses other than prostitution).
   (b) Offenses against property (such as grand larceny, receiving stolen goods, fraud, forgery, embezzlement, extortion, arson, and malicious mischief).
   (c) Offenses against the family (such as nonsupport, abandonment, cruelty, neglect, impairing the morals of minors).
   (d) Offenses against government (such as perjury, bribery, malfeasance in office, counterfeiting, and violating election, internal revenue, and postal laws).

For the horizontal columns the following are suggested:

Complaints entered
Arrests
Convictions

Comparative statistics of offenses known to the police in American cities will also be found in the Uniform Crime Reports published by the Federal Bureau of Investigation.

1. How many complaints in your community last year, five years ago, involving offenses listed above?
2. How many arrests made? How were these distributed by age groups? (Suggested grouping, sixteen to eighteen, nineteen to twenty-one, twenty-two to twenty-five, twenty-six to thirty, over thirty.)
3. How many convictions? Of those convicted, how many had previous convictions against them?

In postwar years there seems to be a tendency toward increased crime rates. The Federal Bureau of Investigation reported a 12 per cent national increase in 1945 over 1944, with crimes against property leading. You

[1] Government Printing Office, Washington.

will want to ascertain what steps have been taken in your community to prevent and combat this increased lawlessness.

There is a widespread belief that the foreign-born contribute a disproportionate number of offenders with whom the law must deal. Studies that have been made quite generally show that the reverse is true, and that American-born criminals (including, of course, American-born of foreign parents) far outnumber the foreign-born in proportion to their numbers in the population. (See NCLOE no. 10, Report on Crime and the Foreign Born; see also Chapter 7 of Criminology, by Donald R. Taft.[1])

II. ARREST

Turning now to machinery which the community provides for dealing with crime, we have first the officials concerned with detection and arrest. An excellent preliminary would be to read The Police and Modern Society, by August Vollmer.[2] This book contains numerous tables showing incidence of various types of crime in different parts of the United States, with which your own findings may be checked. (See also Police Systems in the United States, by Bruce Smith,[3] and NCLOE no. 14, Report on Police.)

In small communities we may find only one or more constables appointed or elected to maintain order in township areas, with the main responsibility taken by the county sheriff and his deputies. In larger municipalities a police department is part of the regular city government. In some instances a state police force is maintained to patrol thinly settled areas; and finally, officials of the federal Department of Justice may be permanently stationed in your community or may occasionally be sent in to deal with violations of federal statutes. In many places the lines of responsibility are not clear, and conflicts of authority may occur at various levels. See, for example, Crime and the State Police, by August Vollmer and Alfred E. Parker.[4]

4. What officials, local, county, state, and national, share responsibility in your community for the detection of crime and the apprehension of criminals? What is the division of responsibility among them?

5. How are the local administrative officers appointed and to whom are they responsible: (a) municipal, (b) county?

6. What are the qualifications leading to appointment of the present chief of police, county sheriff? How are police officers, deputy sheriffs, constables appointed? Is a training school for police officers in operation?

[1] Macmillan Co., New York, 1942.
[2] University of California Press, Berkeley, 1936.
[3] Harper and Bros., New York, 1940.
[4] University of California Press, Berkeley, 1935.

7. Is there a merit system governing appointment and promotion? Is there a retirement system with pension?

8. How many patrolmen (constables), detectives, other special divisions in the police force? How many deputies regularly serving under the sheriff?

9. Has your police department officers specifically concerned with prevention of crime; e.g., policewomen, a crime prevention bureau? How many officers; how chosen; qualifications and experience of officers engaged in crime prevention?

10. How many inhabitants are there per police officer?

11. Has your police department expert facilities for the detection of crime, such as a fingerprint department, chemical laboratory, ballistics expert? Are police cars equipped with receiving sets for radio communication with headquarters? With transmitting sets?

12. What was the budget requested for the police department in each of the past five years? Amount appropriated? Proportion of total expenditures? Per capita cost? (See page 37.)

13. Have there been investigations of the police department within the past five years which have disclosed evidence of corrupt connection with the underworld? Have they resulted in administrative reorganizations? Is the police department generally believed to be involved, or free from involvement, with such influences?

14. Have the state police a post within the area of your community? How many officers? What are their powers and duties?

15. Are federal agents of justice stationed in your community? How many? What are their powers and duties?

(For police powers and duties in the maintenance of public safety, see Chapter 5.)

The difficulty of apprehending criminals has been enormously increased by the availability of automobiles to get them across state lines. Many people believe that the successful control of crime in modern society depends in part upon the breaking down of territorial immunity through the development of a statewide and a nationwide police force with power to make arrests anywhere in the country. At present, offenders against state laws can be apprehended and brought back to stand trial only by cumbersome and uncertain interstate agreements for extradition.

16. For what offenses in your state can persons be extradited from other states? How many persons were extradited to your community last year? How many extraditions were requested and refused? How many criminals are reported to have escaped the jurisdiction altogether?

III. PROSECUTION

The prosecution of criminals is comprised in a complicated set of courts and public bodies. (See NCLOE no. 4, Report on Prosecution, and no. 8, Report on Criminal Procedure.) The constitutions of most states establish certain rights and safeguards under the common law for persons accused of crime. (See NCLOE no. 11, Report on Lawlessness in Law Enforcement.)

17. What safeguards are provided in the constitution of your state?

The public prosecutor in charge of securing indictments and conducting prosecutions is usually a county official. In most jurisdictions he is elected, not appointed. He may summon, from previously prepared panels, a grand jury which determines whether cause for prosecution exists in certain cases, and if so, may indict and hold for further trial.

18. What are the training and experience of the present public prosecutor? What are his political affiliations?

19. How is the panel of grand jurors established? How many sittings last year? How many indictments rendered? How many cases dismissed?

The grand jury has the right to order independent investigations of crime conditions.

20. Has any grand jury in your community taken such action during the past five years? Results?

Superior and inferior courts go under widely varying names in different parts of the country. They are divided into civil courts, which deal with such matters as inheritance, property rights, divorce, contracts, and the settlement of disputes between individuals which do not involve the state; and criminal courts. For the purposes of this study it should be sufficient merely to list the civil courts, and note the number of cases awaiting trial, since overcrowded calendars in these courts may lead to serious delay in administering justice. If the probate court in your community passes upon adoptions, this function should be considered under Chapter 16.

In some communities small claims courts, sometimes called "reconciliation courts" exist, where small claims can be adjusted by voluntary submission of both parties to arbitration, without formal legal process or the engaging of counsel. Where this valuable device is found to reduce costs of litigation for the "little man" and avoid the overcrowding of civil calendars, it should be noted in your study.

In the main, however, this section will consider the means of administering justice in criminal cases—that is, those in which the individual is accused of offenses against the laws of the state. In very small communities a single official, frequently called justice of the peace, may be the only officer administering justice. In larger communities magistrates' courts and police courts function in much the same way. Petty offenses only are dealt with by these courts, but they may hold preliminary hearings on more serious offenses, and detain the accused for trial in courts of superior juris-diction.

The community's criminal courts, however named, handle the bulk of criminal prosecutions conducted in the local area. (Special courts, usually considered part of the criminal courts system, will be treated in other chapters—juvenile courts, as already noted, in Chapter 16 and family or domestic relations courts in Chapter 15.)

Higher courts to which appeals may be taken are usually part of the machinery of state government, culminating in a final court of appeals, differently titled in different states, which reviews only actions coming up from the lower courts. The federal circuit and district courts usually deal only with infringements of federal statutes and with civil cases having interstate aspects. The final court of appeal in this country is, of course, the Supreme Court of the United States, but it considers only appeals involving the federal constitution or law.

21. Make a chart showing all courts operating in your community, both criminal and civil, and indicate higher courts through which appeals may be taken.

22. Are local judges and magistrates elected or appointed? What are the qualifications leading to their appointment? Term of office? Are court fees paid in lieu of salaries to magistrates, court clerks?

23. In which courts, or for what offenses, is trial before a jury obligatory? Optional? How is the panel of jurymen chosen? Are women eligible for jury duty in your state? On what grounds are exemptions from jury duty secured?

24. Visit some of the criminal courts in your community. Are they crowded, ill-ventilated, noisy, or the reverse? Is decorum maintained among frequenters of the courtroom?

25. What is the process of admission to bail in your community? Are professional bondsmen permitted to frequent courts?

26. Is it generally believed that political leaders are able to influence procedure or decisions?

27. How are accused persons who lack means to hire counsel represented in court? Is there a public defender to undertake criminal defenses? Are lawyers individually appointed by the courts, and do lawyers of recognized standing accept such appointments? Has your community established or considered establishing a post of public defender?

28. Is there a voluntary defenders' league undertaking defense of criminal cases? How many did it defend last year? (For legal aid societies, see page 205.)

IV. PUNISHMENT

Conviction results directly in sentence (execution of which may, however, be postponed through appeal for review to a higher court). Sentence may consist of the death penalty, of fine or imprisonment or both, or of probation. (See NCLOE no. 9, Report on Penal Institutions, Probation and Parole.)

29. Does capital punishment exist under the law of your state? For what offenses? Is it mandatory or permissive for these offenses? How many persons from your community have been executed during the past five years?

30. How many were sentenced during the past year to imprisonment (a) in jails, lockups or workhouses, (b) in county or municipal penitentiaries or prisons, (c) in state institutions, (d) in federal prisons?

Conditions in local jails and prisons are frequently one of the darkest blots in our American communities. At this point you may want to read Plans for City Police Jails and Village Lockups, by Hastings H. Hart,[1] and "The Local Jail—Some Substitutes," by William E. Cole, in the October–December, 1945, issue of Federal Probation. A visit to your local jail or workhouse would prove of great value.

31. How does your jail compare with standards in the references mentioned above? Is it clean and sanitary?

32. Is there provision for separating men from women? First offenders from more hardened criminals? Those awaiting trial from those serving sentence?

33. Is there a matron in charge of women prisoners? Are medical examinations given? Are persons with communicable diseases kept separate from other prisoners?

34. Are any children under eighteen being held in jail?

35. What work do prisoners do? If kept indoors, do they have any opportunity for exercise and fresh air?

36. If there are prisons or penitentiaries for men or women in your community, ascertain the same information as above, and in addition learn what opportunities exist for trade training or elementary instruction.

37. Are religious services held? Are prisoners individually visited by a chaplain or other representative of their own religious denomination?

38. Is there a library? Are there organized sports and outdoor or indoor recreation?

39. Are prisoners allowed to converse? Is there any organization of prisoners which co-operates in the management of the prison? What privileges are given to "trusties"?

40. Are psychological examinations given? Is treatment of prisoners in any way related to such findings?

41. What disciplinary measures are used for infractions of rules? Is discipline confined to loss of the time otherwise remitted for good behavior, or to other curtailment of privileges? Or is resort had to severe penalties such as solitary confinement, deprivation of food ("bread-and-water"), corporal punishment?

[1] Russell Sage Foundation, New York, 1932.

42. Is there any system by which prisoners can earn money to be used for the support of their dependents?

43. Are there farm colonies to which inebriates, drug addicts, and others may be committed in your state? Provision for medical and psychiatric treatment? Are the criminal insane incarcerated in institutions which are part of the correctional system, or under the supervision of the mental hygiene authorities of the state?

44. Does your state have the "chain-gang" system, by which gangs of prisoners labor outdoors under guard? Are prisoners "hired out" to contractors?

45. Do the laws of your state require or permit indeterminate sentences? Under what circumstances? How may prisoners be released on parole?

46. Are parole officers appointed under a civil service merit system? What are the qualifications leading to the appointment of the present chief parole officer? For how many prisoners is each parole officer responsible? How frequently are prisoners required to report?

47. How many persons were on parole in your community last year from state and local penal and correctional institutions? How many broke the conditions of parole?

48. Examine the reports of state correctional institutions to which young people from your community are committed. What evidence do they reveal of medical care, attention to nutrition, psychological examinations, psychiatric treatment, occupations given, trade training, educational courses, and so on? Are social workers employed in such institutions?

49. Have any studies been made in your state or community of the after-careers of young criminals? What percentage of recidivism (repeating offenses) do they show? (See page 222.)

50. Is there any privately supported organization in your community devoted to the aftercare of prisoners? What is its program? What results have been reported?

V. PROBATION

Probation is a form of suspended sentence in which the offender is allowed to remain at large in the community as long as he maintains good conduct and reports regularly to a probation officer for a specified term. If he fails to observe the conditions of probation, the sentence originally imposed goes into effect.

Probation, which was first developed for juvenile offenders, has been extended in many communities to adult offenders as well. In cases which might respond to such treatment, reformation through supervision in normal community life is believed by many authorities to be more efficacious and less of a financial burden on the community than incarceration. The National Probation Association[1] can furnish information on standards and procedures. Good reading references are Probation and Parole in Theory

[1] For address see List of Agencies, p. 251.

and Practice, by Helen D. Pigeon;[1] Probational and Criminal Justice, edited by Sheldon Glueck;[2] and the National Probation Association Yearbook.[3]

51. Is there a central probation service for the courts in your community? How many of the courts in your community, other than juvenile and family courts, have probation officers? How many officers attached to each? Are they appointed from civil service lists? How otherwise? What qualifications led to the appointment of the present chief probation officers? How many officers are members of professional organizations?[4] How many are men, how many women?

52. What was the average number of probationers reporting to each officer last year? How frequently were they required to report? What does the report of the probation department show as to (a) total cases on probation last year, (b) number for whom jobs were found or other adjustment services rendered, (c) number who completed probation successfully, (d) number who broke the conditions of probation?

53. Does the probation department make preliminary investigations at the request of the court? In how many cases was a social history furnished the judge in advance of sentence?

54. Are the services of psychologists and psychiatrists available to the probation department? How many results of such examinations were reported to the judge in advance of sentence?

VI. CONDITIONS WHICH CONTRIBUTE TO DELINQUENCY AND CRIME

Finally, the conditions which may contribute to crime and misdemeanors in your community should receive study. Read Preventing Crime: A Symposium, edited by Sheldon and Eleanor Glueck.[5] Some of the conditions contributing to delinquency and crime that can be improved will be dealt with in Chapter 12.

55. Are there any large aggregations of men without families in or near your community, such as military establishments or camps of workmen on construction projects?

[1] National Probation Association, New York, 1942.
[2] Macmillan Co., New York, 1933.
[3] The Association, New York. (Title changes annually.)
[4] In this and subsequent references, professional organizations mean those associations of social workers which impose professional standards of membership, and not simply clubs which any practicing social worker may join. At present, the social work associations are:
American Association of Social Workers, 130 East 22d St., New York 10.
American Association of Medical Social Workers, 1129 Vermont Ave., N.W., Washington 5.
American Association of Psychiatric Social Workers. Address varies from year to year, but can be obtained from the National Committee for Mental Hygiene, 1790 Broadway, New York 19.
American Association of School Social Workers. Address varies from year to year, but can be obtained from the Public Education Association, 745 5th Ave., New York 22.
[5] McGraw-Hill Book Co., New York, 1936. (Out of print but available in many libraries.)

56. Has your community a segregated vice district? What provisions exist in the law for the control of prostitution? Are patrons of prostitutes liable to arrest, compulsory medical examination, or only the prostitutes themselves? How many arrests in connection with prostitution last year? How many paid fines; how many were committed for treatments; sentenced to reformatories?[1]

For obvious reasons, information about the organized promotion of crime in your community by vice rings, associations of gangsters, and racketeers can be secured only if some official body in the community such as a grand jury or a crime commission has assembled evidence and made it public, or if arrests and prosecutions have caused the story to "break" in the newspapers. Your local newspaper should be able to show you classified clippings on the subject, if articles have recently appeared in its columns on underworld activities.

57. Has any body of citizens, organized as an independent committee or as an official crime commission, attempted to study vice and crime conditions in your community in recent years? What do its reports reveal?[2]

58. Consult your local newspaper, and read whatever recent clippings have been classified under crime. Do they point to the existence of promotion of crime for profit in your community?

[1] A general text recommended by the American Social Hygiene Association is Prostitution in the Modern World: A Survey and a Challenge, by Gladys M. Hall, Emerson Books, New York, 1936. Current leaflets on the subject may be obtained from the American Social Hygiene Association, 1790 Broadway, New York 19.

[2] See, for instance, An Outline of the Cleveland Crime Survey, by Raymond Moley, The Cleveland Foundation, Cleveland, 1922.

5. PROVISION FOR PUBLIC SAFETY

INCREASING complexity and urbanization of American life, together with wider use of motor vehicles, have forced communities to devote larger amounts of attention and of public funds to the prevention of physical harm to citizens and their property.

The local police, highway, and fire departments and the local automobile association may be called upon for information as to provision for public safety. General information on safety and accident prevention is issued by the National Safety Council.[1] It may have state or local branches in your community. This national agency conducts annually a "national safety contest."

1. Did your community compete in the last national traffic safety contest? If so, secure a copy of the schedule which was filled in and submitted. It will help you in answering the questions in this section.

Issuance of licenses and of other local ordinances often has as its motive protection of the public safety. An example that readily comes to mind is the license to operate a motor vehicle; but hunting licenses, dog licenses, ordinances that prevent dogs from running at large without muzzles, licenses to conduct a street parade, and many others, may be related to safety.

2. How many types of licenses issued in your community have some bearing upon the public safety?

Prevention of health dangers due to communicable diseases, contaminated water and food supply, and so on, is discussed in Chapter 8; safety inspection of dwellings is taken up in Chapter 7; and measures to prevent industrial accidents are dealt with in Chapter 6. The general organization of the police department and its relation to crime was covered in Chapter 4, but there remain certain functions of that department to be treated under the subject of public safety.

[1] For address see List of Agencies, p. 251.

I. MAINTENANCE OF PUBLIC ORDER

The function of maintaining public order and preventing unlawful assembly is traditionally exercised by the police department. In some communities it is wisely and tolerantly exercised; in others, its exercise involves infringements, sometimes intolerable, upon the civil rights of citizens.

3. What does the Bill of Rights in your state constitution say about the right of peaceful assemblage?

4. Have any groups been refused permission to hold meetings, parades? What groups and for what stated reasons? Have "soap-box orators" been arrested? On what grounds?

5. Have there been riots accompanied by violence in your community in the past five years? What were the points at issue (labor conflicts, race friction)? How well prepared was the local police force to deal with the situation without itself having to resort to violence? Were persons injured, killed, by mob action? Was the state militia called in? Was martial law declared?

6. Are your police officers given special training in the handling of race riots?[1]

II. TRAFFIC SUPERVISION

Safety on the public highways has become a major center of attention due to the increased hazard of accident and death from the operation of motor vehicles. Two publications that will assist your study are: Sudden Death and How to Avoid It, by J. C. Furnas and Ernest N. Smith,[2] and How Cities Protect Pedestrians: Practical Ideas Used by Cities in the Pedestrian Protection Contest[3] and discuss these ideas with the superintendent of the traffic division of your police department.[4]

7. Have any campaigns for the reduction of traffic accidents been staged in your community recently?

The state laws covering operation of motor vehicles should be read before considering methods of local enforcement.

8. Does your state law provide that all drivers of motor vehicles must be licensed? Under what age is driving prohibited? What tests are given before licenses are issued: (a) physical test, (b) examination by questions on traffic regulations, (c) driving tests? By whom?

9. Have any licenses been revoked in your community within the past five years? How many? On what grounds?

10. Has your state a law that all motor vehicles must carry liability insurance? If not, can you learn in what proportion of traffic accidents in your state or com-

[1] See A Guide to Race Relations for Police Officers, by the American Council on Race Relations, Chicago, 1945.
[2] Simon and Schuster, New York, 1935.
[3] American Automobile Association, Washington, 1944.
[4] Consult also A Check List for Surveying Community Activities in Traffic Safety, National Safety Council, Inc., Chicago, 1943.

munity resulting in damage it was impossible for the injured party to collect because the car at fault carried no insurance?

11. Secure from local insurance firms the rate for liability insurance on (a) pleasure cars, (b) commercial vehicles. Has there been any change in the past five years? How does the rate compare with similar communities elsewhere?

12. In what department, local, state, federal, is safety inspection of ferry boats, excursion boats, and other passenger carrying vessels located? To what safety regulations must they conform? How frequently are they inspected?

The agency responsible for removal of traffic hazards is usually the engineering department, or department of highways. The National Safety Council has issued a publication[1] setting forth standards in traffic engineering.

13. Does your community employ a traffic engineer?

14. What traffic studies or observations were made in your community last year? By whom? Give briefly nature and results of each.

15. How well do street signs and signals conform to the standards laid down by the National Conference on Street and Highway Safety? (These standards can be obtained from the National Safety Council.)

The agency chiefly concerned with enforcement of traffic regulations is the police department.

16. What is the division of responsibility between state police and your local police department for patrolling the streets of your community?

17. Has your police department a traffic division? How many officers detailed to it? (See page 42.) Is there a trained accident investigation squad?

18. Are special officers assigned to school zones during school hours? What added safeguards are in effect (e.g., mechanical "slowers" in the pavements, high mandatory fines for exceeding the speed limit in school zones)?

19. What means are employed to reduce the hazards incident to bicycle riding?

20. During the past year, how many arrests were made or tickets issued for traffic violations? How many convictions were secured? (See page 40.)

21. Is there compulsory motor vehicle inspection in your community?

22. Is inspection made by commercial garages and service stations, or by police-operated inspection stations? How frequently? What percentage of vehicles in your community was thus inspected last year?

23. Is an accident spot map available from any of the above-mentioned agencies in your community, showing residence of drivers and pedestrians involved in traffic accidents? If so, compare it with your density map. (See page 26.)

III. FIRE PREVENTION AND CONTROL

Every community has some provision for fighting the ever-present danger of fires. Small communities may have volunteer companies, while fire de-

[1] Engineering for Traffic Safety. Chicago, 1939.

partments in large cities are an important and costly part of the municipal administration. The rates of fire insurance premiums which property owners have to pay are an objective test of the community's success in avoiding fire losses. Any fire insurance company with offices in your community or area should be able to explain how these rates are determined, and furnish information as to increase or decrease of rates in your community, and how these compare with those of similar communities in the region.[1]

24. Secure information as to fire insurance rates similar to that outlined in question 11.

25. Has your community a volunteer fire brigade? How is it recruited, trained, and financed? What equipment does it own? When was this equipment purchased?

26. Has your community a paid fire department? How many employes has it? How were they selected, appointed, and trained? What have been the training and experience which led to the appointment of the chief?

27. What have been the department's expenditures for each of the past five years? What has been the annual per capita cost of fire protection? Percentage of annual public expenditures? (See page 37.)

28. How many fire stations are maintained? Is the equipment motorized? How many pieces are there? How recently were they purchased?

29. How often are hoses inspected? Is any part of your community lacking in sufficient fireplugs, or in water pressure to fight fires effectively? What is being done about it?

30. How many fires occurred during the past year? How many injuries and deaths resulted, and what amount of property loss was due to fires?

31. What are the regulations governing fire and other hazards in moving picture houses, theaters, and places of public assemblage? How and by what departments are these regulations enforced?

32. Is a local "fire prevention week" sponsored by your fire and police departments?

33. What public instruction is given in your schools and elsewhere, in fire prevention, methods of extinguishing, emergency treatment of burns, and so on?

IV. ACCIDENT PREVENTION AND FIRST AID

Accidents are due to a number of causes in addition to those enumerated above. The largest percentage of all accidents occurs in the home, and their prevention is often the object of educational campaigns among children.

34. Are any local groups such as parent-teacher associations sponsoring planned safety programs in your community?[2]

[1] Read Safeguarding the Nation Against Fire, National Board of Fire Underwriters, New York, 1944, and Fire Prevention Education, edited by Charles C. Hawkins, Center for Safety Education, New York University, 1942.

[2] National Congress of Parents and Teachers, A Safety Manual for Parent-Teacher Associations. Chicago, 1944.

Drownings and asphyxiations are also accountable for many deaths.

35. Are the beaches in or near your community provided with lifeguards? Is free swimming instruction given? During what hours are lifeguards on duty?

36. Does the Bureau of Mines or any other state department give instruction in first aid in drowning, asphyxiation?

37. Has your Red Cross chapter a lifesaving service? Does it hold classes in first aid? How many persons received instruction last year from these sources?

38. Are inhalators available for resuscitation? How can they be secured in case of accident?

39. Is domestic electrical equipment subject to any inspection in your community (a) in the shops, (b) in the homes? Do your public utilities supply customers with information regarding dangers to be avoided in the use of gas and electricity? Is any public information given through other sources?

V. CO-ORDINATION OF SAFETY MEASURES

Public safety, involving as it does many different agencies, needs to be co-ordinated. Especially is this true of plans to meet disasters of a catastrophic nature. The American National Red Cross is active in securing the appointment of local chapter committees to explore the hazards of disaster to their communities, to list resources which would be available for housing, transportation, and health care, and to work out in advance the plans to be followed in different types of disaster and the functions to be carried out by different agencies and groups.

40. Has your community Red Cross a committee on disaster preparedness and relief? Have plans been worked out in advance for dealing with the results of major disasters such as fire, tornado, earthquake, and flood?

41. What agencies, public and private, have accepted responsibility under the plan for carrying out what functions? What subcommittees have been appointed? How do the plans of your community compare with those suggested in the manual mentioned above?

42. Is there a safety council in your community? What public and private agencies are represented on it? With what national agencies is it in relation? What are its program and accomplishments claimed?[1]

43. Are there junior safety councils in the schools? In how many (public and private)? What are their programs and accomplishments claimed?

[1] See National Safety Council, Inc., Community Organization for Safety, Chicago [1945].

6. WORKERS, WAGES, AND CONDITIONS OF EMPLOYMENT

IT IS UNNECESSARY to stress the importance to a community of how its people get their living. As has been earlier mentioned (see Chapter 2), the main industries of a community color the entire life not only of those who work but of the whole population. Such things as health, housing, education, and recreation must be geared to what local industry makes possible.

For the purposes of such a study as this, the most important facts to learn in relation to the working population and the conditions of their employment are the following:

Number of people able and willing to accept gainful employment
Number at work
Kind of work they do
Wages they earn[1]
Number who are partly or wholly unemployed
Machinery for placing people in jobs
Means adopted by workers to improve wages and working conditions
Efforts of employers to further the welfare of their employes
Safeguards which government supplies for the workers

The sources from which information is to be secured will depend upon the community to be studied. Only general suggestions can be given here, because what can be secured will differ according to the size and characteristics of the community studied. You will need to refer to the latest available reports of the Census Bureau. Some material may be gained from special or annual reports of the Census Bureau; e.g., the biennial census of manufactures, reports on The Labor Force, and special unemployment censuses.

In addition to census information, the United States Department of Labor publishes the Monthly Labor Review, in which pertinent analyses are made from time to time of conditions in selected industrial centers. Recent

[1] For cost of living as related to average earnings, see p. 198.

issues of the Review should be checked through for possible references to your community or to others similar to yours in size and location. You may find the periodical indexes at the library useful in finding references to industrial conditions in your community.

Many state departments of labor, state employment offices and unemployment compensation agencies publish regular reports on employment conditions within the state. The Social Security Administration also compiles extensive data on unemployment and wages. State federations of labor may also be a source of information.

Finally, there may be local agencies which can help you. Some of them may continuously collect data in this field. The local public employment service should have available information about trends in employment. Banks, especially those in the Federal Reserve System, may have research departments which can supply current information about employment and industrial conditions. A chamber of commerce or manufacturers association may be similarly equipped. The local community chest is likely to have information about the community's larger industrial concerns and the number of persons each employs. Local federations of labor unions can give information about extent of unemployment, membership in labor organizations, and the programs of organized labor.

As a general introduction to the work of this section, we suggest that you read Chapter 8, "Industrial Conditions," in volume 3 of The Springfield Survey directed by Shelby M. Harrison.[1] While this survey took place a number of years ago, the methods followed and the standards set up will be helpful in studying other communities.[2]

I. OCCUPATIONS

General Occupational Information.[3] The census report entitled The Labor Force classifies the population in great detail as to occupations in both public and private employment in cities of 100,000 and over. The data will be found grouped under the following main heads:

[1] Russell Sage Foundation, New York, 1920. (Out of print but generally available in libraries.)

[2] For examples of later studies see Chapter 2, "Getting a Living," in Middletown in Transition: A Study in Cultural Conflicts, by Robert S. and Helen M. Lynd, Harcourt, Brace and Co., New York, 1937; Chapter 3, "The Chances for a Living in Allegheny County," in A Social Study of Pittsburgh: Community Problems and Social Services of Allegheny County, by Philip Klein and others, Columbia University Press, New York, 1938; and Chapter 13, "The Economic Life of the Community," in The Social Life of a Modern Community, by W. Lloyd Warner and Paul S. Lunt, Yale University Press, New Haven, 1941.

[3] Suggestions for conducting community occupational surveys are found in Community Surveys, by Marguerite W. Zapoleon, U.S. Office of Education, Vocational Division Bulletin no. 223, Government Printing Office, Washington, 1942.

Professional and Semiprofessional
Proprietors, Managers, and Officials
Clerical, Sales
Farmers and Farm Managers
Craftsmen, Foremen
Operatives
Domestic Service
Service Workers
Farm Laborers and Foremen
Laborers, except Farm and Mine

1. How many persons were employed in your community at the time of the latest census, in each of the foregoing divisions? How many by race and nativity? What proportion of the total population was "gainfully occupied"?

If your community was one of the 83 included in the National Health Survey, 1935–1936, information concerning the occupations of heads of families may be secured from the bulletin Families Classified by Occupational Class of the Head.[1]

Working Women and Children. Of particular interest in such a study as this are working women and children, because of the special protections thrown around them in industry (for which see page 72); and workers in agriculture, because of interrelationship of the farm and the farm home.

2. How many women, eighteen years of age and over, were gainfully occupied in your community when the latest census was taken? What proportion was this of the total female population? How does the proportion compare with that of similar communities in your state?

3. How were occupations of women classified, according to the headings previously given? If possible, give separate data for white and Negro women.

4. In how many families was the homemaker gainfully employed? What proportion of total families had homemakers?

5. Of homemakers gainfully employed, how many were white, how many Negro? How many were employed at home, in agriculture or other occupations; how many away from home?

6. How many boys, girls, fourteen to seventeen years of age, were gainfully employed in your community at the time of the latest census? What proportion of all the boys, girls, of these ages were employed?

7. How many were employed as apprentices, that is, were receiving training in some skilled occupation? How many were employed in factories? How many in street trades (messengers, newsboys, and so on)?[2]

[1] Division of Public Health Methods, National Institute of Health, U.S. Public Health Service. Preliminary Reports, Population Series Bulletin B. Government Printing Office, Washington, 1938.
[2] For placement of juniors, see pp. 64 and 75. For vocational guidance, see p. 155.

The demands of defense and war production during the years 1940–1945 brought many additional women and juniors into the labor market. Between April, 1940, and April, 1944, the employment of white women increased by 51 per cent and that of Negro women by 40 per cent. During a similar period there were an estimated 2,000,000 young workers fourteen to eighteen years old employed in excess of the number who would normally have been employed in the labor force. Subsequent demobilization and the reconversion of industry to peacetime production dislodged a considerable number of these new workers. If your study is being made before late postwar census information is available, you will wish to correct the picture presented by the answers to the foregoing questions, through the marshaling of such current information as you can gather from employers, the chamber of commerce, or other sources.[1]

Agricultural Workers. The census report on The Labor Force gives the number of men and women, of different age and racial groups, engaged in agriculture within the area of towns and cities. If the area you are studying is rural, you will need supplementary data by counties. This may be secured from the census volumes reporting on agriculture.

8. What was the rural farm population of your county at the latest census? What was the rural nonfarm population?

9. How many farm families, by race and nativity of head, owned their own farms? How many were tenants? What was this distribution for rural nonfarm families?

10. How many acres in your county were devoted to farming? How many different farms were there? What was the average acreage of farms; average value of farm land per acre?

11. What was the total value of farm crops produced in your county? What proportion of this was (a) dairy and meat products, (b) grain and vegetable crops, (c) fruit, (d) other?

From other sources, such as banks, county farm agents, farm bureaus, granges, and local representatives of governmental farm agencies, it should be possible to secure data revealing the financial status of farmers in your county.

12. Can you learn how many farms in your community are owned clear of mortgage? On how many farms are taxes in arrears; mortgage payments? What has been the situation with regard to foreclosures during the past ten years?

Seasonal Workers and Migrants. We depend upon the work of migrants to pick and can our crops and to do other forms of seasonal or intermittent work.

[1] For special protection of working women and children, see p. 72.

13. What industries in your community are seasonal? (See page 28.) Has any study of seasonal workers been made recently in your community?[1] Did it give the average annual income of seasonal workers?

14. Do seasonal workers come into the community from other regions? To do what kinds of work? What occupations do they have at other times?

15. Does your State Department of Labor investigate conditions under which migrants work in your community?

II. WAGES

Wage rates in various occupations are only one factor in the adequacy of family earnings. Others equally important are continuity of employment, living costs, size of family, and number of gainfully employed people per family. The census report on families gives some information on the latter points.

16. What was the average number of gainfully employed persons per family reported for your community in the latest census report on families?

Prevailing wage rates per hour in certain occupations are usually easy to obtain from state departments of labor, but may be published only for the state as a whole. Some state departments also report on average weekly earnings. In connection with this and the following section, we suggest study of Employment Statistics for the United States by Ralph G. Hurlin and William A. Berridge.[2]

17. What are the prevailing wage rates at present for common labor, skilled labor, factory labor, and other occupations, as reported for your state? What were they a year ago?

18. What can you learn from local sources about the rates paid in your community? Are they higher or lower than wage rates prevailing in the state?

19. Does your State Department of Labor publish a monthly bulletin? Can you secure from it the number of people currently employed in selected industries, and their average weekly earnings? How do these compare with a year ago?

(For the effect of collective bargaining on wages see section V, and for working conditions see section VII.)

III. THE UNEMPLOYED

Recurring periods of unemployment have been one of our most pressing domestic problems. During the decade of the 1930's no smallest hamlet escaped its effects, and yet with that experience to guide us no substantial agreement has been reached as to how unemployment may be avoided in

---

[1] One of the most valuable recent reports, The Joads in New York, was issued by the Consumers League of New York in 1945. It is not a study of one community, but of several in the farm and canning area of central New York State.

[2] Russell Sage Foundation, New York, 1926.

the future. Since, however, the causes of recurrent periods of unemployment, rooted as they are in the national economic system and situation, are outside the scope of a local community study, we shall confine ourselves here to an attempt to discover the amount of unemployment, and perhaps something of its intangible effects upon the community.

Extent of Unemployment. There has never been in effect in this country any system of registration by which the number of people unemployed can be currently and continuously known. Censuses of unemployment can be, and have been, taken at certain times, but are difficult and expensive, and produce data concerning only one period. Estimates of the number of persons employed and unemployed are made monthly for the nation by the Bureau of the Census by means of its cross-section survey, the Monthly Report of The Labor Force, using as a basis the changing employment status of individuals and families as represented in a carefully controlled national sample. Unemployment insurance claims data, available for states and localities as well as nationally, are useful to show trends in registered unemployment and in the characteristics of those who are unemployed. Claims data can be secured on a local basis. The same is true regarding the characteristics of unemployed persons registered for unemployment insurance benefits. However, as already noted, these data will not yield information on total unemployment until all workers are covered by unemployment insurance through the entire period of their joblessness.

The federal government has from time to time conducted special censuses of unemployment. These naturally represent only the situation at the time the census was taken, and vary in reliability according to the methods employed.[1] If you wish to make a detailed study of unemployment in your community in the depression of the 1930's, the data from these census reports should be consulted and tabulated. They are by no means complete, however, even for that period.

20. What estimates can you secure from local sources (as suggested in the introductory paragraphs of this chapter) as to the current amount of unemployment in your community?

[1] In addition to the data from the Fifteenth Census (Unemployment, vol. 1) there were, for example, two special censuses of unemployment conducted during the 1930's. One, in January, 1931, was made in 19 industrial cities, and appears as the final chapter in the Fifteenth Census, Unemployment, vol. 2. The other, a nationwide inquiry depending upon a voluntary return by unemployed or underemployed people of questionnaires delivered by postal employes, was made in November, 1937, and the returns were published in four volumes under the title Census of Partial Employment, Unemployment, and Occupations: 1937.

The latest available unemployment data are found in the 1940 census report on The Labor Force and periodic reports issued by the Bureau of the Census on the basis of sample reports made to it.

Generally speaking, two groups emerge as being those most seriously affected by unemployment. These are, first, the workers of forty-five and over, many with their vigor and accumulated skills intact, who if they lose their work find it difficult or impossible to get new jobs because of employer preference for younger men, especially in the highly mechanized industries. The second disadvantaged group consists of young people directly out of school or college who enter the labor market with no experience to offer prospective employers.

21. Can you secure any estimates as to the age distribution of the unemployed? What can you learn from employment bureaus or other informed sources concerning employer preferences about the ages of people they hire?

Effects of Unemployment. The *cessation of income* due to unemployment has many evil effects on health, housing, and general standard of living which we have tried elsewhere in this book to touch upon, and to which, so far as possible, we have tried to suggest the application of some measurements from the community standpoint. There remain to be considered, however, apart from financial deprivation, the effects of *involuntary idleness itself* upon the individual affected and upon his family group.[1]

William Hodson, one-time commissioner of welfare for New York City, had these more subtle evils in mind when he spoke of "that neighbor who used to hold his head high. He was up betimes in the morning and off to his job and back at night, complaining joyously of how much work he had to do, and that he could not get it finished. He and his family lived in happiness and self-respect. There is a blight on that household now. This neighbor sleeps late in the morning, his clothes look baggy and old, he shuffles about puttering with odd tasks here and there. The habit of work leaves him, the skill which he had is falling into disuse and he does not like to see and talk with his neighbors any more. The family life is twisted and distorted by the fear of destitution, and hatred born of love and fear destroys the normal relationship between the husband and wife—between the parents and their children. America . . . has never really understood what happened to 30 or 40 million people when the flood of unemployment descended and swept men, women and children into the swollen rivers of despair."

Objective data concerning such human tragedies as these cannot readily be assembled. There are no yardsticks for measuring damage to human personalities and emotional relationships. Subjective judgments of teachers, pastors, medical and court workers, labor leaders, and social workers

---

[1] We suggest that you read at this point a book with a satirical title—Some Folks Won't Work, by Clinch Calkins, Harcourt, Brace and Co., New York, 1930.

who have known many families under the stress of unemployment will probably have to be relied upon for information in this field.

22. What, in their judgment, is the effect of prolonged unemployment upon family relations, particularly upon the status of the jobless person within his own family group?

23. Do unemployed fathers or sons, to their knowledge, leave home in order to avoid being a burden, or to get away from continued blame for idleness?

24. Do unemployed families show a general tendency to withdraw from church and social contacts? Are they more difficult to draw into church and community activities than they formerly were?

25. What changes have these observers noticed in the attitudes and activities of young people who have not been able to find work since leaving school?

26. Do these informants believe that "the unemployed don't want work"?

27. Is there any positive evidence—other than the general impression to that effect—that prolonged unemployment destroys or seriously lessens the worker's special occupational skills; his ability to turn out a full day's work; his desire to secure or retain a job?

Public Works to Relieve Unemployment. Genuine public works are those which draw upon the labor market without reference to the workers' need for relief. In genuine public works the costs are paid from public funds appropriated or borrowed for the purpose, and not from funds allocated to relief. Wages and hours are those current in the community for similar jobs. Public works may be said to be those undertaken to relieve a condition of unemployment which exists in a community. Work, even though carried out by public authorities, primarily directed toward relieving the needs of individual unemployed persons is termed work relief. (See Chapter 14.)

There is no one place where information concerning genuine public works is brought together. These latter generally take the forms of (1) public construction of roads, sewers, bridges, airports, parks, buildings, and the like; (2) maintenance and repair of such publicly constructed facilities.

28. What genuine public works have been constructed in your community during the past ten years?

29. Has your community a shelf of public works in readiness for the next period of unemployment?

30. In which will the costs be borne entirely by your community? In which will the work hinge upon whether state or federal money is available?

31. Has your community taken advantage of federal legislation under which federal funds are available for the advance planning of local public works?

IV. PLACEMENT

There is no single organized channel through which people find jobs. However, recent years have seen a vast expansion of public employment offices which have been increasingly relied upon by both workers and employers. Nevertheless, in securing private employment and public appointive jobs not under civil service, great reliance is still placed on advertisements and word-of-mouth notifications between friends or associates that a job is available, and upon the recommendation or pressure of interested friends of the applicant. Many industrial concerns maintain their own employment departments and certain employers still prefer to "hire at the gate" from among applicants who present themselves, rather than to fill jobs through an organized placement service. The unguided job hunting which workers are thus forced to do is a laborious, hit-or-miss process, attended by repeated rebuffs and discouragements.

The key importance of comprehensive public employment services has gained widespread recognition in recent years, however, as a result of the inauguration of a nationwide system of unemployment compensation administered through the states, together with wartime labor market organization through the United States Employment Service (USES).[1] As a byproduct of the creation of a national unemployment compensation program all communities are now within reach of a public employment office or an itinerant point which undertakes to bring together jobs and qualified workers, thus reducing in part the waste of time and money involved in fruitless job hunting and cross-purpose activities under the traditionally chaotic procedure of the labor market.

The employment services of a community, in addition to the public employment office, may comprise commercial employment bureaus, and privately sponsored nonprofit agencies. In addition, labor unions generally carry on a more or less formal placement function for their members. Some professional organizations, schools, and colleges also attempt to place members or graduates. (For special placement services for the handicapped, see Chapter 10.)

The Public Employment Service. Prior to the close of World War I public employment services were entirely under state and local auspices. In response to wartime pressure from industries, the United States Employment Service was created in 1918, but functioned for only about a year. This experience, together with the principles upon which good employment service must be founded, is discussed in Public Employment Offices: Their Purpose, Structure and Method, by Shelby M. Harrison and Associates.[2]

Early experience was enough to demonstrate the need for federal assist-

[1] See also pp. 74–75.
[2] Russell Sage Foundation, New York, 1924. (Out of print, but generally available in libraries.)

ance and regulation, and agitation of interested groups kept the question alive until, in 1933, an act was passed reorganizing the United States Employment Service and appropriating funds to be allocated to states in aid of their public employment services.[1] Subsequently, under the requirements of the Social Security Act and state unemployment insurance legislation, public employment offices or itinerant service points have been established within reach of every community in the United States.

During the war federal jurisdiction over the USES was shifted first to one agency and then to another. State employment services were temporarily nationalized by Presidential Order following Pearl Harbor, but by act of Congress in 1946 were returned to state operation. Continuing federal responsibility for the USES has now been lodged in the Department of Labor.

32. Where is the public employment office in or nearest to your community? What supervisory and financial relation has the state employment service to it? What was its total budget last year?

33. How is the manager of your local public employment office selected? What have been the training and experience of the present manager?

34. How many persons on the staff are engaged in placement? How are they selected? What were the qualifications and training leading to the appointment of the present staff?

35. Are there any advisory committees in connection with your public employment office? How appointed? What are their functions?

36. Is the office located in publicly owned or rented quarters? Visit it and ascertain whether the rooms are clean, well lighted, well ventilated, and attractive. Are there separate rooms or cubicles to insure privacy during employment interviews? Is there adequate seating space in the waiting rooms? Are there separate facilities for workers of different occupations?

37. Does the employment service place workers of all types including professional workers? What separate divisions are there for placing different types of workers?

38. What special provision is made for vocational counseling and placement of juveniles and other inexperienced persons? Of handicapped persons and those who have to change their occupations and industries?

39. Are employment interviews by appointment? Do interviewers specialize in related groups of occupations? Secure a copy of the card used in registering applicants. What information does it call for?

40. What does the employment service do to interpret its functions to the community? To interpret to employers the kinds of work that can successfully be done by handicapped workers, women, Negro workers, or others who may experience particular difficulty in securing employment?

[1] For detailed discussion of this move see Public Employment Service in the United States, by Raymond C. Atkinson and others, Public Administration Service, Chicago, 1938.

Information will be available for your state as a whole about numbers of persons registered, but you may not be able to secure all the detailed data you would like for your own community. Effort should be made, however, to secure the number of calls from employers, number of registrants referred to fill calls, and the number of placements made.

41. Can the public employment office tell you how many different persons were registered last year in your community as wanting jobs? How many men, women, twenty-one to forty-four, forty-five and over, by race? How many boys, girls, under twenty-one, by race?

42. How many are on its "live register" at present, in these same classifications? How many of these are unemployed? How many are employed, but looking for other jobs? How do these numbers compare with those for a year ago?

43. Under what circumstances are registrations refused, canceled, because of unemployability?

44. Are medical examinations demanded or procured for any registrants?

45. Are persons requiring medical care to fit them for employment referred to appropriate medical or social agencies?

46. What information does the public employment service secure from employers about the jobs they wish to fill? What is done to verify claims of applicants that they possess certain skills? Are applicants for any types of employment screened for possible police or court records? How?

47. How many calls for workers did the public employment office receive last year? Can you secure any estimate of the proportion of vacancies which employers sought to fill through the public employment service?

48. How many persons were referred to employers in answer to these calls? What method is followed in selecting registrants for referral to employers? Does your employment service now have requests to refer more workers than are available? Why? What is done to assure referral of qualified Negroes (or other minority group workers) on the same basis as other qualified workers?

49. How many placements were made last year (a) in private employment, (b) in public employment other than public works, (c) on public works, (d) in work-relief jobs?

50. Does the public employment service notify other placement agencies of jobs it can not fill? What agencies? The public employment service in other communities?

51. Of placements made last year, how many when made were presumed to be permanent? How many were known to be temporary?

52. Among private placements made, what types of jobs predominated?

53. Of persons placed, how many boys, girls, by race, under twenty-one? Men, women, by race, twenty-one to forty-four, forty-five and over?

54. How many members of the staff, if any, are assigned to make contacts with employers in the effort to find vacancies or place individuals with special skills? If none is so assigned, what portion of the time of the staff is spent in making field contacts? How many calls made last year upon employers?

55. If public works or work-relief programs are being carried on in your community, is the public employment service responsible for placement of

workers? Is there any means of maintaining liaison between the employment service and the other public agencies concerned? Are representatives of one agency stationed in the offices of the other?

56. What are the arrangements for notifying the agencies responsible for administering work relief or public welfare when their clients register or re-register with the employment service? When they are placed in jobs? When they are offered and refuse a job?

57. To what extent is the public employment office responsible for administering or co-operating in the administration of unemployment insurance? Is unemployment insurance administered in the same quarters and with the same staff as is the placement service?

58. What co-operative relations does the public employment service maintain with the placement services of labor unions, noncommercial placement agencies?

59. Has the public employment office a department of statistics and research? Does it issue information to the public at regular intervals? Through what channels? Has it made any special studies of employment problems? Describe.

Other Employment Services. Private nonprofit employment agencies generally serve some particular age or membership group. Agencies which give social service to families and individuals quite generally find jobs occasionally for their clients, but this is part of the informal job finding which is continually going on.

60. What schools and agencies in your community conduct nonprofit employment services? For each ascertain auspices, source of support, whether fees are charged to employers, to registrants, amount of fee, eligibility requirements for service, number of present registrants, number of calls received last year, number of temporary, permanent, positions filled.

Commercial employment agencies differ widely in their standards. Those placing professional people (e.g., teachers, nurses) serve needs in their special fields, which a general public agency, at least at present, could probably not do so well. Many of those placing common labor and domestic servants are managed ethically and possess the confidence of employers and registrants, but compete directly with the public employment service. Others in this group may be no better than rackets, charging exorbitant fees, placing workers at substandard wages, and conniving with employers to defraud them.

61. How many commercial employment agencies in your community place workers (a) in professional fields, (b) in common labor and domestic service?

62. What laws regulate fee-charging employment agencies in your state? Must all fee-charging agencies be licensed? By what agency?

63. How frequently is their work inspected? By a state or local agency? Have any licenses to employment agencies in your community been revoked within the past five years?

V. WORKERS' ORGANIZATIONS

The right of employers to organize into associations to promote their own interest has never been questioned in this country. Also, our courts and public opinion have generally upheld the theoretical right of workers to organize, but for many years the efforts of unions to develop and pursue their normal functions of improving work conditions were seriously impeded. The public has sometimes failed to see, especially when strikes interfere with public convenience, that labor's efforts to improve wages and working conditions were as logical and defensible as an employer's or farmer's right not to produce and sell goods below what he considers a fair return for his efforts. Unions were also handicapped by injunctions and other court and police actions, as well as opposition of employers who were in a stronger political and financial position than unions.

Misuse of injunctions and the privilege of employers to require their employes not to join unions were made illegal in 1932 by the Norris-LaGuardia Act. Inequality in bargaining relations was legally remedied in 1935 with the passage of the National Labor Relations Act which not only gave workers a right to organize but made it illegal for employers to interfere with that right. The act established the National Labor Relations Board which holds elections among employes to determine which union, if any, they wish to have represent them; also it protects employes from unfair labor practices by employers.

With these legal protections, unions have been able to expand greatly, both in membership and influence. In 1946 about 14,000,000 workers belonged to labor unions. More than half of all employes in private industry were working under agreements negotiated by unions and employers. In some of the most important industries, such as railroads, steel, automobile, mining, and building construction, practically all employes were working under collective bargaining contracts.

As significant as these accomplishments are, labor unions face many serious problems both in their relations with employers and among themselves. Rivalry between different unions and jurisdictional disputes are not only detrimental to the unions concerned, but frequently work a hardship on employers and the general public. There is also the problem of internal union administration—how to preserve maximum democracy within the union and at the same time have strong, effective leadership. The question of how much and in what way unions shall participate in local and national politics is also an important issue. Within the factory or work place there is the unresolved question of what matters shall be reserved for employer control alone, and what are subject to joint determination by the employer and union.

Some recently published books which will throw light on the history, aims, and activities of organized labor are listed below.[1]

64. Is there in your community a federation (sometimes called central labor union) of craft organizations which are members of the American Federation of Labor? How many locals belong to it? Total membership claimed?

65. Has the Congress of Industrial Organizations a central committee in your community? How many locals in its membership? Total membership claimed?

66. How many of the principal industries of your community operate on the closed shop principle, i.e., employ only union members, with agreements as to wages, hours, and conditions of labor?

67. In what other important industries have employers negotiated agreements with unions as to wages, hours, and conditions of labor for union members? In what important industries have employers refused to negotiate with or recognize labor unions?

68. Have elections under the auspices of the National Labor Relations Board been held in any industry in your community during the past several years? With what result?

69. What percentage of the workers in open shops do the labor unions claim organized?

70. Of union members in your community how many are women? Are Negroes eligible for union membership in all unions? How many Negroes are members?

71. What are the principal objectives which organized labor is seeking to obtain in your community, as stated to you by their representatives? What principal grievances do they express?

72. What unions are able to control placements in their trades? What placement machinery have they set up?

73. What unions control entrance into the trade through apprenticeship? Do any unions provide vocational education?

74. Is there a labor college, labor forum, in your community? Auspices, source of support, attendance claimed, type of education offered? (See page 161.)

75. What labor unions provide sickness, death, unemployment benefits for their members? Describe. Do they render health, employment, or other services to members?

76. Are dues remitted for unemployed members? For how long a period?

77. How many strikes took place in your community during the past two years? What unions, what employers, were involved? What were the points at issue? Duration? Number of workers involved?

[1] American Labor, by Herbert Harris, Yale University Press, New Haven, 1939; Union Rights and Union Duties, by Joel I. Seidman, Harcourt, Brace and Co., New York, 1943; Trends in Collective Bargaining, by Samuel T. Williamson and Herbert Harris, Twentieth Century Fund, New York, 1945; and American Labor Unions: What They Are and How They Work, by Florence Peterson, Harper and Bros., New York, 1945.

78. What gains are claimed, what losses admitted by unions? By employers?

79. What machinery is available in your community for arbitration of labor disputes? Are there arbitration boards for particular industries? How many strikes were settled by arbitration? In how many instances was it refused (a) by employers, (b) by organized labor? For what stated reasons?

80. Were any injunctions issued by the courts in connection with strikes?

81. Were any labor disputes attended by violence? Describe. Were the United States Army, state militia, or state police called in during any strikes?

82. What part do unions play in the broader life of your community? Do they co-operate in your community chest drive? In other social welfare activities? Are they active in politics? In other community activities?

VI. PERSONNEL ADMINISTRATION

Personnel administration is that phase of management which is concerned with the effective use of human beings in an organized enterprise—business, governmental, educational, or social.[1] It deals with the human relationships within the organization—the relationships between the worker and management, between the worker and his job, and between the worker and his fellow workers. By centering attention on the worker's well-being, morale, and capacity to produce, it increases the effectiveness of management.

Professional workers in this field may act in an advisory capacity to management in formulation of policies with respect to employes or may themselves have responsibility for carrying out personnel policies. To attain these ends they must be familiar with the basic operations and purpose of their organization; they must provide for the full development of employes' interests and capacities, and they must utilize special methods and procedures that make the personnel aspect of management more precise and measurable.

In industry and government they are generally concerned with the staffing of operating departments and agencies with competent, trained personnel and are thus responsible for the development of policies affecting placement, training, transfer, discipline, rate setting, wage payment plans, counseling, grievances, health and safety, labor relations, compliance with federal and state laws, separations, and so forth.

Personnel administration is concerned with procedures affecting employes both during and outside of working hours; with formulation of a harmonious relationship between management and workers. In industry this field is usually designated as union relations or labor relations. Elements in-

[1] For a summary description see "The Profession of Personnel Administration," by the National Roster of Scientific and Specialized Personnel, in the Personnel Journal, January, 1946, which has been heavily drawn upon in the preparation of this section. For a longer treatment of the subject see Human Relations in Industry, by Burleigh B. Gardner, Richard D. Irwin, Chicago, 1945.

volved are collective bargaining with employe representatives; arranging for mediation, conciliation, and arbitration of disputes between management and labor; devising procedures for hearing and settling grievances; and maintenance of discipline.

Personnel workers are concerned too with discovering and utilizing sources of labor; devising techniques for attracting applicants; setting up requirements for various positions; preparation of tests to determine intelligence levels, achievement, and aptitude. Placement, which means finding the right job for the right man, is another responsibility of personnel workers. The placement of the physically handicapped is a specialized aspect of this activity.

Training is yet another function of personnel administration which seeks to cultivate ability, interest, and goodwill among employes through an effective leadership and improved on-the-job instruction. Further responsibilities include the development of pay plans which frequently involve negotiations with union officials; study of reasons why employes are separated from service; and the attempt to effect adjustments necessary to retain workers requesting releases.

83. What principal private or public employers in your community emphasize personnel administration? What has been accomplished? Is there an association of personnel managers in your community? How many members has it? By what industrial and mercantile firms are they employed?

A primary concern of personnel workers is with the working environment and the maintenance of adequate standards of health and safety of employes. The goals here are to provide adequate medical and nursing facilities; optimal lighting and ventilating conditions; a minimum of unnecessary noise; clean, pleasant surroundings; first-aid facilities; and protection of workers against accidents.

84. In what industrial establishments is an active safety campaign carried on (more, that is, than the state labor law demands)?

85. What plants have a first-aid room where minor as well as major injuries can receive prompt treatment?

86. What firms in your community make provision for periodic medical examinations of employes? What firms employ physicians, nurses, to give medical or nursing care to employes and their families? Upon what terms?

87. What firms provide hospital facilities, under group insurance plans or otherwise, for their workers? Under what circumstances?

88. Are medical services available to workers during periods of layoff?

89. What is the attitude of organized labor in your community toward such programs?

There are many other forms of industrial welfare programs which, when in operation, are part of the varied responsibilities of personnel management. These may comprise counseling, maintaining centers for recreation and education at an employer's expense, providing low-cost housing near the plant, sharing profits through various bonus or insurance plans, organizing credit unions, and so on. Workers sometimes contend, however, that employers' welfare schemes are endeavors to avoid paying wages high enough to permit individual employes to provide these services for themselves, or so to control the living conditions of employes that organization will be discouraged.

90. What firms in your community have supervised recreational or educational programs for their employes? Buildings devoted to social, recreational, and educational purposes?

91. What employers provide means for their employes to buy goods at less than retail prices, either through a company store or otherwise? What employers provide low-cost housing in company-owned dwellings? Sell houses to their employes on easy terms?

92. What employers provide regular vacations for manual workers as well as for clerical and administrative personnel? For how long a period? With or without pay?

93. What employers offer their employes a guaranteed number of weeks' work per year, or guaranteed annual income? A bonus dependent on company earnings? Dismissal pay (bonus paid on dismissal)?

94. What employers have set up some form of social insurance paying (a) sickness or death benefits, (b) unemployment benefits, (c) old-age benefits? Is part of the premiums deducted from wages? What part? What has been the effect on company insurance plans of the passage of the federal Social Security Act? When employes leave, go on strike, or are laid off or discharged, what becomes of the equities they have built up in the form of insurance or property?

95. Do any employers provide for employes a counseling service? What employers engage, or secure from community agencies, social workers or other professional personnel for the administration of industrial welfare measures? Are arrangements made for referring to the appropriate community agencies those workers having special social or health problems?

96. Are employes given any voice in the control of industrial welfare measures established for their benefit?

VII. GOVERNMENTAL SAFEGUARDS

This section of the inquiry will take you into the area of state and national legislation for the protection of workers, and the means of local enforcement of these laws. The State Department of Labor is usually the body responsible for enforcing statutes relating to conditions of employment, hours, and wages. A standard text on this subject is Principles of Labor Legislation, by John R. Commons and John B. Andrews.[1]

[1] Harper and Bros., 4th rev. ed., New York, 1936.

97. Read the law creating your State Department of Labor and defining its duties. Is the department governed by a board? How appointed? Does the board appoint the administrator? Is he appointed directly by the governor? Is he appointed under a civil service merit system? What are the experience and training of the present administrator?

98. Into what divisions is the work of the State Department of Labor divided?

99. How many inspectors on the staff? How chosen? What are the training and experience of the inspector (s) working in your community?

Safety and Sanitation

100. What does your law prescribe as to safety in places of employment? In regard to sanitation? What penalties does it lay upon employers who violate these provisions?

101. How many violations of regulations relating to safety and sanitation were reported in places of employment in your community last year? How many were corrected without resort to punishment under the law? In how many instances were penalties enforced?

102. Try to secure information from state or local sources about industrial accident rates in your community over a period of years. Is there evidence to show that they have been materially reduced?

103. What changes were sought in the law or its administration regarding safety and sanitation at the last session of your state legislature? What groups supported, opposed, this legislation? What changes in the law were enacted?

Hours of Labor

104. What are the provisions of your law in regard to number of hours of labor per day, week, which employers may demand of employes: (a) children, (b) women, (c) men? Are any industries excepted? Which? What are the penalties for violations?

105. How many violations of the labor law were corrected without resort to penalties in your community last year? In how many cases were penalties imposed upon employers?

106. If your state does not now have a law regulating hours of labor for children, women, men, has there been recent agitation for one? Has a bill been before your legislature? What groups supported, opposed it? What were the lines of argument advanced by each side?

Wages

107. Is there a minimum wage law in your state? To what classes of workers does it apply? What occupations are excepted? What scale of minimum wages is prescribed?

108. Has your state revised its minimum wage rates since 1940? Have qualified agencies in your community made a study of how much it costs to maintain a single person or family in health? How does the present minimum wage scale compare with the cost of a minimum standard of living in your community?

109. If your state does not now have a minimum wage law, has there been recent agitation for one? Has a bill been before your legislature? What groups supported, opposed it? What was the line of argument advanced by each side?

110. Is extra compensation for overtime prescribed in your law? How much, and for what classes and occupations?

111. Has your state a mechanics' lien law? Any other law which provides (a) that wages must be paid in legal tender, (b) that wages must be paid at regular intervals (weekly, bi-weekly), (c) that wages constitute a prior lien on income of employers? How are these provisions enforced in practice? Does your State Department of Labor have a bureau for the collection of wages due individual workers?

Governmental agencies especially interested in working conditions of women and children are the Women's Bureau, the Wage and Hour Division, both of the United States Department of Labor, and the Children's Bureau of the Federal Security Agency. State departments of labor also often have special bureaus for women and children in industry. Nongovernmental agencies particularly interested in these fields are the National Women's Trade Union League of America, the National League of Women Voters, and the National Child Labor Committee.[1] The National Consumers' League has branches in nine states. If your state has a consumers' league it will be a valuable nonofficial source of information about hours, wages, and conditions of industry, particularly as they affect the employment of women and children.

Protection of Working Women. For a brief discussion of changes affecting women workers, obtain a copy of Patterns of Women in Industry, by Frieda S. Miller.[2]

112. Has your state an equal pay law for women? To what industries does it apply? How is it enforced? If there is no law, has a bill been introduced in the legislature? What are the arguments advanced by supporters, opponents?

113. Is the labor of women prohibited in certain occupations considered dangerous to their health? What occupations? Are there restrictions upon night work by women? Describe. Are there any provisions in your labor law governing work by women during pregnancy? Describe.

114. What other types of women's laws are there in your state that would protect health of workers? Are there laws requiring rest periods? Lunch periods? Is seating for women workers required?

Protection of Working Children. References which will help you in studying the protection of working children include two publications of the Children's Bureau: Why Child Labor Laws,[3] and Information Kit: 16-Year Minimum Age for Employment.[4] Two pamphlets published by the National Child Labor Committee will also be useful: The Changing Picture of

---

[1] For addresses see List of Agencies, p. 251.
[2] U.S. Women's Bureau, Washington, 1945.
[3] Publication 313, Government Printing Office, 1945.
[4] Government Printing Office, 1946.

Child Labor, by Gertrude F. Zimand,[1] and The Case for Sixteen Year Employment Laws.[2]

115. Below what age may children not be gainfully employed in your state during school hours? Outside of school hours?

116. Between what ages must a minor obtain a permit in order to take a job? What agency issues these permits? Visit this office and find out what procedure is followed to establish legality of proposed employment, proof of age, completion of required school grade, physical fitness for employment, parental consent. How long does it take a child to secure a work permit?

117. How many full-time working permits were issued last year to children under sixteen? To minors of sixteen and seventeen? How many were denied? How many were issued for part-time or vacation work? Has there been an increase or decrease over the number issued last year?

118. How many cases were reported of children working illegally last year? How many involved violation of age provisions? Hours? Night work? Hazardous employment work permits? What action was taken in these cases?

119. Does your law prohibit employment of minors in dangerous occupations? Which ones? Below what age?

120. Are there special provisions governing public stage performances by children? Street trades? Agriculture? Describe. What agency is responsible for their enforcement?

121. What other provisions limit daily and weekly hours for minors under sixteen? Under eighteen? Night work?

122. Are minors paid extra compensation if they are injured while illegally employed? In case of permanent disability to minors is compensation based on probable future earning capacity if injury had not occurred?

123. Has there been recent agitation for raising the standards of your child labor and school attendance laws? Have bills been presented to your legislature? What groups supported, opposed them? What were the arguments advanced by both sides?

VIII. SOCIAL INSURANCE

Compensation for Industrial Injury. By 1946 laws had been passed in all but one state, providing compensation according to definite scales for workers injured during the course of their employment. About two-thirds of the states also have laws providing compensation for some or all occupational diseases. However, only about half the workers in the United States are covered by workmen's compensation laws. Workmen's compensation was the first form of social insurance established in this country and still remains the only form of health insurance provided by law for any considerable number of American workers. Nevertheless, workmen's compensation is today the stepchild of American social assistance schemes, being the only one in which the federal government assumes no financial or

[1] New York, 1944.   [2] Publication no. 392, New York, 1945.

administrative responsibility. A guide that will prove particularly helpful to you at this stage of your study is the pamphlet How Good Is Your Workmen's Compensation Law?, issued by the United States Department of Labor.[1]

124. By what agency is your state workmen's compensation law administered? Is the act compulsory upon employers? What occupations are excepted? Are domestic workers included? How does the number of workers covered compare with the numbers covered by your state unemployment compensation scheme? What legal process is open under the laws of your state to injured employes in noninsured occupations?

125. Is a state insurance fund established? What options are allowed employers as among (a) insurance under the state fund, (b) insurance by private carriers, (c) self-insurance? Are employes required to contribute toward their workmen's compensation insurance?

126. What regulations govern reporting of industrial accidents? What waiting period is introduced between date of accident and date payments may begin? If occupational diseases are included, what diseases are compensable?

127. Are benefits limited to cash benefits or is medical care directly provided? By whom? For how long? Are there any limitations on the duration or cost of medical care provided?

128. What does the law specify as to maximum payments, minimum payments, duration of payments for death, total permanent disability, partial permanent disability, total temporary disability, partial temporary disability?

129. What is the relation of compensation to earnings? How do benefits compare with unemployment compensation benefits in your state?

130. Under what conditions may lump-sum compensation be awarded?

131. What is the machinery in your community for administering workmen's compensation?

132. How many claims for compensation were presented last year? How many granted? How many disallowed? For what causes?

133. What provision exists for appeal in case the worker is dissatisfied with the award?

134. What measures are suggested in your state for the improvement of your workmen's compensation program? Has a bill been before your legislature? What groups supported, opposed it? What were the lines of argument advanced by each side?

Unemployment Compensation. The Social Security Act[2] created a method by which states could be assisted in the operation of state plans for unemployment insurance, and by which taxes were to be collected from employers in certain occupations and paid into the unemployment trust fund of the

[1] Division of Labor Standards, Bulletin no. 70, Government Printing Office, Washington, 1944.

[2] A convenient form in which to study the Social Security Act is the Compilation of the Social Security Laws, issued by the Social Security Administration for reference purposes and revised from time to time as new legislation is enacted.

United States Treasury. By January 1, 1938, all states had unemployment insurance plans approved by the Social Security Board. Read *Unemployment Insurance and You*, an informational leaflet issued by the Social Security Board.[1] See also the regular monthly section on this subject in the *Social Security Bulletin*.[2]

135. What state agency is charged with the operation of unemployment compensation? Is this agency administered by a commission or board which includes representatives of employers, workers, and the public?

136. Read your state unemployment insurance law, and determine what groups of workers are not covered. Which of the excluded groups are important in your community? What proportion of the gainfully employed workers in your state are protected by the law?

137. Does your state law contain experience-rating provisions allowing lower tax rates to some employers on the basis of unemployment experience? Are benefits paid to specific workers used to measure an employer's unemployment experience?

138. How is the weekly benefit amount determined? What minimum and maximum amounts are provided? How does the maximum compare with that of neighboring states?

139. How is duration of benefit fixed? What is the maximum number of weeks during which benefit may be drawn? The minimum number of weeks? How does the number of workers who exhaust their benefit rights compare with the number in neighboring states?

140. For what causes may insured persons be disqualified or lose their right to benefit under the act? Describe.

141. Is your local unemployment compensation office operating on a full-time basis?[3]

142. How many persons received payments during the past year, or other period for which figures can be secured? Total amount of payments? The average weekly benefit paid? The average duration of payment?

143. What is the procedure for handling complaints and appeals from decisions of unemployment insurance officials in your community?

144. What changes in the unemployment insurance law or its administration are being advocated in your state?

(See page 70 for private schemes for unemployment insurance.)

Old-Age and Survivors Insurance. In addition to providing for federal grants for old-age assistance (see pages 182–183) the 1935 Social Security Act set up a new system of federal old-age insurance benefits. The original act provided only for monthly benefits to insured employes at age sixty-five, a lump sum to those not insured at that age, or a lump-sum payment to their survivors. In 1939 the program was expanded to include dependents

[1] I.S.C. 22, Government Printing Office, Washington, 1945.
[2] Government Printing Office.
[3] Since the office is also the local office of the U.S. Employment Service, see also questions on p. 64.

and survivors benefits. Benefits were made payable in 1940. Conditions of eligibility and methods of payment are set forth in federal law.

Old-age and survivors benefits are unlike old-age assistance in that:

(1) They are based on contributions paid into the insurance fund by the worker and his employers in covered employment.

(2) The amount of benefit is determined by the average monthly wages of the employe and by the length of his employment.

(3) The benefits are paid on application when a fully insured individual attains age sixty-five, without regard to his income (except wages of more than $14.99 a month earned in covered employment) or resources, and need is not a factor in establishing eligibility.

In general, a person is fully insured if he has spent at least one-half of the time after 1936 (or after his twenty-first birthday, if that is later—and before he reaches age sixty-five or dies, or at least ten years) in employment covered under old-age and survivors insurance.

(4) Those employed in certain occupations stated in the Act are not insurable, and will not be eligible to receive benefits at age sixty-five unless the law is amended.

(5) State and local governments participate in no way in the administration of old-age insurance, and all dealings are directly with the United States Department of the Treasury and the Social Security Administration.

145. From the office of the Social Security Administration in your community, learn how many retired workers are on the primary benefit rolls. Average amount? How does this compare with average old-age assistance grants in your community? (See page 190.)

Payment of primary benefit ceases with the death of the insured person.

146. What is the method of determining that beneficiaries are still alive?

The amended act provides monthly benefits to the following survivors of a "fully insured" worker: (1) his unmarried children under sixteen or under eighteen if still in school; (2) his widow of any age while she has children in her care who are entitled to benefits; (3) his widow when she reaches the age of sixty-five; (4) his dependent parents, if the worker leaves neither children nor widow. For children under eighteen and widows with such children in their care, benefits are also payable if the worker was only "currently insured." He is "currently insured" if he worked in a covered job approximately half of the last three years of his life.

Where monthly survivors benefits are not payable, lump-sum death payments are made to certain relatives, or to others who have paid the funeral expenses. Details of the old-age and survivors insurance program are set forth in the following pamphlets obtainable from the Social Security Administration: Federal Old-Age and Survivors Insurance for Workers and Their Families,[1] and Social Security—A Brief Explanation of the Social Security Act.[2]

147. To how many of the following, and in what average amounts, are supplementary benefits being paid:

> Wives of retired workers who are receiving benefits?
> Children of retired workers who are receiving benefits?
> Widows of persons who died fully or currently insured?
> Children of persons who died fully or currently insured?
> Parents of persons who died fully insured?

148. How do average benefit payments to children compare with average aid to dependent children grants in your community? (See page 190.)

149. During the past year, how many lump-sum benefits were paid? Average amount?

150. What is the method of dealing with complaints and grievances concerning old-age insurance and survivors benefits?

Employes of railroads are not eligible for old-age benefits under the Social Security Act; but a separate scheme has been set up for them under the federal Railroad Retirement Act, passed in 1937. It is improbable that you can secure information regarding the number of employes in your community benefiting under the Railroad Retirement Act unless it can be secured from the offices of individual railroad companies.

(For retirement plans of private employers, see page 70.)

[1] I.S.C. 35, Government Printing Office, Washington, 1945.
[2] I.S.C. 1, Government Printing Office, 1945.

7. HOUSING, PLANNING, AND ZONING

DESPITE the advances made within our generation in the mechanical arts pertaining to housing, a shockingly large proportion of our population are compelled by economic necessity to live in substandard quarters. From the dingy tenement of the crowded city to the squatter shack of the open plain, a wide variety of improper and inadequate housing exists. The fact that most of it is occupied should not be taken as proof of the preference of the tenant for that kind of shelter, but rather as evidence of his necessity for accepting it in the absence of better facilities at a price that he can afford to pay.

Housing is a matter of public concern because of its social implications. It has long been noted that evils such as ill-health and juvenile delinquency seem to form an interrelated nexus with bad and crowded housing. In the interest of the people whose lives are thus affected, governments have found it necessary to zone and plan urban communities, restricting certain areas to residential use, others to purposes of recreation, and still others to the uses of industry and trade. Through building codes and by specific order, government has done much to protect society from the most serious hazards of poor housing, notably in the field of safety and sanitation. However, until recently, it has accomplished little correction of faults of overcrowding, obsolescence, disrepair, and squalor. Frequently there exists legal authority to attack and remove nuisances, but until recently government has had little power, and has made small attempt to adopt a positive or constructive policy. The Wagner-Ellender-Taft General Housing Act, which, despite the President's approval, has not been acted upon,[1] is intended to establish an adequate base under a balanced program of public and private housing.

Because of the lack of effective positive measures, there are to be found in every community dwellings which violated no law when they were erected, but which, judged by modern standards, are entirely inadequate, and which could not be erected under any modern building code. Changes in housing standards have been so rapid that some dwellings which were considered

---

[1] As of the adjournment of the 79th Congress.

models in their time have become part of the slums of today. Under the housing patterns which are now characteristic of our communities, the mistakes and the discards of the well-to-do in one generation become the outmoded, poorly adapted, and overcrowded homes of the poor in the next. It was estimated in 1946 that some 35 per cent of urban housing was below a minimum health and safety standard. According to the National Committee on Housing,[1] the rural housing situation was even more critical, with two-thirds of the farm homes in need of major repairs. Except for some public housing developments of the 1930's, new housing has been made available only for the financial middle and upper classes. For the lowest income groups, even after years of agitation for it, new housing has not been provided by private capital because anticipated financial returns from such investments do not tempt private investors. Although government, at the price of having its workers decently housed, can provide housing either at small profits or no profits at all—inasmuch as possible deficits may, in the public interest, be made up from tax funds—this country has been slow to embark upon the sort of public housing program which has long been accepted abroad.

While the need for better housing has been apparent for several decades, the postwar years confront us with a very critical situation. After approximately fifteen years of deficit housing activity, we now have not only the needs created by the normal rate of new family formation but also by the increased marriage rate among servicemen and veterans, plus the rapid growth of most urban centers. In 1946 it was estimated that the United States urgently needed about five million new homes for returned veterans, former war workers, and citizens in general. To meet our continuing obligations to veterans and others in need of housing, each community should tackle not only its acute housing needs but should also make long-range plans. An increasing number of cities and towns are establishing housing committees. Many of these are assisted by local expediters employed by the National Housing Agency.[1] These committees serve as a channel through which the Agency assists communities.

Questions suggested for this section[2] of the study do not require any such impracticable step as a house-to-house canvass. However, it would be advisable if you who are responsible for this portion of the study could make personal trips on foot through the various residential areas of the community in order to become familiar with general conditions. As you make this tour of inspection consider how many residential sections there are that you would

[1] For address see List of Agencies, p. 251.
[2] See also section on Home Ownership, in Chapter 15.

enjoy showing an out-of-town visitor, and how many sections (such as row house districts, "shanty towns," slum areas) you would prefer visitors not to see.

Part of the data required for this study may be secured from public agencies concerned with housing, sanitation, and taxation. In your community, for example, there may be a local housing authority or local office of the National Housing Agency or the Federal Housing Administration.[1] Social agencies, public or private, whose workers visit the humbler homes in your community can give valuable descriptive and illustrative information. Many communities have some private agency or group actively engaged in the promotion of better housing. This may be an independent agency or a unit of some other agency, such as a council of social agencies. If such a group exists in your community, it will probably be your best source of information about both state and local conditions and housing programs. A number of national organizations promote public interest in better housing, such as the National Association of Housing Officials, the National Public Housing Conference, and the National Committee on Housing.[1] In 1945 the Committee on the Hygiene of Housing of the American Public Health Association published a guide that would be useful to any community attempting to appraise its own housing.[2]

Detailed information on housing conditions in all cities and incorporated places of 1,000 inhabitants or more is to be found in the reports of the Bureau of the Census on housing.[3] If your community was one of the 64 cities included in the Real Property Inventory issued by the United States Department of Commerce in 1934,[4] it might be used at least to check more recent information and to indicate changes since that study was made.

In suggesting materials to be read as preparation for this part of your study, the widely varying views of experts in the field of housing have to be kept in mind. One of the most comprehensive recent volumes is American Housing: Problems and Prospects, by Miles L. Colean.[5] Another recent and useful volume is A Million Homes a Year, by Dorothy Rosenman.[6]

---

[1] For addresses see List of Agencies, p. 251.
[2] An Appraisal Method for Measuring the Quality of Housing: A Yardstick for Health Officers, Housing Officials and Planners. New York.
[3] Sixteenth Census, Housing. Government Printing Office, Washington, 1943. Data include total number of dwelling units, color of inhabitants, number of persons per room, state of repair, plumbing equipment, and rental values.
[4] Government Printing Office.
[5] Twentieth Century Fund, New York, 1944. A popular pamphlet has been based on this survey: Houses for Tomorrow, by Thomas R. Carskadon, Pamphlet no. 96, Public Affairs Committee, Inc., New York, 1944.
[6] Harcourt, Brace and Co., New York, 1945.

I. PUBLIC HOUSING

Residential construction in the United States has traditionally been a field which private capital and enterprise have occupied largely to the exclusion of public effort.

Two opposing schools of thought exist on the question of public versus private housing. Whichever view may be correct, there can be little doubt that private enterprise has so far failed to provide adequate housing for low-income groups. This fact has recently led the federal government to undertake a public housing program. To understand current public housing measures it is suggested that the following be read: The Seven Myths of Housing, by Nathan Straus,[1] and Modern Housing, by Catherine Bauer.[2] A striking report, The Social Effects of Public Housing, was made by the Housing Authority of the City of Newark, New Jersey, in 1946.[3]

Federal and state laws, passed only within recent years, have paved the way for governmental action toward better housing, whether the local problem is one of slum clearance, demolition of dangerous firetraps, rehabilitation of blighted areas, or construction of new low-cost single or multiple dwellings. To facilitate public housing programs, Congress enacted the United States Housing Act of 1937, and it is still the basic social legislation in American housing. This Act provides for a permanent public housing program, with loans and subsidies from the federal government. Planning, construction, ownership, and operation are all under local agencies which must meet federal government standards as to costs, wages of building labor, rents, and selection of tenants.

If there are in your community or its vicinity any public housing projects a visit and inspection would undoubtedly repay you.[4]

1. Does your state have enabling legislation to permit local governmental units to construct, maintain, or sell housing constructed at public expense? To co-operate with the appropriate federal housing authorities?

2. Is there a public housing authority or comparable agency in your community authorized to construct or operate public housing? To co-operate with any other governmental agency toward these ends?

3. Has the housing authority used the right of eminent domain to procure sites for public housing projects? Has it the right to acquire or secure long-term options on neighboring tracts? Has the right been used?

4. Have condemnation proceedings been used to provide land for public housing projects?

5. How are appraisals for condemnation made on (a) land, (b) existing dwell-

[1] Alfred A. Knopf, New York, 2d ed., 1945.
[2] Houghton Mifflin Co., Boston, 1934.   [3] This study was conducted by Jay Rumney.
[4] Read Where Housing and Welfare Meet, by the National Association of Housing Officials, Chicago, 1940.

ings in good condition, (c) existing dwellings adjudged unfit for human habitation, (d) nonresidential buildings?

6. Has the public housing authority or other governmental agency constructed any dwellings in your community? Has it leased or otherwise gained control of housing projects? How many units? Temporary or permanent? How many units of one room? Two, three, four, or five rooms? What plans are being made for future construction of public housing in your community?

7. From what sources are funds secured to provide housing? Federal? State? Local?

8. What is the average rental per room? Is income from rentals sufficient to meet costs of operation of these public housing enterprises? If not, from what funds are deficits met?

9. Who is eligible to rent or purchase housing constructed at public expense? What is the method of selecting tenants or purchasers? What special right have veterans? Workers in particular industries? Others?

10. What provision is made for play space outdoors and indoors? How near are the buildings to public schools? Transportation facilities? Parks? Playfields? Churches?

11. What special facilities are integral parts of your public housing projects? Child health stations? Central laundries? Supervised play groups? Preschool day care centers? Adult education forums? Branch libraries? Recreation rooms for adults? How are these services financed and managed?

A large housing project is a community within a community. The tenants must learn to live together and, in behalf of their communal interests, work together. For this reason, the housing manager should have not only practical training and experience in building management, but should have a social point of view and some background in community leadership. A new profession combining these qualifications has been emerging during the past decade. Also, social workers or other professional personnel are sometimes employed to help promote the well-being of residents in public housing units.

12. What are the qualifications of the managers of your public housing projects? Of other professional personnel? Are they selected under the civil service merit system? If not, how selected?

II. GOVERNMENTAL AID TO PRIVATE HOUSING

This section is meant to apply only to large-scale commercial or limited-dividend housing projects. Measures for financing the individual home-owner will be taken up in Chapter 15, together with other aspects of family credit and income management.

Authorities agree that the most difficult problem to solve in connection with housing is that of finance. High interest rates on capital, short amortization periods, low appraisals of land and buildings as a basis for first mortgage loans, costly fees for search of title and negotiation of the loan, have all militated against low-cost housing under even the most favorable conditions of construction costs, land values, and taxation, to say nothing of the problems involved when land values are high or land difficult to procure.

Governmental aid of many forms has been developed to combat these difficulties. It may take the form of (a) loans, (b) tax exemption, (c) mortgage insurance, (d) exercise of the right of eminent domain or condemnation in acquiring property, or (e) outright subsidy in the form of clearing sites, subsidies for building or maintenance. These types of assistance are sometimes available for new construction, or for the repair and rehabilitation of property which has not outlived its usefulness and social value.

13. Have public authorities in your community exercised the right of eminent domain or condemnation proceedings to secure land for private housing enterprises? Under what circumstances?

14. Are limited profit corporations themselves permitted to exercise the power of eminent domain? Under what restrictions?

15. How extensively have these provisions (questions 13 and 14) been used?

16. Is demolition carried out at public expense to pave the way for the erection of new housing by private enterprise? How much demolition accomplished in recent years?

17. How many families had to be moved prior to demolition? Where were they housed after removal?

18. Have any measures been enacted in your state or community to exempt from state or local taxes any housing provided or modernized by private corporations? From what taxes were exemptions granted? For how long? Upon what conditions? To what extent has private enterprise taken advantage of these tax exemptions?

19. Are loans or subsidies from public funds (federal, state, or local) available to private corporations in your community for demolition? For new construction? For improvements, repairs, or modernization? Upon what conditions? To what extent has private enterprise taken advantage of available loans and subsidies?

20. To what extent have insured mortgage loans been utilized in your community to facilitate new construction for rental purposes? To facilitate repairs, improvements, and modernization? Upon what terms? What proportion of these loans have been foreclosed?

21. Are corporations which take advantage of any of the above-mentioned governmental aids subject to investigation, approval, or supervision by any governmental agencies? What agencies? What powers do they have over the corporations concerned?

III. PUBLIC CONTROL OF HOUSING

However important and desirable it may be to provide new housing, many millions of people will have to continue to live in existing houses until something better can be provided. Control over the kinds of houses in which people are compelled to live has long been recognized as a governmental responsibility. In the main, however, attempts to regulate existing housing in this country have not been conspicuously successful. Diffused responsibility for administering various regulations and public apathy or opposition toward their vigorous enforcement have combined to render ineffective even some well-drafted housing codes. Helpful information about the nature of building codes, how they work, and what communities can do to make them more effective may be found in Your Building Code, by Miles L. Colean.[1]

22. Has your state a housing department, board, or authority which has regulatory powers over local housing? Read the law under which it operates.

23. Read the law and administrative regulations which fix standards for housing in your community. Do they apply only to new buildings constructed or old buildings remodeled? Or do they set standards to which all dwellings must conform? Do they apply to single as well as to multiple dwellings?

24. How do the requirements compare with those suggested by the Committee on the Hygiene of Housing[1] as to (a) light, air, and ventilation, (b) fire protection, (c) plumbing, drainage, (d) garbage and waste removal, (e) structural provisions in relation to site and neighborhood, (f) proportion of building site which must be left open?

25. What agency in your local government is responsible for enforcement of these provisions? For continuous inspection of structures used as dwellings? How many inspectors? Do they visit only on complaint?

26. What kinds of violations were reported last year in occupied buildings? How many? How many removed? Has the department the power to order unsafe buildings (a) vacated, (b) repaired, (c) condemned and demolished? How many vacated, repaired, demolished, last year?

27. What are the chief difficulties encountered in the enforcement of the housing code? What suggestions are offered by informed people for improvement of the law or of its administration?

28. What agency is responsible for inspection of mechanical hazards (elevators, boilers, and so forth) in dwellings? In other buildings?

29. What agency in your local government issues building permits? How many inspectors has it? How frequently does it inspect buildings in course of construction? Has it power to stop operations? Has it exercised this power within the past five years?

30. How many permits for dwellings were issued last year? What proportion was this of total building permits issued? How many separate dwelling units did they provide?

[1] National Committee on Housing, Inc., New York, 1946. Since health factors loom large in housing codes, see also Basic Principles of Healthful Housing, issued by the Committee on the Hygiene of Housing, American Public Health Association, New York, 2d ed., n.d.

IV. URBAN DWELLINGS

The United States census reports on population and housing for 1940 contain much information for cities, towns, and counties about the number and characteristics of homes and about the characteristics of families.[1]

In using census data regarding dwelling houses it is important to keep in mind that a dwelling house, for census purposes, is a place in which, at the time of the census, one or more persons regularly sleep. It need not be a house in the usual sense of the word, but may be a room in a factory, store, or office building, a loft over a garage, a boat, or even a tent. A tenement or apartment house counts as only one dwelling house, no matter how many persons or families live in it. Thus, dwelling houses are not always separate dwellings nor are they necessarily separate dwelling units.

31. How many of the dwelling units in your community were in 1-family, 2-family, 3-or-more-family structures? How many were in converted structures?

32. How many families, by race and nativity of head, owned their own homes? How many lived in rented quarters?

33. Of owned homes how many were valued at less than $1,500; $1,500 to $5,000; $5,000 or more?

34. Of rented homes how many rented for less than $15; $15 to $29; $30 to $49; $50 or more?

35. What were the rental values of vacant dwelling units in your community?

36. How many of the dwelling units did not have:
  a. Running water?
  b. Private flush toilet?
  c. Private bath?
  d. Electric lights?
  e. Mechanical or ice refrigeration?
  f. Central heating?
  How many did not use gas or electricity as cooking fuel?

37. Examine the housing characteristics by blocks and census tracts and the analytical housing maps for your community and note the areas where the oldest homes, the greatest number of homes in poor condition, and the greatest number of homes with more than one and one-half persons per room are located. Are these the areas of lowest average rental? The areas inhabited by Negroes? By foreign-born persons?

38. How many of the households in your community are "doubled up" (more than one family in space intended for only one)?

[1] U.S. Bureau of the Census, Sixteenth Census, second series housing bulletins contain limited statistics for all urban places; third series housing bulletins contain characteristics of dwelling units classified by rent groups for places of 50,000 inhabitants or more. Block supplements to the first series housing bulletins contain statistics by city blocks for cities of 50,000 inhabitants or more. Population and housing bulletins on characteristics by census tracts contain statistics for the 58 tracted cities. Population and housing bulletin on Families, General Characteristics, contains statistics for cities of 100,000 inhabitants or more. Analytical housing maps are available for cities of 100,000 or more.

Information will have to be secured from other sources, such as your local association of real estate operators, local housing association, local housing authority, or the local representative of the Federal Housing Administration, to answer the questions that follow.

39. Are the undesirable areas, as determined in question 37 above, close to industrial plants or to quick and easy means of transportation to industrial centers? (Many people will put up with bad living conditions for the sake of being able to reach their work quickly.)

40. Are smoke, gases, odors, sounds from industrial plants, noises of traffic, noticeable?

41. How do these areas compare with the more desirable residential areas in such features as:
    a. Proximity to schools, playgrounds, and parks (see pages 89 and 168–169)
    b. Width of streets and sidewalks
    c. Paving and repair of streets
    d. Lighting of streets
    e. Frequency of garbage and refuse collection (see pages 98–99)
    f. Promptness of snow removal

42. Do these areas contain special hazards (see Chapter 5), such as:
    a. Unprotected railroad crossings at street level
    b. Streetcar and bus lines, or other "through traffic," permitted on crowded residential streets
    c. Unsafe, abandoned buildings where children can enter and play, at risk of life and limb
    d. Deserted buildings, "jungles," frequented by vagrants
    e. Houses of prostitution existing in residential blocks

Increase in congregate nonfamily living is characteristic of many urban communities. Single people of all ages live in quarters ranging from high-priced hotels and furnished apartments, through boarding and rooming houses down to shelters and "flophouses" for homeless men.

43. Are lodging, boarding houses licensed? Inspected? By what agency? To what regulations must they conform?

V. RURAL DWELLINGS

In some respects the situation as to rural housing in the United States is even worse than that of urban housing, but unlike urban housing it has received scant attention and study. Of the nation's farm families it is estimated that some two-thirds of them are ill-housed, half of them living in dwellings "beyond repair."[1] Furthermore, within the rural group, migratory farm laborers and their families present an especially deplorable hous-

[1] Read Farm Housing—A Case Study, National Committee on Housing, Inc., New York, 1946.

ing problem. Some live in trucks, box cars, trailer camps, outlying "shanty towns." At best, some receive accommodations in migrant camps ranging from those with very inadequate facilities to a few with relative decency as to sanitation, conveniences, and provisions for family living.

Among federal agencies concerned with rural housing are the Farm Security Administration, Federal Housing Administration, and Home Owners' Loan Corporation.

44. On the basis of the United States Department of Agriculture indexes[1] how many rural dwellings in your community seem to be in need of major repair and improvement?

45. How many seem "beyond repair"? Do many of the dwellings lack running water, good sewage disposal, plumbing, central heating, electricity and gas?

46. Are the roads and highways leading to these homes properly lighted? Is snow promptly removed?

47. Is your community availing itself of the facilities offered by the federal agencies?

VI. PLANNING AND ZONING

Planning. Recognition of the need for preventive measures to assure the improvement of living and working conditions has led to the establishment of public controls over private development. There are, for example, zoning ordinances and subdivision regulations as well as the building codes mentioned in a previous section. To be applied intelligently these controls require a thorough study of a community to determine its probable future needs. Planning takes on a special urgency after a period of war, economic depression, or high prices which result in widescale deferral of construction and set the stage for an ensuing building boom.

To conduct surveys and make plans for future development many states, counties, regions, and municipalities have appointed planning commissions or boards. Voluntary and unofficial groups often organize for this purpose where it is not feasible to have an official body appointed.

The extent to which community plans can be put into effect depends not only upon the passage of legislation, but also upon the degree to which the public imagination can be fired and public opinion aroused to back the proposals put forward. Their success depends upon the voluntary co-operation of public authorities and private enterprise in carrying them out. Three references that will prove helpful at this stage of your study are Planning

[1] The Bureau of Agricultural Economics of the Department of Agriculture has developed three 1940 rural level of living indexes: a rural farm index, a rural nonfarm index, and a composite rural index. See also Minimum Requirements for Farmhouses Recommended by the United States Department of Agriculture, Miscellaneous Publication 475, Government Printing Office, Washington, 1941.

Your Community: A Manual of Suggestions for Practical Community Planning, by C. Earl Morrow;[1] Neighborhood Design and Control;[2] and Action for Cities: A Guide for Community Planning, by the National Resources Planning Board.[3]

48. Has your state legislature passed enabling legislation to permit the making and execution of plans to serve as a guide for the future development of local communities, counties, or regions within the state? Of the state as a whole?

49. Is there a state planning commission or state agency of similar name? Is it engaged in the formulation of a state plan? Are there regional planning agencies? County planning boards? Do they furnish encouragement and guidance to local planning bodies?

50. Is there an official planning commission or comparable agency in your community? How is it constituted? Who are its members and what are the qualifications which led to their appointment? How far into your surrounding areas does your planning agency's control extend?

51. Is a general plan for the future development of your community being formulated? Does it include such features as (a) location and extension of transportation facilities, including streets and automobile parking areas; (b) control of land uses for residential, recreational, business and industrial purposes; (c) provision of water supply, sewage disposal, and other public services; (d) provision and location of public buildings such as schools and hospitals; (e) neighborhood rehabilitation? What provision has your plan for assuring an appropriate balance between low-cost or low-rental housing and, on the other hand, higher-cost housing?

52. Does any voluntary and unofficial planning body exist in your community? If so, analyze its plan as under the foregoing question. If your community lacks a formal planning body, is any attempt made to induce local builders, banks, and others concerned with building voluntarily to co-ordinate their activities in the public interest?

53. What powers exist for putting into effect recommendations of an official planning body? Of an unofficial body?

54. In any plans which have been developed for your community, has provision been made for beauty or appropriateness of architectural design? For preservation of historic structures and places of natural beauty?

55. Has your local government adopted a plan for its own use to guide the designing, planning, location, and erection of public buildings? Are there proposals for purchase by the appropriate public departments of designated pieces of land for parks, parkways, parking areas, schools, playgrounds, and other public uses, in advance of intensive development of undeveloped areas?

[1] Regional Plan Association, Inc., New York, 1945.
[2] National Committee on Housing, Inc., New York, 1944. A summary of this volume has been published by the Committee under the title Your Stake in Community Planning, 1944.
[3] No. 86, Public Administration Service, Chicago, 1943. See also You and Your Neighborhood: A Primer for Neighborhood Planning, by Oscar Stonorov and Louis I. Kahn, Revere Copper and Brass, Inc., New York, 1944.

That part of city planning and zoning which most closely affects the lives of citizens relates to a community's residential areas. It is generally accepted that the only practical way of laying out large residential sections is to divide them up into more or less self-contained units. There is, however, no general agreement as to the composition of the unit district. The architects of the "greenbelt" communities, erected by the United States Resettlement Administration, have arranged their super-blocks around a sort of combined store and civic center. A number of developments approved by the Federal Housing Administration have consisted mainly of groups of apartment buildings, well spaced by garden courts and play spaces, but depending upon the surrounding territory for their shopping districts, schools, and other neighborhood institutions. A volume dealing with this moot question of neighborhood planning is Housing for the Machine Age, by Clarence A. Perry.[1]

56. In new residential developments in your community have the streets been laid out with the aim of cutting down risk from vehicular accidents? Describe. (See Chapter 5.)

57. Has it been possible to zone residential areas in your community so that facilities for neighborhood shopping and recreation are adequate and convenient? At the same time, has it been possible to keep other forms of business out of residential areas?, Does your community plan provide for locating home areas close to places of employment so as to reduce the transportation problem of workers? If so, what provision is made to protect the residential sections from traffic, noise, and similar by-products of adjacency to work places?

58. When attempts are made to rezone residential areas for business purposes, what agencies in your community are ready to make disinterested representations to the zoning authority?

59. Has your school department been successful in locating school buildings with relation to future needs of the school population? Have still useful school buildings had to be closed because intrusion of business has caused families to move away from the region? Are there any residential areas where children have to attend school on part-time? Are forced to travel out of the area to reach a school building? In planning new schools, is thought being given to providing the conditions which will favor their use as community centers?

Zoning. The controls over development permitted by zoning represent an extension of the power to abate nuisances and include the ability to specify what areas may be used for different purposes and the intensity of such uses. Usually a zoning commission is appointed to map restricted areas and draw up an ordinance, going out of existence when this has been done. A board of adjustment is set up to interpret the ordinance and vary it in minor ways

[1] Russell Sage Foundation, New York, 1939. For a shorter treatment of this question see "Good Neighborhoods," by Catherine Bauer, in The Annals of the American Academy of Political and Social Science, November, 1945, pp. 104–115.

if its application results in undue hardship to property owners. The local building department is usually charged with enforcement. When zoning regulations are passed they cannot in themselves be applied to structures already in use. Usually the code is amended by the legislative body, so that its passage does not necessarily insure a permanent policy. To reduce the disappointments resulting from this procedure it is advisable to have proposed changes reviewed by the planning board, whose recommendations may be overridden only by a large majority of the governing body. A discussion of the whole problem of zoning may be found in Zoning: The Laws, Administration, and Court Decisions During the First Twenty Years, by Edward M. Bassett.[1]

60. Has your community a zoning ordinance? What official bodies are concerned with zoning in your community?

61. How much of the land in your community is zoned for business? How adequate would this area be if population changes expected during the next ten years were to come up to expectations?

62. For what business purposes may premises in restricted areas be used? How many dwellings are there in areas open to business and industry? Do these coincide with those areas on your density map (see page 26) the most densely populated?

63. Does your community have a regulation excluding garages and service stations from the areas near schools and public auditoriums?

64. By what type of restrictions are various kinds of residential areas differentiated? What restrictions are there in regard to (a) such factors as space about buildings, percentage of lot that may be occupied by building, minimum lot frontage, (b) density of population in terms of square feet per family or families per acre?

65. Are there large undeveloped subdivisions, possibly with streets and utilities already completed? Is there a regulation to make the subdivider pay for these streets and utilities or have they been added to the general tax rate?

66. What are the current provisions regarding existing structures and uses which do not conform to zoning regulations? Do these nonconforming uses give rise to any special problems in your community? Is your community attempting in any way to assure the gradual extinction of nonconforming uses? How?

67. What agency is responsible for the enforcement of zoning ordinances and regulations in your community? How many prosecutions last year and with what results? What difficulties encountered in enforcing these provisions?

To prevent a repetition of the mistakes of the past in laying out streets, blocks, and lots some states have passed legislation enabling the municipality to place subdivision control in the hands of its planning board.

The other main control over development is the building code which is concerned with building materials and practices.

[1] Russell Sage Foundation, New York, 1940.

Abatement of Nuisances. Conditions under which people live have such an important effect upon the public welfare that even ancient law gave public authorities power to control and abate "nuisances" which endangered public health, safety or morals, offended the senses, or interfered with the legitimate use of neighboring property.

68. What can you learn through your health department, police, and court officials as to the extent to which governmental control over nuisances has been utilized to improve living conditions in your community? What types of nuisances were abated last year? How and by whom was action brought? With what results?

When you have finished this section, ask yourself the questions:

69. Are the people in my community on the whole well housed?

70. In the opinion of the best-informed people interviewed in the course of this study, has construction of dwellings during the past five years been sufficient to meet the community's needs? If not, what reasons were mentioned most frequently: (a) current land valuation, (b) excessive taxation, (c) high construction costs, (d) no effective demand, that is, the inability of people needing housing to pay the required rentals or purchase price, (e) other reasons?

71. What did they think ought to be done, and through what agencies (a) to improve existing housing, (b) to provide more low-cost housing, (c) to assure the wisest possible planning for your community as a whole?

8. HEALTH CONDITIONS AND RESOURCES

THE HEALTH of the American people, for many years now, has been improving greatly. Death rates from certain diseases in recent years have fallen some 80 to 90 per cent. In very recent years, for the first time in American history, the average life expectancy at birth was more than sixty-five years.

Significant as these gains have been, they are, unfortunately, very spotty. Success attained in overcoming certain diseases has not been achieved in combating others against which gains might have been realized. Successes have varied widely in different geographical areas and among different socio-economic groups.

Infant mortality rates for the United States as a whole have improved materially yet, in certain states, are still three times that in the state having the lowest rate. Although life expectancy in the United States has increased notably, there are still sections of our country in which the chance of survival is no greater than it was sixty years ago. Also, the average length of life for colored males was more than eight years less than the average for white males and the average for colored females ten years less than that for white females.

Despite impressive recent gains in the nation's health, one authority, upon comparing selective service rejections in World War II with comparable data for World War I reluctantly concluded that there is no evidence of improvement in the physical status of young men during the intervening period. Of 17,000,000 registrants between the ages of eighteen and thirty-seven examined between Pearl Harbor and the end of the war roughly 30 per cent were rejected as physically unfit. During earlier stages of the war, before physical standards were lowered, the rates were even higher. As in the case of other health indices, rejection by Selective Service examiners varied widely from one state to another, ranging from less than 30 per cent in some states to more than 50 per cent in others.

Among women, too, physical disabilities have loomed large. Of those examined for service with the Women's Army Corps some 33 per cent were rejected on physical or mental grounds.   As with other data, differences in rejection rates for various socio-economic groups are striking.   During the year ending with March, 1943, Selective Service examiners rejected approximately 37 per cent of the white males and 56 per cent of the Negroes examined.   Study of a limited number of eighteen- and nineteen-year-old registrants revealed that rejection rates for emergency workers and unemployed youths were half again as high as the average.   Contrary to widely held beliefs about the healthfulness of farm life, the rejection rate, on physical grounds, for farmers was even higher.

Sobering as recent findings may be, they only confirm what had been known earlier.   The National Health Survey of 1935, for example, showed that more than 23,000,000 people in the United States had chronic diseases or physical impairments.

Fortunately, many of America's physical troubles are remediable.   According to officials of the Selective Service system, one-sixth, or more, of the ailments for which men were rejected could have been corrected.   That at least large numbers could be helped is evidenced by the Army's success in rendering fit for military duty over 1,500,000 men despite major defects. Nevertheless, in spite of both this success and of the careful screening that was done, more than a million men had to be discharged from the Army and Navy for physical or mental disabilities, not resulting from wounds.

Sickness and disabilities also exact a heavy toll from the American people as a whole.   In 1943 the average male industrial worker lost more than eleven days of work as the result of sickness or injury.   The average female worker lost more than thirteen days.   For the country as a whole this meant a loss of more than 600,000,000 man-days annually.   On an average day, according to one estimate, illness or injury prevents one person in every 20 from carrying on his normal duties.

Again, sickness rates are known to vary widely among different socio-economic groups.   The National Health Survey of 1935, for example, showed that low-income groups had twice as much sickness as high-income groups.

To compute the costs of sickness and injuries one must take into account not only the losses in wages and in diminished production, but also the expenditures required to restore health.   To these must also be added the intangible costs of worry and insecurity resulting from sickness.

A community can, within certain limits, have as good health as it wishes to pay for.   However, many communities in this country, although willing and eager to have better and more adequate medical facilities, cannot have them because the total income of the people and the total revenues of local government are too low.

Recent estimates indicate that perhaps one-third of the American people live in areas with substandard local health services. Only through increased subventions from larger governmental units, or through some complete reorganization of our methods of providing medical care, can some communities receive what they need and want. (See Chapter 9.) In other communities, where the amounts expended may be adequate, some of the funds may be wastefully spent. Most communities, even if their health services are reasonably adequate, have still not found the way to integrate the preventive services of public health sufficiently closely with private practice or with the diagnostic and treatment services of institutional medicine.

I. HEALTH INDICES

Through analysis of various indices the state of health of a community can be measured. Health conditions may be appraised and compared with those in other communities. Comparison may also be made with conditions prevailing in the same community in previous years. The effectiveness of individual health procedures can be evaluated and the adequacy of community health services determined. It should be borne in mind, however, that the statistical method measures mass events and reveals quantitative facts. Figures must never be used uncritically and certainly not to interpret events unless all the underlying facts are known.

Among the indices that may be used in the appraisal of a community's health and health services are data on: natality, stillbirths, infant and maternal mortality, general mortality and causes of death, morbidity, and invalidity. Further significant data which, if available, are also useful as indices of community health are those relating to insanity and mental defects, alcoholism and drug habits, and examinations of physical fitness.[1] Accident rates, which are discussed elsewhere, are also an important index to community well-being.[2]

Births and Deaths. Registration of births and deaths is required by state law. Annually, statistics on population, births, deaths, and the major causes of deaths have been published by the Bureau of the Census for the individual states as well as for the nation as a whole.[3] Reports are also issued

[1] See "Health Indices: A Study of Objective Indices of Health in Relation to Environment and Sanitation," by K. Stouman and Isidore S. Falk, in Quarterly Bulletin of the Health Organization (League of Nations), December, 1936, pp. 901–1081.

[2] See Index.

[3] Vital Statistics—Special Reports, State Summaries. Washington, 1945. For changes

periodically by other official agencies, such as the health departments of the states, the larger cities, and many counties.

Birth and death rates give the annual number of births and deaths, respectively, per 1,000 population; specific death rates give the number of deaths from specific diseases per 100,000 population; the maternal death rate gives the annual number of deaths due to maternity per 1,000 live births; the infant mortality rate gives the annual number of deaths under one year per 1,000 live births; and the fatality rate gives the proportion of cases of a disease resulting in death.

1. What are the provisions of your state law concerning registration of births and deaths? Compare them with those suggested in the Uniform Vital Statistics Act.[1]

2. What were the birth and death rates in your community during the past five years? Were there differences between various racial groups? Can you find out if there were differences between economic groups? What was the excess of births over deaths? How do the rates in your community compare with those observed in similar communities and in your state as a whole?

3. Is there reason to believe that some deaths in your community are not registered? What were the principal causes of death during the past five years? What were the diphtheria, tuberculosis, and cancer mortality rates? How much is believed to be preventable?

4. What were the maternal mortality and infant mortality rates in your community during the past five years? Principal causes of death? Any differences between racial and economic groups? How did these rates compare with those in similar communities and in the state as a whole? How much is believed to be preventable?

5. How widely known in your community are the facts about birth and death rates? What is being done to improve conditions indicated by these facts to be necessary?

Morbidity. Statistical data on morbidity are an important measure of health conditions in a community. They provide information on the incidence, severity, and prevalence of illness, defects, and gross impairments. They give insight into the socio-economic factors causing or contributing to illness and into the effect of illness upon the socio-economic conditions of individuals, families, and communities. Many diseases and accidents do not result in premature death. If they occur frequently, are serious, and

in mortality rates and causes of death see Vital Statistics Rates in the United States, 1900–1940, by Forrest E. Linder and Robert Grove, Government Printing Office, Washington, 1943. The U.S. Children's Bureau periodically publishes sets of tables, charts, and maps giving details on births, maternal deaths, and infant deaths. As of July, 1946, the Division of Vital Statistics of the Bureau of the Census was transferred to the Federal Security Agency.

[1] For a brief description see Physicians' Handbook on Birth and Death Registration, by the U.S. Bureau of the Census, Government Printing Office, Washington, 1943.

necessitate prolonged care, however, they indicate that the health record of the community is unsatisfactory, even if the death rate is relatively low.

Legal requirements to report on cases of illness are limited to "notifiable diseases," most of which are communicable diseases. State laws and regulations regarding notification differ greatly. The weekly Public Health Reports of the United States Public Health Service carry data on notifiable diseases.

In order to obtain information on the incidence (or frequency) and severity of illness in general and on the prevalence of sickness, defects, and gross impairments, special studies of selected diseases or selected population groups have been made in some communities[1] and nationwide surveys have been made by studying a small number of representative areas.

Sources of information on morbidity other than that from communicable diseases are (a) the studies made, during the period 1928–1931, under the auspices of the Committee on the Costs of Medical Care;[2] (b) the National Health Survey,[3] covering sickness experienced in 1935 and 1936; (c) the Selective Service examinations;[4] (d) studies made by federal agencies such as the National Youth Administration and the Farm Security Administration; and (e) school health examinations.

Rates showing the incidence of morbidity give the annual number of cases of illness per unit of population, such as 1,000 persons. Disability rates give the annual number of days of disability (defined in various ways) per person in the population. Severity rates show the average number of days of disability per case of illness.

6. What diseases are reportable in your state? What was the incidence of all notifiable diseases in your community during the past five years? Which communicable diseases occurred most frequently? How many cases of diphtheria, malaria, measles, poliomyelitis, scarlet fever, tuberculosis, typhoid, syphilis, reported in the past five years? Have there been epidemics? How do your morbidity rates compare with those in other communities comparable with your own?

7. What was the frequency of notifiable occupational diseases during the past five years and which of these diseases occurred most frequently?

8. Was your community included in the nationwide studies made by the Com-

---

[1] Pertinent material is assembled in Medical Care and Costs in Relation to Family Income: A Statistical Source Book, Bureau Memorandum no. 51, Social Security Board, Government Printing Office, Washington, 1943.

[2] Falk, Isidore S., and others, Incidence of Illness and the Receipt and Costs of Medical Care Among Representative Families: Experiences in Twelve Consecutive Months During 1928–1931. University of Chicago Press, Chicago, 1933.

[3] Division of Public Health Methods, National Institute of Health, U.S. Public Health Service, Sickness and Medical Care Series, Bulletins nos. 1–11. Government Printing Office, 1938.

[4] U.S. Senate, Subcommittee on Wartime Health and Education, Report no. 3 (Pursuant to S. Res. 74). 78th Congress, 2d Session. Government Printing Office, 1945.

mittee on the Costs of Medical Care or in the National Health Survey? Have special morbidity studies been made in your community? What did these studies reveal? From employers or labor unions can you secure some estimate of how much time workers in your community lose each year on account of sickness or injury? What is the best estimate as to resultant wage losses? What is being done in your community to effect changes, shown by morbidity statistics or studies to be needed?

Physical examinations of school children and of persons called up for military service yield a wealth of material regarding your community's health. Reference already made to rejections of men examined under the Selective Service Act and to numbers discharged from the Armed Services because of health reasons (other than service-connected disabilities) makes it clear that great improvement in our community health services is needed.

Findings in respect to selectees examined in your community may be secured from your state Selective Service headquarters and possibly from your local headquarters office. Reports on examinations of school children should be available from your local school authorities.

9. What have physical examinations of school children, of persons called up for military service, or of other representative groups disclosed about the health of your community? What disabilities appeared most frequently? What do these findings teach with respect to the adequacy of health services in your community? What has been done as a result of these findings to secure needed improvement?

II. THE COMMUNITY AS A HEALTH ENVIRONMENT

Weather and the topographical conditions of a community have relation to its health. Your nearest meteorological station can undoubtedly help you with this part of your study.

10. Is your community in hilly country, or is the problem of drainage complicated by a level, low-lying situation? Is it free from stagnant water or marshes which breed insects?

11. What is the average temperature, the average rainfall, by months? Is the community subject to (a) periods of drought, (b) periods of excessive heat, cold, (c) seasons of rain or fog? How many full days of sunshine last year? What are the prevailing winds at different seasons? Has it, within recent years, experienced disastrous floods, tornadoes? How do these factors affect the health of your community?

The means taken by a community to guard its own health are of utmost importance. Information on water supply, sewage and refuse disposal, control of smoke nuisance, and supervision of milk and food can probably all be secured from your local and state departments of health. You can secure from the United States Public Health Service statements on standards for many services, such as the provision of safe drinking water, the sanitary distribution of milk, and the regulation of eating establishments, and finally, standards for the construction of privies. Progress made to date in the field of sanitation should not blind us to the fact that standards in some communities are still deplorably low. According to estimates of the Public Health Service, nearly 5,000 communities currently need new water systems and approximately 6,500 need water extensions or improvements. New sewerage systems are said to be needed in about 7,700 communities with a combined population of nearly 9,000,000.

Water Supply. A community's water supply is one of the most important factors in its public health.

12. Has your community a public water supply? Is it municipally owned, or furnished by private enterprise? What department administers or supervises it?

13. What is the source of the water? What system of purification is employed? Is the water hard or soft? (This question, generally neglected in technical works, is of great importance, if not to health, at least to the comfort, convenience, and cleanliness of homes.)

14. Has it been necessary to limit use of water during recent years? For what periods? Have there been additions to capacity during the past five years? What reserves can be called upon in case of shortage? What is the basis of payment for water? How do costs compare with those in neighboring communities?

15. How frequently are bacteriological tests made of your water supply? By what agency? Have any epidemics of typhoid fever or other water-borne diseases been traced to the water supply during the past five years?

16. Is drinking water bought from other sources than your water supply by any considerable portion of the population? Is it inspected by any governmental authority?

17. Is any portion of your community without water connections? Approximate area and population? How do its inhabitants obtain water?

18. Are wells, cisterns inspected and tested by your authorities? How frequently? What regulations exist in your sanitary code governing private water supplies?

19. What types of public drinking fountains are used in schools, railroad stations, elsewhere? What provisions in your sanitary code concerning them?

Sewage and Refuse Disposal. Proper disposal of human excreta is essential to the health of a community. Solid wastes, such as garbage and animal excreta, have no such direct relation to health, except as they breed flies, which are transmitters of certain diseases. Comfort and sanitation, however, demand that these wastes also be efficiently disposed of.

20. What department of government is charged with maintaining the sewerage system? With collection and disposal of garbage, ashes, and rubbish?

21. How many miles of sewers are there in your community? Is there a sepa-

rate system for storm water? If not, are there any portions of your community where sewage backs up in cellars during heavy storms?

22. Is there a sewage disposal plant? Where is sewage residue discharged? If into a lake or river, does it create a nuisance? Have shellfish, public bathing beaches, been found to be contaminated? Does it contaminate the water supply of other communities? Have epidemics in your own or neighboring communities been traced to it?

23. Is any part of your community not served by the sewerage system? Approximate area and population? What provision made for sewage disposal? In the portion served by sewers, are there any dwellings which are not sewer-connected? How many?

24. Has a count been made of outdoor privies in your community? How many were found? How many met the specifications (if any) of the State Department of Health? Is there any system of night soil collection in any part of your community? Are human excreta used as fertilizer by market gardeners in your community? What does your sanitary code provide regarding private disposal of sewage?

25. Are there public comfort stations in your community? Do you find them clean? Equipped with washbowl, soap, towels? How supervised? Any inspection made of private comfort stations in restaurants, depots, filling stations, and so on? By what agency?

26. What ordinance governs sanitation of auto and trailer camps? What department enforces it?

27. Are there public baths, laundries for public use? Auspices? Sanitary inspections? By what agency?

28. What is the schedule for collection of household garbage, ashes and rubbish, in different parts of your community? At different seasons? Does your sanitary code demand the separation by the householder of different types of waste?

29. Is there a local ordinance that cans containing garbage be kept covered? Is it enforced? Are carts or trucks used in its collection kept covered?

30. What are your local ordinances covering private dumping or incineration of garbage and waste? Are they enforced?

The Smoke Nuisance. Contamination of the air we breathe, by smoke and fumes, is a health hazard in many communities, as well as a tax on the strength and tempers of housewives, and a detriment to the appearance of public buildings.

31. Has your community any ordinance which attempts to abate the smoke nuisance by (a) prohibiting use of certain fuels by householders, and by industrial and transportation concerns, (b) directing use of mechanical devices to prevent ejection of smoke and noxious gases? Is this ordinance enforced? By what agency?

32. Has a study been made of air contamination in your community within recent years? By whom? How did it show your community's ranking with other similar places in air pollution? What did it recommend? What steps have been taken to put its recommendations into effect?

Milk and Food Supply. Protection of the food supply is a community function to which far too little attention is commonly paid. Continuous opposition by manufacturers of patented food and drug preparations to measures for nationwide control has made impossible effective national legislation. Moreover, staple food supplies are produced so largely in the region where they are consumed that measures of state and local control are called for in addition to the limited amount of supervision which the federal government can exercise over articles in interstate commerce. Owing to its importance in the dietary of children, the milk supply receives the closest attention.

33. Read your state law and any local ordinances that exist regarding milk production and distribution. By what agency are they locally enforced?

34. What agency issues permits to milk producers and distributors? Are permits ever revoked? How many revoked last year?

35. How frequently must cows be tuberculin-tested? What is done when a herd is found to be infected?

36. Is milk bacterially tested? What percentage of butterfat must it have to be sold as whole milk in your community? Are the results of tests made public?

37. Are laws and regulations specific on such points as pasteurization of milk, sterilization of utensils used, rapid cooling and keeping at low temperature, cleanliness and construction of dairies, sale of unbottled milk in stores? Is the phosphatase test used?

38. How many dairies supply milk and milk products to your community? From how many is the milk delivered directly to the customer? What proportion of the entire supply is thus delivered?

39. By what agency and how often are dairies inspected? (Authorities state that it should be not less than four times a year for producers; weekly for dairies that distribute direct to customer.) Distributing points? Ice-cream producers? (Authorities state that it should be not less than once a week.) Secure a copy of the score card used by your milk inspectors, and note the points used in scoring.

40. What is the daily per capita consumption of milk in your community for any convenient period? What percentage of the milk supply is pasteurized?

41. Have any epidemics in your community been traced to the milk supply?

42. What agency in your state is charged with the inspection of food and drugs? What agency in your community is charged with the inspection of bakeries, restaurants, ice-cream and soda dispensers, food stores and markets?

43. Do all these have to have permits, licenses, to operate? What agency issues permits? Are they ever revoked? How many revoked last year? What other penalties may be imposed for failure to comply with laws or regulations? As a last resort, can offending eating establishments be closed?

44. Are your local ordinances specific on such points as fitness for consumption of materials used or exposed for sale, cleanliness of premises and utensils, sterilization of dishes used by patrons, protection of food against flies and dust?

45. Are all eating places licensed? How frequently inspected? Secure a copy of the score card used by the inspectors and note items used in scoring.

Danger to the public health from food handlers who are diseased, or who, while apparently in good health, are "carriers" of certain diseases, has been increasingly recognized in recent years.

46. Is there a state law or a local ordinance which demands that handlers of milk or other food handlers must receive regular medical examinations? How frequently? Are the examinations free? Where are they given? By what agency? Are laboratory tests included?

III. HEALTH FACILITIES

A community's health and its medical care programs are necessarily dependent upon the doctors, nurses, hospitals, clinics, and other facilities available. The key to the whole health problem, however, is the physician.

Although it has been maintained that in peacetime the United States as a whole has nearly enough doctors, there are many areas in which this would not be true. In 1944, for example, Massachusetts had about three times as many physicians in proportion to population as did South Carolina. Disparity is clearly noticeable in rural as opposed to urban, and in poor as compared to wealthier, areas. In large cities the national average in 1940 was one physician for approximately 800 persons. In sparsely settled rural areas the average was sometimes as low as one physician to every 3,000, or even more, persons.

The distribution of nurses and dentists varies even more widely than does the incidence of physicians. Although medically rich states, on the average, had only about three times as many physicians in proportion to population as did the least favored states, they had more than four times as many dentists and five times as many nurses.

Medical Personnel. The basis of medical care is, of course, the trained physician. Suggested reading at this point is Physicians and Medical Care, by Esther L. Brown.[1] The American Medical Association's annual directory of physicians in the United States will also be of help to you. It can doubtless be consulted in the office of your county medical society.

47. How many physicians in your community are listed in the American Medical Directory? How many of these are actually practicing in your community? What is their ratio to the population?

48. How many are graduates of approved medical schools? How many belong to the county medical society?

49. How many are general practitioners? How many are in specialized practice? In what specialized fields?

The American Dental Association may be in position to inform you as to

[1] Russell Sage Foundation, New York, 1937. See also Factual Data on Medical Economics, by the Bureau of Medical Economics, American Medical Association, Chicago, 1940.

the number of dentists in your community. Or, count the number of dentists listed in your classified telephone directory.

50. What is the ratio of dentists to population? How many dentists are members of your county dental society?

51. Of other persons who treat diseases, how many are listed in your telephone directory as osteopaths, chiropractors, and the like? How many optometrists?

Your state health law carries provisions regarding persons who may treat sick people.

52. Is it necessary to obtain a license to treat the sick in your state? Are licenses issued to persons other than physicians and dentists? What form of permit to practice is given to osteopaths, chiropractors, naturopaths, and so on? What tests do they have to meet?

53. What restrictions does the law place upon pharmacists and others in prescribing or furnishing drugs without a physician's prescription? Is there any provision of law governing prescription, sale of glasses, by optometrists without medical training? In short, who may not treat or prescribe for the sick in your community, and what penalties accrue if they do?

In bedside nursing (in hospitals or in private homes), the nurse works under the physician's direction. In public health service, the public health nurse also works under medical direction from a health officer, a medical advisory committee, a clinic physician, or a private physician. In addition to giving skilled nursing care, she provides instruction in the preservation of health and the prevention of disease. She may also offer assistance in adjusting family problems which affect health.[1] Unfortunately, there is often no easy way to discover the number of nurses in your community as there is in the case of doctors and dentists, since there is usually no one place where all nurses are listed. However, the state representatives of the American Nurses' Association, and the National Organization for Public Health Nursing can probably supply you with information you will need.

54. Is there a nurses' registry in your community? How many graduate nurses registered for private duty?

55. How many graduate nurses in your community are employed in hospital nursing? How many in private-duty nursing? How many doing public health nursing? What is the proportion of each to the population?

56. How many nurses belong to the American Nurses' Association and the National Organization for Public Health Nursing?[2] How many nongraduate nurses ("practical nurses," untrained midwives) do these agencies believe to be practicing in your community?

---

[1] For a discussion of the importance of nursing services, see Nursing as a Profession, by Esther L. Brown, Russell Sage Foundation, New York, 1940.

[2] For addresses see List of Agencies, p. 251.

57. What provisions in your state law govern the practice of nursing? Are graduate nurses required to be registered? Are practical nurses, midwives, required to be licensed? What test of their competence is made before a license is issued?

The hospital is the center about which community medical care programs revolve. In the opinion of experts there should be five or six general hospital beds per 1,000 population to provide adequate care. In 1943 the national average was less than four beds per 1,000 and many states fell below even that low average. In 1946 there were in the United States some 1,200 counties (in which lived 15,000,000 persons) having no hospital registered by the American Medical Association. Evidence of the uneven distribution over the country of hospital facilities is evidenced by the fact that in states with the lowest per capita income the ratio of general hospital beds to population was one-half that in the states with the highest per capita income. The lack of hospital facilities not only deprives a community of needed hospital care but also tends to lower the whole standard of community health services. Competent physicians understandably are reluctant to practice in communities lacking hospital facilities.

According to estimates of the United States Public Health Service the nation in 1945 needed some 60,000 tuberculosis beds, 166,000 general hospital beds, and 191,000 mental hospital beds to meet unmet needs and replace obsolete facilities. It was to help meet this national hospital need that Congress enacted the federal Hospital Survey and Construction Act of 1946 and appropriated funds to assist states in providing construction of either public or private hospitals.

In 1941 registered hospitals owned by public agencies provided nearly half of the beds in general hospitals, more than four-fifths of the beds for patients with tuberculosis, more than nine-tenths of the beds for patients with communicable diseases, and provided for all but 3 per cent of the beds in mental hospitals. However, one in every four governmental hospitals and one in every five beds in those hospitals was for particular types of patients and therefore not available for general use. Between 1942 and 1946 the number and proportion of beds in public hospitals have increased greatly, largely because of additions provided for the Armed Services and the veterans. This fact must be borne in mind in interpreting recent statistical data. In order to appraise the adequacy of hospitals in a given community the facilities not available to the general public must be viewed in the light of this fact. At present nongovernmental hospitals provide for the greater part of all general hospital beds for community use.[1]

[1] For statistical data see the annual Hospital Number of the Journal of the American Medical Association.

The increase and expansion of hospitals, over the years, has taken place without over-all planning. The result is that hospital beds are very unevenly distributed and that governmental and nongovernmental activities in the hospital field are not well co-ordinated. To remedy this situation various steps have been urged.[1]

In studying the hospitals of your community you will need to secure access to two valuable compilations: the List of Approved Hospitals issued annually by the American College of Surgeons, and the report on hospital service in the United States which appears annually in the Journal of the American Medical Association.[2] Some of the hospitals or private practitioners in your community will doubtless have these publications.

58. List the hospitals and related facilities in your community, classifying separately the general hospitals, special hospitals (such as isolation, tuberculosis, children's, orthopedic, and chronic disease hospital), convalescent homes, and custodial institutions with infirmary or hospital unit.

59. How many beds are provided by all hospitals and by each type? Are there communicable disease, tuberculosis, or psychiatric divisions in the general hospitals? How many beds in each? How many beds are in (a) registered and (b) approved hospitals?

60. What agencies administer these facilities? Which are administered by local, state, or federal governmental authorities? Which by private: (a) religious groups, (b) racial groups, (c) fraternal organizations, (d) particular employers or industries, (e) other?

61. Which hospitals are nonprofit; which unrestricted as to profit? Any not approved by the American College of Surgeons? Why? Which are approved by the American Medical Association for the training of interns? Which are approved by your state board of nurse examiners for training nurses?[3]

62. For each hospital:

How is its governing board appointed?

How is its superintendent appointed? Qualifications which led to appointment of present superintendent?

How many resident physicians and interns, how many visiting physicians on its staff?

How many graduate nurses and student nurses on its staff? How long is their working day?

If a public hospital, what positions are under a civil service merit system?

---

[1] See, for example, the Hospital Survey and Construction Act of 1946.

[2] Additional references that will be found useful include Small Community Hospitals, by Henry J. Southmayd and Geddes Smith, Commonwealth Fund, New York, 1944; and Health Service Areas: Requirements for General Hospitals and Health Centers, by Joseph W. Mountin and others, Public Health Bulletin 292, Government Printing Office, Washington, 1945.

[3] The National League of Nursing Education will supply a List of Schools of Nursing Meeting Minimum Requirements Set by Law in the Various States. This list is revised every three or four years.

Is there a social service department? How many social workers? How many are members of a professional association? (See page 47n.) How many cases given social service last year?

63. Who is eligible for admission to these hospitals and institutions? Upon what conditions can hospital or institutional facilities be utilized by patients from your community and by local public agencies? What requirements must be met by the patient and his family? What agency or hospital official authorizes admission? Is authorization given for a definite period of time? Is there any control of the length of stay?

64. Are there special hospitals in your community for particular groups such as veterans, Negroes, or others? How do standards of these hospitals compare with others in the community or vicinity?

65. Do any hospitals in your community refuse admission to Negroes? To other groups? If so, what provision is made for such persons who need hospital care?

66. What rates are charged by the hospitals? Are they adjusted to the patient's ability to pay? What collection procedures are in use? Who determines patients' ability to pay?

67. Are voluntary hospitals in your own community or in adjacent communities utilized by public agencies (such as the department of public welfare)? If so, is there an agreement regarding (a) admission of patients for whom the public agencies pay the bill in full or in part, (b) the rate of payment, (c) the control of length of stay, and (d) the settlement of disputes? What is the rate of payment by public agencies and on what basis is it computed? Does the voluntary hospital or the public agency collect the portion which the patient is able to pay? What agency authorizes care in such hospitals?

68. Has any move been made to secure through your state health authority federal funds for the construction of hospital facilities needed in your community? For a public hospital? Private? How much of the total income of voluntary hospitals is derived from tax funds paid by public agencies?

Nursing Service. Many institutions and agencies provide nursing services offering health care and instruction for persons in their own homes. Nurses rendering these services are sometimes employed by public, sometimes by private agencies. A good idea of the work of a public health nursing service can be obtained by reading Public Health Nursing for Your Community, published by the National Organization for Public Health Nursing.[1]

When a patient can afford to pay it, visiting nurse associations often charge a fee based upon the actual cost of a visit. If the patient is unable to pay, part payment may be accepted, or the care may be rendered free. In many communities nursing organizations have undertaken by contract with life insurance companies to render this type of nursing service to their policyholders at the expense of the companies.

[1] New York, rev. 1945.

69. Is there a publicly or privately financed visiting nurse association in your community? Auspices? Source of support? Who is eligible for care?

70. How many nurses does it employ? How many meet the standards of experience and training laid down in Recommended Qualifications for Public Health Nursing Personnel.[1] Is the agency approved by your state board of nurse examiners for field work for student nurses?

71. On what basis are families accepted for nursing care: (a) free, (b) on a fee basis? How many different families given service last year? How many visits made? What percentage of these made free?

IV. THE PUBLIC HEALTH AUTHORITY

The basic tasks of public health authorities are to improve community sanitation and health, and to reduce both morbidity and mortality from causes which affect large sections of the population. Recommended as preliminary reading at this point are two publications of the Commonwealth Fund, Community Health Organization, edited by Ira V. Hiscock,[2] and Local Health Units for the Nation: A Report, by Haven Emerson and Martha Luginbuhl.[3]

Beginning with communicable diseases, especially those causing devastating epidemics, public health work has expanded to include some of the chronic noncommunicable diseases which affect large groups of the population; or which seem to be on the increase. The attack has been concentrated at different periods and places upon different types of diseases. As new discoveries have been made about the cause of a disease, the method of its transmission, modes of discovering individual susceptibility, ways of immunizing against it, and finally, specific treatment, these discoveries have been made the basis of new public health measures. Many diseases formerly epidemic or endemic in this country have been thus controlled or virtually eliminated.

From mass prevention through environmental sanitation the public health movement has advanced to personal service for the prevention of illness and the promotion of good health. Some public health services have gone even farther, adding provisions for the care of the sick, health guidance of individuals, and consultant service to professional persons and recognized agencies, private as well as public. This trend in public health work is most marked in the field of communicable disease control (particularly in venereal disease and tuberculosis control), and in services for persons with physical handicaps. The liberal determination of eligibility for care at public ex-

[1] National Organization for Public Health Nursing, New York, rev. 1942.
[2] New York, 3d ed., 1939.
[3] New York, 1945. See also Desirable Minimum Functions and Organization Principles for Health Activities, American Public Health Association, New York, 1943.

pense, which characterizes the recent development of provisions for patients with communicable diseases, contrasts sharply with policies followed in most other fields of health service.

Both state and local departments of health operate under state law. In addition, your community may have local ordinances or other legislation, including a sanitary code, which should be read in connection with this part of your study. The American Public Health Association issues an evaluation schedule for appraising local health work. Local health departments are urged to submit these periodically, whereupon the Association suggests ways in which departments can improve their work. Summaries of the evaluation schedules are published from time to time by the Association.

72. Does your health department fill out and send in these evaluation schedules? What suggestions have been received on the basis of these reports? How does your health department compare with departments reported in Health Practice Indices, 1943–1944, published by the American Public Health Association?[1]

73. Has it taken part in activities promoted by the American Public Health Association?

The official in charge of public health is usually, though not always, a medical man. He may be heavily burdened with a private practice and his public duties confined to reporting the vital statistics of the community to the state health department, placarding communicable diseases, and giving free medical treatment to the "town poor." At the other extreme we may find a large health department with an active citizen board, an administrator who is a trained public health officer, department heads and inspectors likewise trained in public health and appointed under a civil service merit system, numerous bureaus concerned with various phases of health protection, provision for the isolation of cases of contagious disease, public health nurses and medical social workers employed wherever they can give effective service, clinics and dispensaries for diagnosis and treatment, a chemical and bacteriological laboratory, departments of vital statistics and research, and a department which vigorously promotes public health education. Questions suggested below touch lightly upon the public health authority's responsibility for the care of sick persons and the control of communicable diseases. These subjects are considered in Chapter 9.

The American Public Health Association fixes the figure of $1.00 per capita as essential for a minimum public health program. However, it is estimated that in larger cities annual expenditures of approximately $2.50 per capita are necessary to permit officials to do effectively what they are capable of doing.

[1] New York, 1945.

74. Is your community part of a public health district? Does it maintain its own department of public health?

75. Is there a board of health? Administrative or advisory? Paid or unpaid? How appointed and for what terms? Qualifications which led to appointment of present members? How many physicians, laymen? What are its powers and duties? Does it appoint the director? What other appointments does it control? What advisory or administrative subcommittees has it?

76. What is the title of the director? Is he appointed under civil service? How otherwise appointed? For what term? On full or part-time? Is the present incumbent a physician? What special training has he had for public health work?

77. How many persons on its staff other than clerical or manual workers? How many (a) physicians, (b) nurses, (c) sanitary inspectors, (d) other professionally trained persons?

78. Do the physicians on its staff belong to the county medical society? To what other professional medical associations? What staff members are members of the American Public Health Association?

79. How many of the nurses meet the minimum standards laid down by the National Organization for Public Health Nursing? (See page 106.)

80. How are staff members appointed? How do salary scales, vacations, sick-leave, retirement allowances, compare with those of other public departments in your community?

81. What duties has the health department in your community in regard to inspection of water, milk, food supply? In regard to street sanitation, sanitation of dwellings? (See pages 97–98, 100.) Is it or the department of education responsible for school sanitation and hygiene?

82. What responsibility has your department of health for public health nursing service? (See page 105.)

83. Does your department of health maintain a laboratory? On what terms may examination of specimens be procured by (a) public agencies, (b) private hospitals, (c) private physicians?

84. Does your department of health maintain (a) a general hospital, (b) other hospitals, (c) clinics and dispensaries for general treatment, (d) diagnostic or treatment clinics for special diseases such as tuberculosis, syphilis and gonorrhea, cancer, cardiac conditions? Specify.

85. Does it maintain instructional clinics (e.g., "well-baby clinics")? Health centers?

86. Does it offer diagnostic or consultation services to private physicians? Are medical-social consultative services provided?

87. Does it provide health education or information service? Does it maintain a nutrition service? Does it publish an annual report or other regular publications? Specify.

88. What has been the budget submitted by your health department for each of the past five years, and the amounts appropriated? Percentage of total governmental expenditures spent for health? Cost per capita? How does this compare with the minima suggested above?

Not only local, but state health officials have definite responsibility for the maintenance of the public health in their areas. One of the duties of the United States Public Health Service is to allot funds to each state for the purpose of assisting not only the states but also the health districts, and other political subdivisions in establishing and maintaining adequate public-health services.

89. What are the powers, duties, and responsibilities of the State Department of Health and other state health agencies or officers in regard to health work in your community? Have they power to supervise and set standards? To take over any of the local health authority's responsibilities in case these are not being properly carried out?

90. Are funds allotted to your community by the State Department of Health? Upon what terms?

V. VOLUNTARY HEALTH ORGANIZATIONS

In addition to technical personnel, hospitals, clinics, other medical facilities, and public health authorities there are in many communities a wide variety of private agencies promoting better health of the population and better understanding by the public of health and hygienic measures. A recent survey of these organizations indicates that some 20,000 of them are working throughout the country.[1]

In many instances local voluntary health organizations are units or affiliates of national organizations such as the following:

American Cancer Society
American Committee on Maternal Welfare
American Foundation for the Blind
American Hearing Society
American Heart Association
American Hospital Association
American Social Hygiene Association
National Committee for Mental Hygiene
National Foundation for Infantile Paralysis
National Organization for Public Health Nursing
National Society for the Prevention of Blindness
National Tuberculosis Association

Additional national agencies which stand ready to co-operate with local health organizations are:

[1] See Voluntary Health Agencies: An Interpretive Study Under the Auspices of the National Health Council, by Selskar M. Gunn and Philip S. Platt, Ronald Press, New York, 1945.

American Medical Association
American National Red Cross
American Public Health Association
Health Council of the National Social Welfare Assembly
Maternity Center Association
Medical Administration Service
National Society for Crippled Children and Adults

91. What voluntary health agencies are there in your community? In what diseases are they particularly interested? Are there important health needs in your community in which no private agency is particularly interested?

92. What voluntary health agencies have paid executives (full-time, part-time)? What are the qualifications which led to the appointment of these executives?

The complexity of the various means, both public and private, for promoting the public health makes some form of organized co-operation and planning a necessity in most communities. Sometimes this is brought about through a privately organized health association or the health section of a council of social agencies. (See page 235.) Sometimes a separate health council is set up. Co-ordinating machinery is particularly necessary in view of the limited interests of many voluntary health agencies which are often concerned with only a single disease.

Occasionally, a "pressure group" of citizens is organized to secure the passage of a specific piece of legislation or to bring about a given change in which the members are interested.

93. Under what auspices do health workers in your community meet for joint counsel and planning? What agencies are represented in the membership? What staff does it have? What have been its accomplishments?

94. Are there in your community neighborhood health committees concerned with studying and publicizing health needs, improving the administration of local health agencies and interesting citizens in improving their own health?

95. Is there in your community any fund other than the community chest (see Chapter 18) from which voluntary health work can be financed? How large is the fund? How raised? How administered?

VI. INFORMING THE PUBLIC ABOUT HEALTH

In a true democracy, the controlling factor on any given issue is public opinion. Upon community opinion, therefore, depend in large measure both the level of health in the community and the nature of a community's health services.[1]

[1] See "How Lay Citizens Can Influence the Local Administration of Health," by Carmen McFarland, in Proceedings of the National Conference of Social Work, 1940, Columbia University Press, New York, 1940, pp. 508–516.

The importance of public education in health matters is all the more important in view of modern emphasis upon the positive attainment and preservation of health for the entire population. This goal, obviously, can be attained only as people learn to co-operate in keeping their own bodies fit, by taking advantage of the teachings of modern hygiene and sanitation. An important part of the work of progressive health agencies consists in teaching people how to be well and how to stay well. Recommended as preliminary reading at this point are several booklets in the National Health Series:[1] Food for Health's Sake, by Lucy H. Gillett; The Common Health, by James A. Tobey; Staying Young Beyond Your Years, by Howard W. Haggard; and The Human Body, by Thurman B. Rice.

Health education is in part directed toward special groups and related to specific problems such as tuberculosis, cancer, gonorrhea and syphilis, and of informing the public about the importance of receiving care promptly. Recent emphasis in health education is upon more inclusive programs directed toward the whole community. The leadership in such a program may come from the local health department, a health council, or a single private health agency. Read Ways to Community Health Education, by Ira V. Hiscock and others.[2] Methods of teaching health to school children and other special groups are also vital aspects of health education but are discussed elsewhere.[3]

96. What agencies in your community sponsor health education programs?

97. On what health topics have they supplied single lectures, courses of lectures, and radio talks or sketches during the past year? Does any local agency, such as your public health department, sponsor regular radio programs, newspaper columns, or other media presenting local health needs and steps for the attainment of better health?

98. What special days (such as Mother's Day or Child Health Day) have been devoted to intensive efforts to disseminate health information?

99. Do local newspapers carry regular health columns or departments?

100. On what health topics is informative free literature distributed? Through what channels? In what other languages besides English?

101. What educational films have been shown (a) in commercial motion picture houses, (b) before other audiences? Under what auspices?

102. On what topics have popular health exhibits been prepared and where were they shown?

[1] Funk and Wagnalls Co., New York, 1937. While these are now quite old and out of print they are still useful and will be found in many libraries.

[2] Commonwealth Fund, New York, 1939. See also Community Organization for Health Education, American Public Health Association, New York, 1941. A useful report on the Cleveland Health Museum is Making Health Visible, published by the museum in 1945.

[3] See p. 241.

103. What efforts are being made, and by what agencies in your community, to fight medical misinformation? To restrict the advertising and sale of harmful drugs and proprietary medicines? To combat medical inaccuracies in sponsored radio announcements and programs?

Current emphasis upon positive attainment and preservation of health places increasing importance upon the relationship of nutrition to health.[1] Nutrition education is frequently a responsibility of state or city health departments. Local chapters of the American Red Cross frequently offer nutrition service.

104. What agency or agencies in your community provide public information on food values and the relationship of nutrition to good health?

When you have finished this section of your study, ask yourself the questions:

105. Are sufficient funds being appropriated to provide needed health resources in my community?
106. For what areas of the health field, and for what age groups do resources appear to be most adequate? Least adequate? Are the health services in my community well co-ordinated?

[1] See The Road to Good Nutrition, by Lydia J. Roberts, U.S. Children's Bureau, Publication 270, Government Printing Office, Washington, 1942. For a more extended treatment see Feeding the Family, by Mary D. Rose, Macmillan Co., New York, 1940.

9. ORGANIZED CARE OF THE SICK

AMERICA is rich in resources for the care of the sick and injured. If you have followed the study outlined in the previous chapter you have a good idea of the health resources of your community. Unfortunately, even adequate medical facilities do not of themselves assure communities of proper medical care since many persons in need of care are unable to pay for it. This has been clearly evidenced by a number of important studies.[1]

As we have already seen, families in low-income groups suffer more than their proportionate share of disabling illness. Yet, extensive studies reveal that the average low-income family spends for medical care only a fraction of what the average family in higher income groups spends. Nevertheless, the amount paid by the low-income groups was a much larger proportion of their income than the higher income groups paid for medical care.

Studies made by the Committee on Costs of Medical Care also show that persons in low-income groups received less than half as many physicians' calls and included only about a fourth to a fifth as many dental cases per 1,000 persons as did persons in higher income groups. The inadequacy of the dental services available to the American people is indicated by the fact that the dental care provided by the Army in 1942 and 1943 required the production of three and a half times the total quantity of dental supplies and equipment normally produced in the United States in an entire year.

Current estimates indicate that adequate medical care could be provided for American families at an average cost representing about 4 per cent of their incomes. This would be about as much as the American people, before the war, were already spending for medical care. What is indicated, then, is not an increase in total expenditures but a pooling of costs so that these are more equitably distributed not only among different income groups but

---

[1] Some of these are summarized in Need for Medical-Care Insurance, Social Security Board, Bureau Memorandum no. 57, Washington, 1944. See also Health Care for Americans, by Charles-Edward A. Winslow, Pamphlet no. 104, Public Affairs Committee, Inc., New York, 1945; and the Interim Report by the U.S. Senate Subcommittee on Wartime Health and Education, Report no. 3 (Pursuant to S. Res. 74), 78th Congress, 2d Session, Government Printing Office, Washington, 1945.

also between families which, in any given year, suffer disabling sickness and those which are not thus affected.

Organized care of the sick is of two types: general care for a wide variety of illnesses and disabilities and special care for particular diseases such as tuberculosis, venereal diseases, and the like. Medical care programs, whether general or more highly specialized, may be provided by government or through voluntary effort.

I. GENERAL PUBLIC MEDICAL CARE

Public medical care in the United States has developed from humble beginnings in colonial times to a social movement steadily gaining in impetus. The principal features of this advance are the growth of public hospitals, the development of public clinics, the introduction of organized programs of medical care for selected socio-economic groups, and the adjustment of the administrative organization to modern requirements. Since the 1930's public medical care has increased greatly.[1] At present this care, widely varying in scope and quality, is available to various groups of more or less self-supporting civilians (such as merchant seamen, Indians and Eskimos, certain employes of the federal government, the wives and infants of enlisted men in the four lowest pay grades), to "medically needy" persons and to that large group of persons dependent upon public assistance.[2] Particularly extensive and varied public medical care services are available to members of the Armed Services and veterans.

The more advanced public medical care programs include, to a varying extent, home, office, clinic, hospital, and custodial care. In many instances provision is also made for certain specialist services outside of hospitals and clinics, for bedside nursing in the home, for a variety of drugs and appliances, including eyeglasses, and for ambulance service and transportation to clinics. However, the traditional policy of providing primarily for hospitalization, out-patient department service, and care in institutions of the almshouse type is still widespread.

In the fiscal year 1943–1944 the total expenditure of tax funds for public medical care for civilians exceeded $900,000,000. The magnitude of this sum in itself demonstrates that wide and effective use of the money provided by taxpayers is imperative.

[1] The policy followed in developing public medical care in the United States is analyzed and appraised in Public Medical Care: Principles and Problems, by Franz Goldmann, Columbia University Press, New York, 1945. The functions of various government agencies administering medical care programs are discussed in Medical Services by Government: Local, State, and Federal, by Bernhard J. Stern, Commonwealth Fund, New York, 1946.
[2] See Chapter 14.

Medical Care for Needy Persons. The recent development of general programs of medical care for needy persons and the recognition of medical care as an essential part of public assistance is characterized by liberalization of eligibility requirements, improvement of the quality of service rendered, efforts to achieve co-ordination of professional and institutional services, and reorganization of the administrative structure.[1] In many parts of the country, the responsibility for organization of general programs of public medical care has been transferred recently from small political units such as towns, to larger units such as counties and states. Several states have come to assume broader responsibility than in the past. Most important is the development of systematic state-local co-operation in financing and operating public medical care.

Pertinent examples of modern legislation are the New York State social welfare law, which makes the public welfare district "responsible for providing necessary medical care for all persons under its care, and for such persons, otherwise able to maintain themselves, who are unable to secure necessary medical care"; and the Rhode Island public assistance laws which declare eligible for aid any needy individual in the state "who has not available sufficient income and resources to maintain a reasonable standard of health and well-being," regardless of citizenship, residence or settlement, and availability of small resources.

1. Is there in your community an organized program of public medical care for persons in need? Is it local, countywide, or statewide? Is it organized on the basis of a local or state law, such as a welfare law, or a special law dealing with health service? By what agency is it administered? How much was spent for this purpose last year? Source of funds?

2. Who is eligible for care at public expense? Recipients of public assistance? Recipients of subsistence payments? The medically needy? How is eligibility determined and by whom?

3. What requirements must be met in regard to residence, citizenship, disposal of small assets, liens on property, repayment? What agency is responsible for the final decision? What is the procedure in the case of emergencies and of transients? Is a signed affidavit or a sworn statement of destitution required? Is the recipient of service classified as a pauper? Is he disfranchised?

4. Are persons accepted for public medical care expected to contribute to the costs of the service? If so, how much for the various services in question? What collection procedures are in use?

5. Does the beneficiary of public assistance receive services as needed or does he

---

[1] For details see the books by Franz Goldmann and Bernhard J. Stern, cited on p. 114. See also the following three reports by the Joint Committee of the American Hospital Association and the American Public Welfare Association: Institutional Care of the Chronically Ill, American Public Welfare Association, Chicago, 1940; Out-Patient Care for the Needy, the Association, 1942; and "Hospital Care for the Needy: Relations Between Public Authorities and Hospitals," in Hospitals, August, 1938, pp. 17–24.

receive a special cash allowance to pay his doctor or druggist bills? What are the practices in determining the amount and supervising the proper use of the cash allowance? What is the experience with this method?

6. What services are available? What services of specialists? What diagnostic and laboratory services? How are special services provided for patients with communicable diseases, mental diseases, physical handicaps, dental defects, and so forth, co-ordinated with those provided under the general program?

7. Is free dental care provided and, if so, what type of service (extractions, fillings, dentures, and so forth)? Who supplies this service — dentists in private practice or salaried dentists? What agency pays for this service, on what basis, and how much?

In providing for clinic and hospital services, certain public agencies have come to use tax funds to pay nongovernmental agencies for service rendered to the needy and medically needy. The old practice of allotting a lump sum for such service is gradually being supplanted by payment methods which relate compensation to the volume of service actually rendered.

8. What hospital care is available? What clinic care? Provision for calls to physicians' offices? What method of organization is employed in providing for home care by (a) physicians, (b) nurses? By what method and how much are the physicians and nurses paid? Is payment on a fee for service or on a salary basis? What effect does the method of payment have upon the quality of health services rendered? How many physicians are employed in the general public medical care program full time? Part time?

9. What are the provisions for patients with chronic diseases other than mental diseases and tuberculosis? Are the facilities adequate in regard to physical plant, equipment, medical staff, nursing service, medical social service, occupational and recreational services? Are private nursing homes utilized? Is home care provided?

10. What are the provisions for convalescents? What facilities are utilized? Are they adequate? What types of conditions are excluded from admission?

11. Has any study been made in your community of the effectiveness of existing provisions for the medical care of the needy?

12. Are there any statistical data on the frequency of medical care at public expense, broken down by specified types of service; the average amount of service rendered, by types of service; the total average cost of public medical care, the average cost of specified types of service, and the proportion of (a) the public assistance budget and (b) all local tax funds spent on medical care?

13. Are there any statistical data on the services rendered to, and the expenditures made for, needy persons by voluntary agencies?

Compulsory Health and Disability Insurance.[1] As early as 1798 the principle of compulsory insurance against sickness was accepted in the United States by the passage of the Act for the Relief of Sick and Disabled

---

[1] Discussion of workmen's compensation and other social insurance measures is included in Chapter 6.

Seamen. A compulsory plan has been in operation among city workers in San Francisco since 1937.

In Congress as well as in many state legislatures proposals for establishment of compulsory health insurance have been introduced frequently. In 1945 and 1946 the National Health Bill (the so-called Wagner, Murray, Dingell Bill) aroused much interest. Among the states Rhode Island in 1942 adopted the first compulsory disability insurance law in this country, and in 1946 California followed suit. These programs compensate certain classes of employed persons for part of their income losses sustained as a result of disabling illness.

14. What forces in your community are working for and against national or state health insurance? What arguments are advanced by proponents and by their opponents?

15. If you live in an area having compulsory insurance, what groups are covered? Who pays the cost? By whom is the scheme administered? What medical benefits are available? In the opinion of beneficiaries, physicians, and others directly associated with it, how has the plan benefited your community? If you live in an area where proposals for compulsory insurance are under discussion, what is recommended with respect to the questions suggested here?

II. VOLUNTARY MEDICAL CARE

Voluntary health measures, like those administered under public auspices, are of two types: more affording cash benefits in time of sickness and those providing medical care rather than cash for sick persons. Service plans provide the subscriber with direct service ranging from hospitalization or surgical service in the hospital to more or less complete medical care, including clinic, office, or home visits. Such plans are made available mainly by nonprofit organizations set up for this purpose.

Cash Benefits. Traditionally, the average American has secured his medical care from a privately engaged physician to whom he then paid the fees demanded. Even families which could normally afford to pay for medical care found that it was difficult to budget these costs in serious illnesses, involving heavy costs likely to arise infrequently and without warning. The obvious answer, therefore, was to pool risks. Accordingly, fraternal organizations, mutual benefit associations, labor unions, and commercial insurance companies developed a wide variety of schemes under which contributors could pay regular, stipulated fees and, in time of sickness, receive prescribed cash benefits.

Cash indemnity plans reimburse the subscriber up to a certain amount for bills for professional services (medical or surgical expense indemnity insurance), hospital bills (hospital expense indemnity insurance), loss of income due to disability (disability insurance, often called "sickness benefit"), or a combination of various specified expenses or losses.

In addition to individual insurance policies commercial insurance companies recently have offered group insurance contracts covering medical expense indemnity, hospital expense indemnity, or both. Master contracts, underwritten by a commercial insurance company, are often sponsored by industrial corporations or business firms, or purchased by them for their employes. In some instances coverage is extended to dependents of the employes covered. Lately labor unions have placed emphasis on the inclusion of health insurance provisions in collective bargaining agreements and, in some instances, obtained a contract charging employers with payment of the full contributions.

16. What fraternal organizations, labor unions, or other groups maintain sickness funds for any considerable numbers of persons in your community? What rates are charged? What benefits paid? Are these sufficient to assure necessary medical care as well as maintenance during sickness?

17. How are these sickness funds administered? What safeguards to protect funds?

18. What group insurance plans with commercial companies cover significant numbers of persons in your community? Who is eligible for inclusion?

19. What is the annual cost per family covered? Do employers contribute to this cost? What benefits are paid? Are they sufficient to pay medical costs as well as maintenance in time of sickness?

Hospital Service Plans.[1] Hospital service (commonly known as Blue Cross Plans) provides for hospitalization up to a certain period of time, such as three or four weeks, and, not infrequently, a 50 per cent discount for an additional number of days. Group enrollment of employed persons is the prevailing policy, although lately individual enrollment has been made possible by some plans. A good example of a relatively advanced Blue Cross Plan is the Michigan Hospital Service.

On January 1, 1946, there were nearly 20,000,000 persons enrolled in plans approved by the Blue Cross Commission of the American Hospital Association, family members constituting more than half of all participants. In order to meet the needs of subscribers more fully and to prevent hospital service plans and medical service plans from working at cross purposes the co-ordination of hospital service plans with prepayment plans covering professional services has received increasing attention lately.

[1] See The Story of the Blue Cross, by Louis H. Pink, Pamphlet no. 101, Public Affairs Committee, Inc., New York, 1945. See also Non-Profit Hospital Service Plans, by C. Rufus Rorem, American Hospital Association, Chicago, 2d ed., 1944.

20. Is there a hospital service plan in your community or state? Who is eligible to enroll? Are Negroes eligible? Groups of employed persons only or also individuals? What services are covered and for what period of time? What are the most widely needed services *excluded* under the plan? Is there a ward service as well as a semi-private service plan? What is the rate of prepayment?

21. What hospitals participate in the service and what are their standards? How is the administration organized and who is represented on the administrative bodies? Are the consumers represented?

22. What is the experience with the operation of the plan? What proportion of the population in your community is enrolled and to what economic groups do these persons belong? How many participants are subscribers? How many family participants? Does the plan meet the needs of subscribers?

23. How much of the total income of the participating hospitals is derived from payments from the plan? To what extent has the plan increased the use of hospitals in your community?

24. Is the plan co-ordinated with a prepayment plan covering physicians' services? For what groups ineligible for membership in the hospital service plan is medical care particularly needed?

Prepayment for Medical Care. Nonprofit prepayment plans covering selected professional services or a combination of various professional and institutional services have been developed under a variety of auspices. In 1945 plans were providing services for approximately 6,000,000 members.[1] More than half of these members were provided for under plans sponsored by medical societies (as, for example, those in Michigan and California); 1,500,000 came under industrial plans (such as those of the Tennessee Coal, Iron and Railroad Company and the Kaiser companies). Smaller numbers were served by plans organized by private group clinics (such as the Ross-Loos Clinic in Los Angeles); consumer-sponsored plans (as, for example, that of the Group Health Association, Washington, D.C.), and governmental plans of which that of the War Food Administration was by far the largest.

The scope of service varies greatly. The majority of the medical society plans cover only surgical service in a hospital. However, some (including those in Washington and Oregon) provide for most of the essential services. The majority of the plans established by organizations other than medical societies include hospitalization as well as a variety of professional services in the home, office or clinic, and hospital, and auxiliary services.

Eligibility requirements usually include group enrollment. Further widely applicable requirements relate to residence in a defined geographic

[1] For a description of programs and statistics see Prepayment Medical Care Organizations, Bureau Memorandum no. 55, Social Security Board, Government Printing Office, Washington, 3d ed., 1945.

area, physical examination upon admission, age restrictions, and income limits.

25. Is there a nonprofit prepayment plan for medical care in your community or state? Who is eligible to subscribe? What requirements must be met? Are Negroes eligible? What rates of prepayment are charged? Do employers bear any or all of the cost? How many persons are enrolled? How is the administration organized? Are consumers represented in the controlling body?

26. What services are covered, and for what period of time? Hospital care? Surgery? Physicians' services in hospital, clinic, office, home? Services of specialists? Dental service? Maternity care? Nursing service? Diagnostic and laboratory service?

27. How many physicians participate in the plan and what specialties are represented? Are participating physicians authorized to make extra charges for service to patients earning more than a certain amount?

28. Is there a group practice prepayment plan in your community? What is the basis of payment? Who is responsible for its administration? What is the size and composition of the staff? Does the group use a clinic or a hospital as base?

29. Who may subscribe for care? How many persons are enrolled in this prepayment plan? Does the group also accept patients who are not subscribers? What is the experience as to quantity, quality, cost, and administration of the service?

30. What provision is there for continuing in effect the benefits of prepayment plans during periods of unemployment or economic need? Do public assistance or other agencies help temporarily needy persons to keep their benefits in effect? In the opinion of physicians and consumers how well do prepayment plans in your community meet the need for such measures?

III. SPECIAL MEDICAL CARE PROGRAMS

In addition to general medical care programs already described there are in operation a variety of programs for special groups such as pregnant women, nursing mothers, infants and school children, veterans, and finally, sufferers from particular diseases or handicaps, notably communicable diseases and physical disabilities.

Mothers and Children. Recent years have seen tremendous progress in safeguarding the lives and health of mothers and young children. Nevertheless, these gains are still very uneven over the country and vary widely among different social and economic groups. Negro infant mortality rates, for example, are still nearly twice as high as those for white babies. Despite significant progress, some 200,000 mothers each year receive no medical care at childbirth. Competent authorities estimate that our present infant mortality rates could be cut in half if necessary funds, facilities, and services were provided.

Promotion of direct methods of guarding the health of mothers and babies is of such national importance that federal legislation empowers the United States Children's Bureau to help finance approved state plans for extending and improving local maternal and child health services.[1]

Publications which will assist you in your study of maternal and infant health services include: Child-Health Conference: Suggestions for Organization and Procedure;[2] Standards of Prenatal Care: An Outline for the Use of Physicians;[3] and Standards and Recommendations for Hospital Care of Maternity Patients.[4]

A summary of health and medical measures for children is included in the final report of the 1940 White House Conference on Children in a Democracy.[5]

31. Has the United States Children's Bureau approved your state's plan for maternal and child health? When? Date of first grant? Has the program been improved and extended since that date? What services are now offered under the plan?

32. Does your local health department receive from the State Department of Health subsidies in aid of its maternal and child health program? How much?

33. What has been accomplished in your community under the emergency maternity and infant care program (administered by state departments of health in co-operation with the Children's Bureau) for families of Army and Navy enlisted personnel of the lower pay grades?

34. What supervision of midwives is provided for in your state? What supervision of maternity homes? How is this supervision given in your community? Are maternity homes licensed and inspected? What facilities have you for the care of Negro patients?

35. Of births in your community last year, what proportion was in hospital, what proportion at home?

36. Of home births reported, what proportion was attended and reported by a physician? A midwife? What provision is there for medical or nursing service for home births in families unable to pay for such care?

Increasing emphasis in recent years has been laid upon the importance of hospital care for maternity cases. Experience gained under the emergency maternity and infant care program during World War II demonstrated that the majority of women concerned preferred hospital care if it could be made available to them.

37. How many hospital beds are available in your community for childbirth? How many available for free care? How many patient-days were used last year

---

[1] Various measures such as the provision of a safe milk supply and community sanitation (discussed in Chapter 8) have an important bearing upon infant and maternal health.

[2] U.S. Children's Bureau, Publication no. 261, Government Printing Office, Washington, 1941.

[3] *Idem,* Publication no. 153, 1940.   [4] *Idem,* Publication no. 272, 1942.

[5] *Idem,* Publication no. 314, 1946.

for maternity care? Is there a sufficient number of hospital beds for maternity care available to all racial groups?

38. What special hospital facilities and home nursing services are available in cases of premature birth? Is incubator service available? Is there any organized means in your community of obtaining breast milk when mothers are unable to nurse their babies? Is it supplied free? Under what conditions?

Because births out of wedlock involve a whole series of special social, health, and personal problems, particular provisions are required if the interests not only of the mothers but also of their children are to be safeguarded.[1]

39. What provisions are there in your community for care of unmarried mothers? How many unmarried women cared for last year? Are maternity hospitals and other services available to unmarried mothers of all races? Are social services, including mental hygiene service, available in hospitals or other agencies to insure that the mother and child receive care in accordance with their needs? Are special funds available for foster home care when needed?

40. Do procedures in the registration of births of children born out of wedlock provide the protection of not revealing illegitimacy of the child on the birth certificate?[2]

41. What special services are available to help unmarried mothers keep their babies, to avoid exploitation by persons seeking to adopt children, or to reunite mothers and children if it is found later that a mother can properly care for a child?

Public health agencies stress the major importance of early examinations and proper nutrition for pregnant women in order to assure the best possible health of both the mother and baby.

42. Are there prenatal clinics in your community for the education and supervision of expectant mothers? How early in pregnancy are mothers urged to attend? How long after the child's birth? What efforts are made to induce attendance? Is care given free? How many visits were made to clinics last year? (See page 108.)

43. What routine laboratory tests are carried out? Does your state law require that Wassermann tests be given to all expectant mothers?

44. What agencies do educational work in the field of nutrition for pregnant women, nursing mothers, and infants? Do any agencies help pregnant women, nursing mothers, and young children to secure needed foods not otherwise available?

45. What has been the increase or decrease in the infant mortality rate in your community during the past ten years, for Negro and white children? The maternal mortality rate? (See page 94.)

[1] A suggested reference on this subject is Services for Unmarried Mothers and Their Children, by the U.S. Children's Bureau, Government Printing Office, Washington, 1945.
[2] Read Birth Out of Wedlock, available in mimeographed form from the U.S. Children's Bureau, Washington, 1945.

46. Do any clinics in your community give contraceptive advice? Treatment? At request of physician? Otherwise? What are the legal provisions in your state governing (a) dissemination of contraceptive information, (b) supplying of contraceptive devices?

47. What clinics exist in your community (a) for the treatment of infants, (b) for the routine health supervision of mothers and babies, (c) for pediatric care? Are preventive health services freely available? What hospitals have pediatric beds? How many beds in all? How many for Negroes? Is the number of free beds adequate to the need? Which of the hospitals and clinics serving mothers and babies have medical social workers to deal with social needs?

48. Which of the hospitals and clinics serving mothers and babies have nurses who visit and give instruction in the home? How many nurses assigned to this special service? How many mothers given home instruction last year? What proportion of mothers visited by public health nurses during the first two or three weeks following childbirth?

49. Is Child Health Day made the occasion for emphasizing maternal and child health needs? Has any intensive program of public education in maternal and child health been undertaken in your community during the past year?

50. Are working women of your community allowed sufficient time from work to safeguard their health and that of their children before and after childbirth?

School Children. Health care and education of the school child, whether conducted by the school or the health department, is considered here.

The work of the school health program is both preventive and corrective. Through health education students learn how to prevent disease, how to live healthfully, and how to co-operate with community health agencies. Two standard manuals on the subject are Health Education: A Guide for Teachers in Elementary and Secondary Schools and Institutions for Teacher Education,[1] and Health in Schools.[2] A recent report, Suggested School Health Policies: A Charter for School Health, outlines the scope of school health programs and recommends policies for each phase of activity.[3]

Not only the school physician, dentist, and nurse are involved, but also the classroom teacher through whom most of the instruction in prevention and hygiene will be given to the children. Teachers should be alert to discover and report to the doctor and nurse symptoms of communicable diseases or any physical abnormalities observed.

Important as school health services have been, they do not necessarily assure the correction of disabilities revealed. A recent study in an eastern city has shown, for example, that many registrants rejected by Selective

[1] Joint Committee on Health Problems in Education of the National Education Association and the American Medical Association. National Education Association, Washington, 1941.
[2] American Association of School Administrators, Twentieth Yearbook, Washington, 1942.
[3] National Committee on School Health Policies, Teachers College, New York, 1946.

Service examiners during World War II were turned down because of conditions which had been discovered in school some fifteen years before but which had remained uncorrected.

51. What person on the school staff gives leadership to school health activities and co-ordinates school and community health efforts? Is this person prepared for administrative and supervisory work in health education and other school health activities?

52. How many school physicians are employed? By what department? Full or part time? For how many children is each responsible? How frequently are the children seen by the doctor?

53. How many school nurses are employed? By what department? Full or part time? For how many children is each nurse responsible?

54. Secure a copy of the health record card used, and note the items on it. Is it completely filled out at each examination? Does the child's health record card follow him through his school career? Where are the children examined? With or without clothing? Are parents encouraged to be present at examinations?

55. How does the school nurse report the results of medical examinations to teachers and parents?

56. If families prefer to have children examined by their own family physician, are there means of securing and recording his findings regularly on the child's school record card?

57. Does the school nurse assist the doctor with examinations? Is she responsible for follow-up care between his visits? Has she an office? Regular office hours? How often does she visit the classrooms? What emergency care does she give?

58. What policies guide school personnel in caring for pupils who become sick or injured at school? Does each teacher have a written copy of established policies? Has the school medical adviser prepared *written* directions for the emergency care to be given?

59. What is done to correct defects noted in school physical examinations? What proportion of identified defects are corrected? By whom is the correction made? What is done if the child's family is unable to pay?

60. Is there a school dentist? A dental clinic attached to the school system? What types of dental care are given? Are fees charged? What are they? What provision for free treatment? How often do the children have dental examinations?

61. How many children had dental examinations last year? How many had dental defects corrected (a) by their own dentists, (b) by the school dentist? Is instruction in oral hygiene a part of the regular health education program?

62. How frequently are the children's vision and hearing tested? Is any treatment given by community agencies for children with such defects? (See pages 139 and 141.) Are glasses supplied when families cannot pay for them?

63. What co-operative arrangements has the school health department with other health agencies in your community for treatment and for remedial work for children whose parents are unable to provide such care? Is there a community school health council?

64. Is there a clinic in the community for cardiac children? Diabetic children? Any other special clinics for children? (See page 130.)

65. What special provision is made in your schools for children suffering from physical handicaps, heart or other diseases requiring special attention? Do the schools offer special services to such children in their own homes?

66. What treatment is available for children who appear to be undernourished? Is there a nutrition clinic? What efforts are made to correct faulty food habits, instruct children and parents in the principles of nutrition? Is milk provided? Free or at low cost?

67. What modifications are made in the school routine for handicapped students and other children who are under par physically? Are they given rest periods? Are cots or reclining chairs provided? Extra feedings? Periods for supervised exercise? Describe.

68. What do the reports of the school health department show as to (a) improvement in health, (b) improvement in school progress, of children who have received special health care in school?

69. Are working children attending continuation classes given the same health care as the other children?

70. Are school health programs in private or parochial schools supervised? By what public agency?

71. In what grades is the teaching of health and hygiene begun? Does the school hygiene department supervise the quality of the teaching, choice of textbooks? Are efforts made to present these subjects in terms of the daily lives of the children?

72. Is there a teachers' guide or course of study for elementary school health education? For health education in the secondary schools?

73. How much time is allotted to health education in the secondary schools? Are textbooks, reference books, visual aids, and other teaching helps provided?

74. Who teaches secondary school health education courses? Have these persons had special preparation for their work?

75. Are there resources in your community such as child-guidance clinics or other agencies for education and consultation of pediatricians, doctors, nurses, and others regarding mental hygiene of childhood? Are child-guidance clinics available in your community for mental health services?[1]

76. Is use made in the schools of educational health films, radio programs? Was Child Health Day last year made the occasion of emphasizing school health needs? What part was taken by the school health department?

77. Is co-operation of parents and the school health program developed through the parent-teacher association?

Communicable diseases of childhood have their best chance of spreading among school children whose personal hygiene is not supervised, and who are not excluded from school on the appearance of the first symptoms.

78. How many cases of measles, scarlet fever, chickenpox, poliomyelitis were

[1] See "Coordinating Mental-Hygiene Work for Children," in The Child, June, 1945, pp. 183–186.

reported in your community last year? Were they epidemic? Were any other diseases of childhood epidemic?

79. What has been the increase or decrease in the death rate from communicable diseases of childhood in your community during the past ten years?

80. Are children required to be vaccinated against smallpox before admission to school? What proportion of children entering school are found not to have had during the preschool period (a) vaccination against smallpox, (b) Schick tests for diphtheria, and, if susceptible, immunization, (c) immunization against whooping cough, (d) immunization against tetanus?

81. What responsibility is taken by the school health department for ascertaining and immunizing susceptibles?

82. How frequently are tuberculin tests given to high school pupils? To teachers and other employes? Are those who react positively X-rayed?

Sufferers from Communicable Diseases. State and local public health departments co-operate according to several different patterns in the prevention and control of various communicable diseases. A pamphlet, The Control of Communicable Diseases, published by the American Public Health Association, will be useful for reference at this point.[1]

83. What are the diseases which must be reported by your health department as communicable and dangerous to public health? How many cases of each were reported in your community last year? (See page 96.)

84. What epidemics have occurred within the past five years? What measures to control them were adopted by your health department or by the State Health Department?

85. Is a spot map available in your community showing location of cases of tuberculosis, syphilis, other communicable diseases? Compare it with your density map. (See page 26.)

Isolation hospitals for communicable diseases are no longer felt to be a necessity. Thanks to modern methods of disinfection, wards of general hospitals can now be employed for this purpose.

86. Does your community maintain an isolation hospital for communicable diseases? Isolation wards in the general hospital? How many beds available? What diseases treated there?

87. For what communicable diseases, if any, may removal to hospital be ordered in your community?

88. In general, what regulations are enforced in the home care of communicable diseases? What restraints are placed upon other persons who have been exposed to the disease?

89. Do public health nurses give nursing service and instruction in homes where there are patients with communicable diseases?

90. Have your health authorities legal power to control carriers of communicable diseases? How many carriers are under surveillance in your community?

[1] New York, 1945.

91. For what diseases are vaccines and serums kept on hand by your health department? Are they administered by physicians employed by the department? Can physicians obtain them for use in private practice? Under what conditions can patients obtain free serum and vaccine treatment?

92. To what degree is vaccination against smallpox required of the people in your community? Is any other immunization compulsory?

Two communicable diseases are of peculiar public health interest because of the great numbers of persons affected. These are tuberculosis and syphilis.

The prevention of tuberculosis calls for early and intensive attention to the health of children, as well as for measures which build up the general health of the adult population. This involves better wages and better working conditions, better milk and food supply, better public understanding of nutrition and hygienic habits. Read The Modern Attack on Tuberculosis, by Henry D. Chadwick and Alton S. Pope.[1] Public health workers believe that only through routine periodic examinations with X-rays of supposedly well people, can tuberculosis be detected in its early and easily controllable stages.

93. What agencies in your community are conducting community campaigns for (a) routine annual health examinations of supposedly well people, (b) public information about tuberculosis and its prevention and treatment? (See page 111.)

Since 1900 tuberculosis has been deposed as the leading cause of death in the United States and now rates only seventh. Nevertheless, it continues to take more lives than any other disease among persons between the ages of fifteen and forty-five. Approximately 55,000 persons are estimated to succumb annually to tuberculosis.

94. What has been the increase or decrease in the death rate from tuberculosis over the past ten years in your community?

95. Can you secure from private health organizations such as your state or local anti-tuberculosis association more detailed analysis of the morbidity and mortality statistics in your community for tuberculosis as it affects different age groups, races, and occupations?

96. Can these agencies give you any estimate of what tuberculosis costs your community annually, in actual expenditure, in wage loss, and how this figure compares with that of similar communities?

97. What clinical facilities are there in your community for the early diagnosis of tuberculosis? Is supervision given in these clinics to arrested cases discharged from hospitals? Are any clinics held at night? Is the service free? How many visits were made to tuberculosis clinics last year?

98. Are public health nurses attached to the clinics? Do their duties include

[1] Commonwealth Fund, New York, rev. ed., 1946.

case-finding? Follow-up of patients who need clinic care? Securing examinations of persons suspected of being infected? Are social workers attached to the clinic?

99. Is there an anti-spitting ordinance in your community? How is it enforced?

100. Are wards in local hospitals available for both early and advanced cases of tuberculosis? Is free care available? Is there a tuberculosis sanatorium in your county? Public or private? How many patients from your community? Were any refused last year for lack of beds? Is care provided free?

101. Is there a state tuberculosis hospital which receives cases in all stages? How many patients from your community?

102. If Negro and white patients are separately cared for in your community, how many beds available for each? In the opinion of informed specialists, how adequate are these facilities?

Syphilis, gonorrhea, and the so-called minor venereal diseases constitute major public health problems, despite improved methods of treatment, more widespread treatment facilities, and recent drastic time reduction in therapy. Read What You Should Know About Syphilis and Gonorrhea, by Max J. Exner.[1]

Prevention of these diseases lies in broad public information programs; development of sound family-life education in schools; adult education for responsible parenthood; the combined efforts of social, religious, health, and educational forces to meet the behavior aspects of these diseases; community measures to repress commercialized prostitution; and, of course, early diagnostic, case-finding efforts and prompt, adequate treatment of the diseases themselves.

With awakened active public interest, improved diagnostic and therapeutic measures, and with the growing trend toward prevention, it is possible to attempt some forecasts. We can look forward to an improvement in the economic aspects of the venereal disease problem. Treatment will be less expensive, fewer days of employment lost, and fewer individuals rendered unemployable through the more devastating manifestations of syphilis, in particular. Family life will undoubtedly be strengthened as prevention of venereal disease is stressed.

103. What public instruction is given by your health authorities on avoidance of venereal diseases? On availability of treatment? Have citizen groups been induced to have blood tests for syphilis? If so, have health authorities provided public information and interpretation, so that the experience would have educational as well as case-finding value?

104. What agencies in the community are supporting and complementing the efforts of health authorities in educating the public about venereal diseases? Are

[1] The American Social Hygiene Association, New York, rev. 1945.

these agencies working with parents, teachers, the clergy, and others interested in preventing venereal diseases? What is done among young people to emphasize wholesome standards and to prevent misuse of the reproductive instinct? Does the curriculum in your elementary and high schools include family-life education?

105. What can you learn from your state and local health departments and social hygiene societies about the incidence of venereal diseases in your community? About the prevalence of insanity probably attributable to syphilis? About stillbirths resulting from venereal diseases? About the number of congenital syphilis cases born annually?

106. What diagnostic and treatment facilities for venereal diseases are there in your community? Are these adequate to meet the demands of up-to-date medical practice? Are public health nurses, social workers, employed in clinics or hospitals treating venereal diseases? How many visits made to public venereal disease facilities last year? Are services freely available to all persons in need of them?

Protection of the public health calls for knowledge on the part of the authorities of cases of infectious venereal disease being treated by physicians. The laws and regulations of nearly all states, therefore, require the reporting of venereal diseases, and empower the health authorities to require treatment of infectious cases of syphilis and gonorrhea. Owing to the fact that many venereal disease infections are traceable to sexual promiscuity, the investigation of contacts involves difficulties such as do not apply to other communicable diseases. Continuing emphasis upon social treatment, upon interpretation, and upon need for understanding the emotional problem of the patient, will help to obviate these difficulties.[1]

107. Does the law or sanitary code specifically mention syphilis and gonorrhea among diseases which private physicians must report? Are they required to give the names and addresses of patients? Are they required to make further report when the patient is no longer infectious?

108. Are male and female sex offenders, including prostitutes, required on arrest or on conviction to undergo medical examination for venereal diseases and to submit to treatment if found to have syphilis or gonorrhea in a communicable stage? Are they held in custody until it is determined that they are noninfectious? (See references to prostitution in Index.)

109. What efforts are made by public health authorities to secure examinations of members of patients' families?

Additional communicable diseases which often necessitate special services are found in various sections of the country. These are, for example, hookworm, malaria, Rocky Mountain spotted fever, tularemia, and endemic

---

[1] Suggestions for community action may be found in Challenge to Community Action, Federal Security Agency, Government Printing Office, Washington, 1945. Also see two pamphlets, Suggestions for Organizing a Community Social Hygiene Program, and Social Hygiene Organization and Your Community, both issued by the American Social Hygiene Association, New York, 1944.

typhus. Public health measures against these diseases emphasize the eradication of insect carriers.

110. Have special campaigns been necessary in your community within recent years to eliminate insect carriers of disease? How prosecuted, under what direction, and with what funds? What have been the results, as shown in morbidity and mortality rates?

111. What communicable diseases, other than tuberculosis and venereal diseases, have required special action in your community? What has been done about them?

Noncommunicable Diseases. The interest of public health authorities in diseases not of a communicable nature is a matter of somewhat recent development. The most widespread efforts in this field are those directed against cancer and cardiac diseases.

Among diseases, heart ailments now rank as number one killer in the United States. In 1944 approximately 28 per cent of all deaths were reported as due to diseases of the heart. Read Problems in the Prevention and Relief of Diseases of the Heart, by Irving R. Roth.[1]

Heart diseases are of many different types. Heart disease among children is chiefly due to attacks of rheumatic fever and other diseases of childhood, and its prevention depends upon proper treatment of the predisposing condition. Syphilitic heart disease affects people in middle life, and its prevention depends upon control or eradication of syphilis. The arteriosclerotic type strikes later in life, and its cause is not yet sufficiently understood to make prevention feasible. Social and economic factors, important in relation to other diseases, have an important bearing upon heart disease also. Among children of low-income groups the incidence of heart disease has been found to be higher than among more privileged children. The incidence among Negroes is also higher than that among white persons.

Treatment of cardiac disease often involves complete reorganization of the patient's way of life, with rest and freedom from strain, anxiety, and excitement as the principal goals. Special heart clinics, so far as they have been developed, are usually for cardiac children.

112. What has been the increase or decrease in the death rate from heart disease in your community during the past five years? In what age and socio-economic groups have the changes been most apparent?

113. What special clinics, rest homes, or other facilities for cardiacs are available in your community? What services do they render? Are any particularly concerned with the discovery and treatment of rheumatic fever among children?

[1] American Heart Association, Inc., New York, 1943.

114. What agencies are informing the public about heart disease and the ways of mitigating its dangers? Describe their activities.

Deaths resulting from cancer have seriously increased in recent years and now constitute 12 per cent of all deaths, ranking second only to deaths from heart diseases. The cause of the disease is obscure. Hope of recovery lies in early diagnosis and quick beginning of treatment, and it is toward these ends that public health campaigns are directed. Cancer, A Study for Laymen, by Clarence C. Little,[1] is suggested reading at this point.

115. What has been the increase or decrease in the death rate from cancer in your community during the past ten years?
116. Is there a special cancer clinic in your community? Locally supported or state-aided? Independent, or part of a hospital or health center? Is the service free? Adjusted to patients' incomes? Is there provision for large-scale diagnostic examinations? Is treatment provided? What types? Is radium available for treatment? Are charges made for X-ray, radium, or other treatments? What follow-up care is provided after completion of treatment? Are public health nurses, social workers, attached to the clinic? How many visits made to cancer clinics last year?
117. Is there a special cancer hospital? Are there special cancer wards in general hospitals? Are early cases received for diagnosis? Are hopeless cases taken, or only those which are still operable? How many beds available in your community especially for cancer patients?
118. What steps have been taken in your community to inform the public about cancer and the importance of early examination and treatment? (See page 111.) Is the American Cancer Society or a related organization active in your community?

There are other noncommunicable diseases—including the dietary deficiency diseases such as pellagra, largely in the South, and goiter, particularly in the Middle West—which have led public health authorities to make special efforts to combat their effects.

119. Has it been necessary in your community for public health authorities to supply vitamin-containing foods or other treatment to combat pellagra? To promote use of iodized salt or to iodize the water supply to combat goiter?
120. Are there other noncontagious diseases the prevalence of which in your community has led to special action?

Chronically Ill Persons. With medical service centered mainly on acute illness, chronic illness has been seriously neglected. Helpful suggestions for a community program for the care of the chronic sick are included in The Unseen Plague, by Ernest P. Boas.[2]

[1] American Cancer Society, New York, rev. ed., 1944.
[2] J. J. Augustin, New York, 1940. See also "Combatting Chronic Illness," by Mary C. Jarrett, in Public Welfare. June, 1945, pp. 129–131.

Although generally identified in the public mind with the aged, actually over one-half of those disabled by chronic illness are under fifty-five, in the productive years of life, or even in childhood. Problems raised by chronic illness are those of prevention, early diagnosis, medical care and services, housing, vocational training, retraining, and placement. These are questions of both private and governmental responsibility, to be shared by health and welfare departments, and involving many other agencies and services. Specially trained personnel which, however, is not yet sufficiently available, is required.

Statistics on chronic illness are difficult to secure. Nevertheless, your hospitals, local medical association, visiting nurse association, and welfare department can probably give you estimates of the approximate number of chronically ill persons in need of care in your community.

121. What is being done in your community to prevent those diseases which are the chief cause of chronic illness?

122. Has your community arranged publicity campaigns urging early diagnosis of diseases most responsible for chronic illness? With what success? Have special diagnostic centers been established? Are diagnostic services free to persons unable to pay?

123. Does your public hospital have adequate facilities for study, treatment, and care of the chronic sick? Are there special wards or special divisions, separate from acute cases, where the long-term patient may enjoy a cheerful atmosphere? How many free beds? What private hospital facilities are there for chronic cases? How many free beds?

124. Is case work by trained social workers available to help solve the many social and economic problems of chronic patients and their families? Have these social workers had special training in medical social work?

125. If chronically ill patients are improving but need further medical care and nursing, are there convalescent homes where they may stay for a while before going home? What provision is there for persons who cannot afford to pay the usual rates?

126. If the patients' condition cannot be improved, is there a hospital-affiliated institution where they can be cared for in surroundings with as little institutional atmosphere as possible? Is it well staffed with medical and nursing personnel?

127. Are the institutions and homes referred to in the preceding questions open to Negroes or other minority groups on the same basis as to majority groups? How does the ratio of Negroes, or other minority groups, to the total cared for in these institutions compare with their ratio to the general population? Are there groups such as veterans which receive preferential treatment?

128. Do your public or private institutions and homes carry depressing and outmoded names such as home for incurables, home for incurable cancer, home for aged and infirm?

129. Are these institutions and homes characterized by a spirit of personal and social understanding or are they merely custodial and palliative? Are services of trained case workers available?

130. If chronically ill patients do not want to live in an institution and have homes to which to go, is home medical care available? Nursing care? Has the visiting nurse association sufficient personnel to care for chronic cases? Is the service free if patients are unable to pay? For patients who are not confined to their homes are there out-patient clinics where they may be treated? Are these equipped to give the time-consuming attention chronic patients frequently require?

131. Is there a public nursing home for patients who are unable to pay the usual charges? Are there sufficient private nursing and boarding homes for patients of small or moderate means? Are such homes licensed by the state and regularly inspected?[1]

132. Do chronically ill recipients of public assistance receive special allowances to enable them to enter nursing, boarding, or foster homes? To provide for medical care, special diets, and other needs? How many assistance recipients are living in these homes?

133. Are there opportunities for training, retraining, and placement of chronically ill persons able to work full time or part time? Are there sheltered workshops? Is there any community agency which makes it possible for chronically ill persons to engage in gainful employment in their own homes?

[1] Inspection should include such points as personnel, food, sanitary conditions, fire hazards.

10. PROVISIONS FOR SPECIAL GROUPS

CLOSELY allied to organized medical services discussed in the preceding chapter are the provisions made for a variety of groups requiring special service or care. Among these groups are those in need of shelter or general institutional care, travelers, or migrants needing a highly specialized type of assistance, and finally, physically or mentally handicapped children and adults.

For some of these groups the care provided is much like that for sick persons, discussed in Chapter 9. However, most of the special groups now to be considered require not only medical care and treatment, but also need broader and longer-range social, educational, and rehabilitative services.

I. GENERAL INSTITUTIONAL AND SHELTER CARE

One of the earliest forms of public service was the almshouse. Although originally caring for all ages and conditions of dependent persons, one class after another has been withdrawn to more suitable types of special institutions—children's homes, general hospitals, mental hospitals, shelters for homeless persons, and correctional institutions[1]—until today the general welfare institution, where it still exists, has become largely an infirmary for the aged and sick poor. Many communities have discontinued their almshouses and general welfare institutions altogether, and pay other types of institutions or boarding homes for care provided needy persons for whom the community is responsible.

In a few communities may be found workhouses or farm colonies where dependent persons not entirely disabled may contribute to their own support by labor adjusted to their capacities.

1. In your community does your public welfare department maintain an institution which serves as an almshouse? Location? When built or remodeled? Capacity? Who is eligible for care? Who decides what persons shall be given care?

[1] Discussed in subsequent sections of this chapter and in Chapters 8, 9, and 16.

2. Is it congregate, or cottage type? Separate rooms or wards? Are there rooms which aged couples may share?

3. Is the institution licensed and supervised by a state or other agency? How was it rated when last inspected?

4. How is its superintendent chosen? Qualifications which led to the appointment of present incumbent?

5. How many inmates at present? How many under sixty-five? Are children, mentally ill or defective persons included?

6. What is the per capita cost of operation per day? Obtain and study menus for the current week. How do they compare with approved nutritional standards?

7. Does the institution have a farm? A dairy? What work are inmates expected to do?

8. Is there a resident or visiting physician? How often are medical inspections made? What are the facilities for bed care of crippled or infirm inmates? Are there nurses on the staff?

9. Are social workers employed? If so, what is their responsibility with respect to deciding who shall be admitted to the institution? Whenever possible are inmates transferred to a more appropriate form of care than that provided by the institution?

Homes for the Aged. A more specialized type of institutional care is frequently available for aged persons. This is sometimes provided under governmental and sometimes under voluntary auspices. Private homes for the aged usually restrict admissions to certain definite groups such as members of certain religious denominations or fraternal organizations. Eligibility may depend upon the applicant's residence, citizenship, country of origin, profession, or other factor. The increasing demand for institutional care for persons who are unable to care for themselves is bringing about a discernible shift in the health requirements for admission.

Some private homes for the aged require no entrance fees. Others, however, may charge heavy fees sometimes running into hundreds of dollars and including also the assignment of all the applicant's property. Homes may give free care for life, or be run on a straight boarding basis, like a hotel for old people. Or any combination of these methods of current financing may be found in the same institution. Legislative provisions permitting the payment of old-age assistance to residents of private homes is having its effect upon the plans for financial arrangements in these homes.

Some private homes in this country and abroad, notably in England, Denmark, and Sweden, have pioneered in replacing the institutional plan with more homelike arrangements such as the cottage type or apartments, especially designed for old people, with private living quarters supplied with light, heat, refrigeration, laundry, kitchenette, and if preferred, cafeteria service.

Literature on the subject of homes for the aged, though still slight, is increasing. Among reports which may be useful in your study are the following: Suggested Standards for Homes for the Aged;[1] Old Age in New York City, by Helen Brunot;[2] and Mental Health in Later Maturity.[3]

10. List the homes for the aged in your community exclusive of general welfare institutions or almshouse. For each, give pertinent information listed above regarding general institutions. List also auspices, entrance requirements, admission fee, if any, and number on waiting list.

11. How many beds are available in private homes for the aged in your community (a) free, (b) for a weekly or monthly payment, (c) for life on payment of an entrance fee? How many beds available to persons receiving old-age assistance?

12. What income does each institution have from (a) endowment, (b) payments from residents, (c) other sources? What is the per capita per diem cost of operation for each? How does this compare with that of your general public institution?

13. Is the institution congregate or cottage type? Are separate rooms available for old people, old couples? May they furnish these rooms with their own belongings if they prefer?

14. If two people must share the same room, is effort made to assign those whose personalities will be harmonious?

15. Is boarding care provided for those able to pay it? Are persons receiving old-age assistance (see Chapter 14) or old-age benefits (see Chapter 6) received as residents of old people's homes?

16. Obtain and study menus for a week. How do they compare with recognized nutritional standards?

17. What homes for the aged have social workers on the staff? Resident or visiting physicians? Trained nurses? What provision is made for bed care? For funeral expenses?

18. What recreation is provided for residents? Are clubs, organizations, invited to socials at the homes so as to give residents a chance to mingle with people from outside?

19. Is it the policy of private homes to take care of aged persons regardless of their physical condition or is transfer made to a nursing home, hospital, or general institution?

Care of Homeless Persons and Transients. Still another specialized type of care is that offered to homeless persons normally resident in a given community and to transient persons who may be in transit or only newly established in their place of present residence.

[1] Welfare Council of New York City, 1939. Supplementary recommendations as to standards are to be found in Criteria to Aid in Establishing Board Rates for Care of Old Age Assistance Recipients in Voluntary Homes for the Aged, Welfare Council of New York City, 1946.
[2] *Idem*, 1943.
[3] Papers presented at a conference held in Washington, D.C., May, 1941. U.S. Public Health Service, Supplement no. 168, Government Printing Office, Washington, 1942.

20. Are there public shelters for homeless men? What provision is made for homeless (a) young boys, (b) girls and single women, (c) families? By what department are these services administered?

21. Does your community operate its own municipal or county shelters for transients? What public agency operates these facilities?

22. Does your community provide shelter for transients in the local jail? Through purchase from commercial lodging and boarding houses? Through payments or subsidies to a shelter operated by a private agency?

23. What private agencies give care to homeless or transient men, boys, girls, or women? To families? Describe methods of care available from private agencies for these groups. Is there a central registration bureau for transients? Under what auspices?

24. What is the capacity of your shelters? Are meals supplied? One, two, or three per day? Study the menus. How long are inmates permitted to stay? Maximum, minimum number accommodated on any given night last year? How many days' care given? Cost per person per day?

25. What is the experience and training of the shelter superintendent(s)? How are disciplinary problems handled?

26. Visit the shelter(s) and observe the general sanitation, heating, and ventilation. Are showers available? Facilities for washing clothes? For barbering? Lockers for personal belongings? Is clothing fumigated? What bedding is provided? How frequently changed, aired, disinfected?

27. Are there facilities for care of young and inexperienced men separate from "old hands" on the road? Is a social worker employed? Available from some other agency?

28. What health care is available? Is there a medical examination on entrance? Daily medical inspection? Is there provision to isolate those with symptoms of communicable diseases?

29. What recreation do inmates have? Is there opportunity to play games, read, smoke, on the premises?

30. What work are the lodgers expected to perform (a) in the running of the institution, (b) other work?

31. How many transient persons and families applied for assistance in your community last year?

32. How many were (a) denied relief in any form, (b) given temporary shelter and told to leave the community, (c) assisted to return to some place on which they had a legal claim, and cared for while arrangements for their return were pending, (d) given temporary relief or work assignments to help them establish themselves in the community?

Lodgings for Workers. Congregate lodging for various groups of young working men and women is sometimes provided under private auspices. Special facilities are frequently afforded for migrant workers and their families.

33. Are there noncommercial hostels or boarding homes for working men, women, in your community? For each, list auspices, type of management, age limits, amount charged for board and room, number accommodated. Is the

agency maintained by income from boarders? If not, from what source is its income supplemented?

34. Are there camps or other facilities for migrant workers and their families in your community? How operated? Under what auspices? (See also pages 57–58.)

II. SPECIAL SERVICES TO TRAVELERS AND MIGRANTS

In addition to temporary shelter care, travelers and migrants often require a variety of services usually provided by highly specialized agencies. An agency which offers special service of this type is the Travelers Aid Society, whose particular interest is the family, or members of the family, who are in transit from one place to another. The purpose of this organization is to provide individualized aid including financial assistance, case work, and travel service, as well as information about community resources. The National Travelers Aid Association will supply information about functions and standards of local travelers aid societies.

35. Has your community a Travelers Aid Society? When was it organized? Is it a member of the National Travelers Aid Association? Is it independent, or a department of some other agency?

36. How is its board appointed? Number and qualifications of present board?

37. What was the agency's budget last year? Source?

38. How many workers (exclusive of clerical employes) on its staff? How many are members of a professional association?

39. At what centers of transportation does it maintain workers? During what periods of the day and night? What services are rendered? Does it operate a shelter? Maintain an information service? A community resource file including housing, recreation, churches, employment agencies able and willing to aid travelers and migrants? How many of these services were rendered during the past year? How many travelers given service?

III. SERVICES FOR PHYSICALLY HANDICAPPED PERSONS

Among the physically handicapped persons for whom special services are provided are the partially seeing and the blind, the hard of hearing and the deaf, crippled and disabled children and adults. Services provided range from preventive programs to education, vocational training, provision of employment, medical treatment, the furnishing of prosthetic devices, and financial assistance to persons in need.

The Partially Seeing and the Blind. Persons with limited vision whose handicap is not sufficient to compel them to use tactual rather than sighted methods are called partially seeing. As they are misfits in schools or occupations suited to the blind, their education is provided for in so-called sight-saving classes, and they are guided into occupations suited to their visual abilities. Suggested reading is Education and Health of the Partially Seeing Child, by Winifred Hathaway.[1] The national agency from which information regarding this group can be secured is the National Society for the Prevention of Blindness.[2]

40. Does your state have a law providing for prophylaxis to eyes of new-born infants?

41. In your community, what agencies provide publicity or education on the prevention of blindness? How often are school children's eyes tested? What provision for glasses for children whose parents cannot pay for them? Are there sight conservation classes in the public schools? (See pages 124, 152.)

42. Are there special clinics in which children or adults can obtain free or low-cost corrective treatment for ocular difficulties? How many treated last year (a) children, (b) adults?

43. Has your state a law authorizing and providing financial support for special education of the partially seeing? Are facilities adequate to cover all children needing such?

44. Is there a public or voluntary agency in your state or community actively interested in the prevention of blindness? What is it doing?

45. Are any public or private agencies providing education in eye health? Eye safety? Counseling for partially seeing persons?

Largely because of the difficulty of defining blindness, its extent in the United States is not exactly known. However, it is probable that the total approximates a quarter of a million. A good reference at this point is Blindness and the Blind in the United States, by Harry Best.[3] The American Foundation for the Blind is the national agency serving this group.[2]

46. Does your state maintain a register of blind persons? How active is the responsible agency in discovering new names? In informing registrants of services or benefits available to them?

47. How many blind persons of school age are known to be living in your community?

48. How is education provided in the public school system for blind children? How many children served? (See pages 124, 152.) Are there in your state special educational institutions for blind persons? Publicly or privately supported? Number resident in each? Waiting list? In what occupations is training given? How many local children resident in schools or institutions for the blind elsewhere in the state?

49. Are opportunities for further education or vocational training open on graduation from the elementary grades? Are blind students going to college or university from your community provided with readers? Given other educational assistance?

[1] Columbia University Press, New York, 1943.
[2] For address see List of Agencies, p. 251.   [3] Macmillan Co., New York, 1934.

50. How many adult blind are there in your community? How many of them self-supporting?

51. How many blind or persons with defective vision are registered at the public employment exchange? At private noncommercial employment agencies? How many placed in jobs during the past year? In what occupations? Does your employment office systematically interpret to employers the various ways in which blind persons can be employed? (See page 143.)

52. Are there arrangements in your community whereby blind persons are given special permission to establish vendors' stands in public buildings? Elsewhere? How many take advantage of this opportunity?

53. Has your community any organization primarily concerned with service to blind persons? Does it manage a workshop? How many employed? Is vocational training given? In what occupations? What other services does it render? What is its annual budget? How raised? How many blind people does it serve?

54. Are local governmental agencies or other purchasers required to or do they voluntarily purchase certain types of products from workshops for the blind?

55. Does any agency in your community promote work for blind persons in their own homes? Provide raw materials? Give necessary instruction? Market the products?

56. How many needy blind persons in your community receive public assistance for the blind? (See Chapter 14.) Are assistance grants sufficient to allow for the special needs of blind persons? For guide service? For electric current for operation of radios?

57. Does public assistance or any community agency enable blind persons who are unable to purchase them for themselves to secure radios? Seeing Eye dogs? Typewriters? Braille writers? Braille watches? Medical treatment for the restoration or improvement of sight?

58. What special rehabilitation services are available to blind veterans in your community? In what respects are these superior to services available to other blind persons?

59. Is there a membership organization of blind persons in your community? How many members? What are its chief activities?

60. Does your public library circulate books in Braille? How many? Is there any other local source where they may be obtained? Can talking book records or machines be borrowed from any source in your community? (See page 164.)

61. Are there any local agencies providing services to the blind, such as visits, reading aloud, tickets to concerts, raising scholarships for gifted blind young people? How many blind people served?

The Hard of Hearing and the Deaf. Special public provision for the deaf has long been made in residential schools for the deaf. Apart from provision made for hard of hearing or deaf children in public schools not much has been done for these groups. A standard reference in this field is Deafness and the Deaf in the United States, by Harry Best.[1] Two national agencies concerned with various aspects of deafness are the American As-

[1] Macmillan Co., New York, 1943.

sociation to Promote the Teaching of Speech to the Deaf and the American Hearing Society.[1] There is a Library of Congress compilation entitled The Hard of Hearing and the Deaf: A Digest of State Laws Affecting the Acoustically Handicapped.[2]

62. Does your public school system offer any special facilities for children with hearing defects? How many children affected? How frequently are aural tests given to all pupils? Is the audiometer used?

63. Has your state an institution for training deaf persons? Public or private? How many pupils? How many from your community? Waiting list? Is vocational training given? In what occupations?

64. Are there public or private organizations rendering special services to the deaf or hard of hearing? Do they offer classes in lip reading, speech correction, vocational training or retraining, assistance in procuring appliances, recreation opportunities? How many do they serve? Do they promote the installation of acoustical systems in churches, movies, theaters, schools, and public auditoriums?

65. How many people are registered at the public employment exchange as having auditory handicaps? In private noncommercial agencies? How many placed last year? In what occupations? Does your public employment agency actively interpret to employers ways in which hard of hearing or deaf persons can be employed? (See page 143.)

66. Are aural tests available for persons not in school? Under what auspices? How frequently? Any special clinics for treatment of aural defects? How many patients treated last year? Special hearing centers for the demonstration and fitting of hearing aids? Is assistance available to persons who cannot afford to purchase hearing aids?

67. Are your deafened veterans availing themselves of the Red Cross and Veterans Administration programs designed to aid in the civilian adjustment of the deafened?

68. Is there a membership organization of deaf or hard of hearing persons in your community? How many members? Chief activities?

When you have finished this section of your study, ask yourself the questions:

69. What handicapped groups are receiving reasonably adequate care in my community? For which groups, and in which directions, do further facilities need to be provided?

The Disabled. The extent of disablement in our population is not generally realized although the war centered public attention upon the thousands of servicemen who returned handicapped and disabled. However, regardless of war, we have in the United States several million persons who are handicapped by physical impairments, chronic illness, or accidents.

---

[1] For addresses see List of Agencies, p. 251.
[2] Government Printing Office, Washington, 1943.

Accidents alone permanently disable some 350,000 persons each year. References that will prove valuable are The Crippled and Disabled: Rehabilitation of the Physically Handicapped in the United States, by Henry H. Kessler,[1] and Normal Lives for the Disabled, by Edna Yost and Lillian E. Gilbreth.[2] Two national agencies serving disabled persons are the National Society for Crippled Children and Adults and the National Rehabilitation Association.[3]

At this writing the so-called Baruch Committee on Physical Medicine is outlining plans for integrated community rehabilitation centers to provide broader services instead of the fragmentary service of small agencies which in the past have treated only single segments of the total problem.[4]

National provision for disabled persons dates back to the Vocational Rehabilitation Act of 1920, which was greatly liberalized by the so-called Barden-LaFollette amendments of 1943. Under the federal-state system of vocational rehabilitation federal funds are granted to states for mentally as well as physically disabled persons. The purpose of vocational rehabilitation programs is to restore disabled persons of working age to the fullest physical, mental, social, vocational, and economic usefulness of their capabilities. The Office of Vocational Rehabilitation, a constituent of the Federal Security Agency, is the central instrument in the federal-state program.

Federal grants to states are based upon actual requirements and the amount of state funds available for matching. The federal government, however, assumes the entire cost of administering state programs, and half the costs of medical examinations, surgical and therapeutic treatment, hospitalization, prosthetic devices, transportation, occupational tools and licenses, training and maintenance. The federal government assumes the entire cost of these items for war-disabled civilians.

State programs are administered by state boards of vocational education. During the fiscal year 1945 approximately 161,000 disabled persons received services from 51 state rehabilitation agencies and 25 commissions for the blind. That rehabilitation pays off economically is shown by the work of the Office of Vocational Rehabilitation, which reports that the 44,000 persons having undergone rehabilitation under this agency in 1944 increased their average annual wage from $148 to $1,768. The total cost of this rehabilitation averaged only $300 per case.

Services rendered include medical, surgical and psychiatric care, hos-

[1] Columbia University Press, New York, 1935.   [2] Macmillan Co., New York, 1944.
[3] For addresses see List of Agencies, p. 251.
[4] One example of a well co-ordinated local program is the so-called Peoria Plan. For details write The Peoria Plan, 415 Liberty St., Peoria, Illinois.

pitalization, artificial appliances, vocational guidance and training, maintenance during training, and placement in employment. Physical examination, counsel, and training are provided without cost to the applicant in all cases. Still other services are provided without cost to applicants unable to pay for them.[1]

70. What agency in your state administers funds for vocational rehabilitation of disabled persons? Of blind persons? How many individuals are served? How much was expended during the past fiscal year? What proportion came from federal grants?

71. At the local level, what agency is responsible for vocational rehabilitation? How many persons from your community have received assistance during the past year?

72. What classes of handicapped persons are accepted for vocational rehabilitation: (a) victims of industrial accidents; (b) victims of occupational diseases; (c) nonindustrial cripples; (d) handicapped but not crippled persons, e.g., the blind, the deaf, cardiacs, "arrested tb's"? Are services for any of the above relatively more adequate than for others?

73. What services are provided: (a) medical, surgical, psychiatric care; (b) hospitalization? Are prosthetic appliances provided? Vocational training? Where? Does assistance comprise free tuition? Transportation to training centers? Cash allowance for maintenance, either at home or away from home during training? If training on the job is provided what safeguards prevent employers from exploiting the system to avoid normal wage payments?

74. How do measures for the rehabilitation of disabled veterans in your community differ from those for other handicapped persons? What has been accomplished for veterans?

75. Are there governmental or nongovernmental agencies in your community which offer employment for physically handicapped workers? Are there sheltered workshops? How many persons employed on the average in each? What are their average weekly earnings?

76. Has the bureau of licenses a record of permits issued to handicapped persons to operate vendor stands? How many so employed?

77. How many physically handicapped persons are registered with the public employment office? How many were placed in jobs last year? Is special effort made to induce employers in your community to allocate to handicapped persons a specified proportion of available jobs? Does any agency in your community actively interpret to employers the types of jobs disabled persons can successfully perform?

78. Has your community any noncommerical private employment agencies serving the handicapped? Does any private social agency help to place handicapped persons in jobs? How many registered and how many placed? What agencies in your community actively work to prevent conditions leading to crippling and physical or mental disabilities? To prevent disabling accidents? To refer dis-

[1] For information read the pamphlet A Public Service for Restoring the Handicapped to Useful Employment: Vocational Rehabilitation, prepared by the Office of Vocational Rehabilitation, Government Printing Office, Washington, 1944.

abled persons as quickly as possible to agencies that can assist in this rehabilitation? What have they accomplished?

Crippled Children. The special federal-state program established for crippled children under the Social Security Act originally gave major attention to children with orthopedic or plastic conditions. In 1939, however, the provisions were broadened to extend care to children suffering from heart disease and rheumatic fever. Federal provisions are administered by the Children's Bureau, which is responsible for approval and supervision of state plans aided by federal funds. These plans cover the locating of crippled children, provision for surgical, corrective, and other treatment, and facilities for diagnosis, hospitalization, and aftercare for children who are crippled or suffering from conditions leading to crippling. Important as have been the achievements under existing federal-state programs, the Children's Bureau in 1946 reported that 20,000 orthopedically crippled children already known to state agencies were not receiving needed care.

79. When was your state program for crippled children first approved? How has your state plan been improved in recent years? What state agency administers the program? How much was expended for services in your state during the past year? What proportion of the funds came from federal grants?

80. On the local level what agency administers the program for crippled children? How is the program co-ordinated with other local child welfare services? With your local vocational rehabilitation program?

81. What professional personnel (such as pediatricians, orthopedists, plastic surgeons, nurses, physical therapy technicians, medical social workers) are employed in the crippled children's program?

82. What services are available? Skilled diagnosis and treatment? Hospital care? Care in convalescent or foster homes? Aftercare including medical social and public health nursing services? Is financial assistance available when needed? Are appliances, special shoes, and so forth provided free when families are unable to pay? Does your community have special playground facilities for handicapped children?

83. What children are eligible for aid? Only children who (or whose parents) have lived in the state for a specified period? Are children suffering from heart disease, diabetes, impaired vision or hearing eligible for care? Are facilities for hospital, convalescent, or foster home care of Negro children adequate?

84. What agency decides whether or not a child needs and shall receive care? What methods are used to locate crippled children? Are physicians, nurses, social workers, teachers, and others periodically reminded to refer crippled children for care? Have traveling clinics been employed? Special census taken? Is use made of birth certificates and epidemiological reports?

85. How many crippled children are known to be living in your community? How many of these need services for crippled children but are not receiving them? Why not?

86. Do the schools of your community provide transportation for crippled children living at home? Maintain special classes for crippled children or make special provision in normal classes? Offer school service to crippled children in hospitals, convalescent homes, or their own homes? Do schools provide any special vocational direction or training for crippled children in the upper grades?

87. What agencies in your community work to prevent crippling? What do they do? Attempt to prevent accidents? Rickets? Tuberculosis?

IV. SERVICES FOR MENTALLY HANDICAPPED PERSONS

Scientific and popular concepts about mental health have been changing rapidly during recent years. Increase in knowledge of mental disease, accompanied by greater emphasis upon early detection and preventive treatment, has largely transferred mental disease from the realm of obscure and incurable difficulty to the area of treatability. It is now recognized that the proportion of persons having completely sound minds is probably as low as that having perfect bodies. That the main objective in both instances is to build for positive health, and to prevent faulty habits of thinking and living likely to cause more serious conditions, is now realized.

A tremendous increase in interest in the nation's mental health was experienced during and after World War II when Selective Service examiners rejected some 30 per cent of all men examined because of mental disease or mental deficiency. Of women rejected for service (Women's Army Corps), some 22 per cent were for mental or nervous causes. In addition, a large proportion of men discharged from service before the end of the war were released because of mental or emotional difficulties.

Although half the country's hospital beds already were occupied by mental patients, the United States Public Health Service in 1946 estimated that another 191,000 mental hospital beds were immediately needed. Equally necessary are extended clinical and other treatment facilities and preventive measures. At least one consolation to be derived from this country's new consciousness of its mental health problem is the passage of the National Mental Health Act in 1946. This made possible federal participation in research relating to psychiatric disorders and authorized federal aid in the development of more effective methods of prevention, diagnosis, and treatment. A first goal is to assist states to establish at least one mental hygiene clinic for every 100,000 persons.

Two useful books to read at this stage of your study would be Mental Hygiene in the Community, by Clara Bassett,[1] and The Mentally Ill in America: A History of Their Care and Treatment from Colonial Times, by Albert Deutsch.[2]

[1] Macmillan Co., New York, 1934.   [2] Columbia University Press, New York, 1946.

Prevention and Treatment of Mental Illness.   Among the national agencies to which you may wish to turn in conducting this part of your study are the National Committee for Mental Hygiene and the American Psychiatric Association.[1]   The former has helped to establish state and local mental health societies or committees in various parts of the country.[2]

88. Is there a mental hygiene society in your state?   Has your community a branch?   What is its program, and what methods of public education does it employ?

89. Does your state provide traveling psychiatric clinics?   How recently was one held in your community?   How many persons availed themselves of its services?

90. What facilities for the prevention, diagnosis, and treatment of mental disorders and behavior problems has your public school system?   (See page 125.) Your juvenile court?   (See page 216.)

91. If a child-guidance clinic exists independent of the schools or courts, how many psychiatrists, psychologists, and social workers does it employ?   What has been their training for the work?   What was its budget?   What services rendered?   How many children served during the past year?

92. Are there other clinical facilities in your community for the treatment of mental disorders?   How many psychiatrists, neurologists, psychologists, or others in your community specialize in the private treatment of such disorders?   What is their training?   How closely do the mental hygiene clinics in your community conform to standards prescribed by the American Psychiatric Association?

Care of the Mentally Ill.   Hospitals for the mentally ill were formerly called insane asylums.   That they are now known as mental or psychopathic hospitals illustrates the changed popular attitude toward mental disease. All states (as well as certain agencies such as the federal Veterans Administration) now maintain one or more mental hospitals.   Municipalities or counties may also have their own psychopathic hospitals, or wards in general hospitals may be set aside for mentally ill persons.   Patients usually are classified and segregated according to the nature and degree of their difficulties, and the probability of their responding to treatment.   Facilities exist in the better hospitals for research and study of mental difficulties as well as for the care of mentally ill patients.

An important part of the community's equipment for dealing with mental illness is the observation ward or hospital where individual patients can be studied and diagnosed before being actually committed for treatment.   In

[1] For addresses see List of Agencies, p. 251.
[2] References that will prove helpful in establishing community mental health measures are Child Guidance Clinics: A Quarter Century of Development, by George S. Stevenson and Geddes Smith, Commonwealth Fund, New York, 1934, and "A County Community Mental-Health Clinic," by N. M. Grier, in Mental Hygiene, July, 1943, pp. 394–402.

addition to governmental facilities, private sanatoria operated either for profit or not for profit are frequently found.

93. What department of your state is responsible for care of the mentally ill? What services does it offer? To what institutions may residents of your community be committed, either for observation or for treatment? How many have been so committed during the past five years?

94. List the hospitals, or wards, of general hospitals available in your community for the observation or treatment of mental illness, and follow the pertinent questions for hospitals as suggested in Chapter 9.

95. What is the total number of beds available for mentally ill patients from your community? (Authorities estimate that there should be from all sources at least one bed for every 150 of the population.)

96. How is commitment for mental illness secured in your community? Is voluntary commitment allowed? Encouraged? What type of medical testimony is accepted?

97. Are there provisions for temporary care and observation? Where are committed persons kept until suitable hospitalization can be provided for them?

98. Can you secure any statements as to whether facilities in state or local mental hospitals are adequate? How many persons committed from your community last year failed of admission because of lack of room to receive them?

99. Have there been criticisms of the treatment accorded abusive patients? Are mentally ill persons ever confined in jails or other unsuitable places?

100. When persons accused of crime plead insanity, what procedure is adopted to establish their mental condition? To what institutions are convicted persons committed if found mentally ill?

101. To what extent do the courts avail themselves of local clinics or other psychiatric facilities for the mental examination of prisoners, especially habitual offenders?

102. Is there a social work department in each of the institutions to which the mentally ill are admitted? How many social workers employed in each? How many are members of a professional association?[1]

103. What form of aftercare is provided for paroled patients? Is boarding care in private families provided by any public agency? For how many persons? Are social work services available? How many paroled in your community? How often visited?

104. What is the division of financial responsibility (as between the patient, his responsible relatives, the community, and the state) for the care of mental patients committed from your community to mental hospitals?

105. How does care provided for mentally ill veterans differ from that available to others in your community?

106. What facilities are there for the treatment of alcoholics and drug addicts in your community? What local or state facilities for their prolonged care? How many are undergoing treatment? Has any organization such as Alcoholics Anonymous, interested in the rehabilitation of alcholics, formed a branch in your community? What has been accomplished?

[1] See footnote 4, p. 47.

107. If it is possible to secure comparative figures[1] for your community for different periods during the past five or ten years, see if there has been an increase or decrease in:

Suicides
Sex offenses resulting in arrest, resulting in conviction (see page 40)
Commitments to state and local institutions for the mentally ill
Children presenting behavior problems in the schools
Children appearing before the juvenile court

108. What do competent officials regard as the most reliable estimate of the number of mentally ill persons needing but not now receiving treatment in your community: (a) in institutions, (b) outside of institutions?

Mental Deficiency. Mental deficiency may be associated with mental disease, but is a different condition, usually requiring special treatment and forms of protection.[2] Although feeble-mindedness is ordinarily a condition present from birth, some authorities believe that it may also develop later in life as a result of acute infection. Psychological tests to discover a person's intelligence quotient (I.Q.) are only one of a variety of diagnostic and therapeutic criteria employed to classify persons suspected of being mentally deficient. Emotional attitudes, habit formation, and the social resources of a mentally deficient person's family must all be considered in planning for his future. Read Social Control of the Mentally Deficient, by Stanley P. Davies.[3]

109. Are routine psychological tests given all children in the public schools? All who appear before the juvenile court? What proportion are found to be below normal intelligence? What special education or training is provided for these children? Have teachers for this group received special training?

110. What facilities exist to give psychological tests to adults in your community?

111. To what institutions in your state may mentally deficient children, adults, be committed? Method of commitment? Population? Number of admissions last year? Between what ages are patients admitted? Waiting list? Types of training offered?

112. How many mentally deficient persons from your community are in state institutions? How many paroled and under supervision?

113. Does your community maintain its own institution for the mentally deficient? If so, raise the questions suggested above.

114. Are there in your state or community supervised colonies where mentally

[1] Changes in laws, administration, or resources should be noted in connection with such comparative figures.
[2] For provision for backward, as distinguished from mentally deficient, children in the public school system, see Chapter 11.
[3] Crowell Publishing Co., New York, 1930. (Out of print but generally available in libraries.)

deficient persons no longer requiring institutional care can be accustomed to social living?

115. Are persons known to be mentally deficient cared for in your community's almshouse or county farm for dependents?

116. What is the procedure when persons with no legal residence in your community or state are found to be mentally ill or mentally deficient? Are they kept in custody until arrangements can be made for their care in the home state? Are they sent back with an attendant or allowed to travel alone?

Authorities differ as to the inheritability of mental illness, epilepsy, and mental deficiency, and many scientists and others disagree as to the wisdom or efficacy of legal attempts to prevent parenthood by such measures as (a) forbidding marriage or (b) sterilization of persons thus afflicted.

117. Do the laws of your state forbid the marriage of those afflicted with mental illness or deficiency? How is this law enforced? How many marriage licenses have been refused on this account during the past year in your community? (See page 195.)

118. Has your state a law providing for sterilization? Under what circumstances? How is the law administered? Can sterilization be effected only with (a) voluntary consent of the patient, (b) consent of relatives or spouse, (c) upon order of some public body or official? Is commitment to a custodial institution a necessary prerequisite?

119. How many residents of your community have been sterilized under the law during the past five years? Women? Men?

When you have concluded your study of your community's provision for special groups you will want to ask yourself:

120. Is my community really doing all it should to prevent the need for such provisions as I have been studying?

121. How nearly adequate are existing provisions?

122. Are there still groups (such as sufferers from epilepsy or cerebral palsy) whose special needs are being overlooked? If so, follow pertinent questions in previous sections of this chapter.

11. EDUCATIONAL RESOURCES

IN APPROACHING the subject of the community's educational resources, it is necessary to think in broader terms than merely those of its facilities for the formal education of its youth, important though that is. Education does not stop with graduation from school; and with the shortened working day and working week in our industrial life, considerable leisure is available, some of which can be applied to self-improvement. Facilities for what has been called adult education are likely to receive more attention than in the past, if the new leisure continues to increase.

The convenient place to begin our study is, however, with the public schools. Most of us spend a number of years in them; and while an appraisal of their educational value is a task which requires expert qualifications, there is nothing to prevent the amateur surveyor from assembling certain objective data concerning his community's schools, and comparing them with those elsewhere.

I. THE PUBLIC SCHOOL SYSTEM

In most communities the schools present an increasingly elaborate structure for study. The nursery school and the progressive school have impinged upon the structure of the public school, until scarcely any portion of it has failed to be influenced in some degree. Public education begins earlier and continues later; it has developed special curricula for special groups; it has reached out into the home life of children through the parent-teacher associations, as well as through the development of visiting teacher service and child-guidance clinics. Not only the conduct of the schools, but the training of teachers for them, has undergone great changes.

For people not close to developments in education, and themselves separated by a period of years from their own school days, it would be well to begin the study by reading a modern work on public education. New Schools for a New Culture: Experimental Applications for Tomorrow, by Charles M. MacConnell and others,[1] is suggested. Read the laws of your

---

[1] Harper and Bros., New York, 1943. Further suggestions are Planning Schools for To-

state covering conduct of the schools. You may be able to secure from your State Department of Education a statement concerning any significant divergences between your education law and that of other states.

1. During what months, and for how many days, are schools in your community in operation during the year? Between what ages are children required to attend? How do the requirements of your state law compare with those of other states in these respects?

2. Do reports of the State Department of Education for the past five years show comparative standing of the schools in the different communities? How do the schools of your community compare with those of similar size in such matters as curriculum, increase or decrease in school population, teaching force, and building facilities?

In most communities, administration of the public schools rests in the hands of an unpaid school board.[1]

3. Is the school board in your community elected or appointed? How many members? How divided as to sex? What are the qualifications which led to their appointment?

4. Are there provisions in local ordinances or in the state law which attempt to keep elections or appointments nonpartisan? Is the school board in your community generally regarded as politically dominated, or free from the influence of graft and politics? Is it representative of all sections of the community, economic, political, racial, and geographic? Does it include some young members as well as older?

5. How is the superintendent of schools chosen? For what term? How many incumbents have there been during the past ten years? What has been the professional experience of the present incumbent? In what fields may he make independent decisions; in what must he secure the approval of the school board?

While the United States spends more than any other nation for its schools, and Americans pride themselves upon their educational system, school expenditures are very unevenly divided, resulting in millions of children being in inferior schools and for so brief a time that it leaves them unprepared to take their places as citizens to help make democracy work. Many children are still denied an equal educational opportunity. Half of our brightest and most talented youth leave school too early; some two million, aged six to fifteen, were not in school in 1940, and this number increased during the war.[2]

---

morrow: The Issues Involved, by John G. Fowlkes, Education Leaflet no. 64, Government Printing Office, Washington, 1942; and also We Can Have Better Schools, by Maxwell S. Stewart, Pamphlet no. 112, Public Affairs Committee, Inc., New York, 1946.

[1] See Know Your Board of Education, U.S. Office of Education, Education Leaflet no. 47, Government Printing Office, 1939.

[2] Read the findings of an investigation sponsored by the U.S. Office of Education, and several other national educational agencies, entitled Unfinished Business in American Edu-

6. In what proportion have expenditures for public schools increased or decreased during the past decade? What have been the sources of revenue? Is there a special tax levy in your community or state for the support of the schools? On what is it levied?

7. Has there been support from state funds toward the schools of your community? How much in each of the past five years? Has state aid to education been commensurate with amounts spent on other activities?

8. Is the budget discussed in meetings open to the public? How has the budget submitted by the school board in each of the past five years compared with amounts actually made available by your community? How much per capita, what proportion of total public expenditures, has been spent on the schools? (See page 37.) Can you learn how your community compared with others in these respects?[1]

The Schools

9. How many schools are comprised in the public education system of your community?

> Nursery schools and kindergartens
> Play schools for the vacation period
> Elementary schools
> Junior high schools
> Trade schools
> High schools
>> Academic
>> Vocational

10. How many special classes—e.g., classes for gifted or for backward children,[2] fresh-air classes, classes for children with physical handicaps, vacation schools, continuation classes, adult education classes?

11. Do the zoning regulations of your community provide for laying out school districts according to residential population? Do they protect these areas from later alienation to other uses? (See pages 88, 90.)

12. Are there any school buildings in which overcrowding of classrooms is a serious problem? Describe.

13. For each separate school building in active use, list the following information:[3]

> Date of construction
> Area of grounds (sufficient to supply outdoor exercise and recreation for pupils of all ages)

---

cation: An Inventory of Public School Expenditures in the United States, by John K. Norton and Eugene S. Lawler, National Education Association, Washington, 1946. State charts give "Current Expenditure Per Classroom Unit."

[1] See Expenditures Per Pupil in City Schools, a publication issued annually by the U.S. Office of Education, Government Printing Office, Washington.

[2] See Needs of Exceptional Children, U.S. Office of Education, Education Leaflet no. 74, Government Printing Office, 1944.

[3] Read The School Plant: Trends, Present Situation, and Needs, U.S. Office of Education, Government Printing Office, 1945. (This is a reprint from Chapter 9, Volume 1, of Biennial Survey of Education in the United States, 1938–1940.)

Method of heating, artificial lighting, and ventilating
Number and location of windows in classrooms
Type of desks and seats (adjustable, nonadjustable; fixed, movable)
Toilets and washrooms, adequate, sanitary, properly separated as to sexes
Infirmary or first-aid room
School library[1]
Assembly rooms or auditoriums
Laboratory facilities for science classes
Sanitary drinking fountains, cafeteria for pupils, restroom and lunchroom
    for teachers
Space and equipment for outdoor and indoor games and play
Gymnasiums, swimming pool, showers, lockers
Cleanliness of halls and classrooms
Attractiveness, decorations, and so on

14. See how the newer buildings compare with the older in these respects. Is progress shown?

Fire is an especially dangerous hazard in the public schools.

15. Are there fire escapes or fire chutes in all upstairs classrooms? Do all doors open outward? Are halls and stairways kept clear of impediments? How rapidly can the building be emptied in case of fire? How often are fire drills held?

Teachers and Curriculum. The teacher is one of the chief determining factors in a good school program. The personal qualities, the education, and professional training of teachers should be the concern of every citizen. Quality of instruction given is difficult for laymen to appraise. The equipment and working conditions of the teachers themselves are, however, capable of concrete description.

16. How many classroom teachers are employed (a) in kindergartens and grades, (b) in high schools? For how many pupils on the average is each responsible? How many are teachers of special subjects?

17. Is the teaching force in your community selected under civil service? If chosen by the superintendent and school board, what criteria are demanded in education and experience for the different grades? What is the salary range? Is it adequate to assure trained and competent personnel and to afford them a reasonable standard of living? How does it compare with that of other similar communities in the state? In the nation? With that of other professional people in your community?

18. Does promotion depend upon securing additional training? Are leaves of absence obtainable for this purpose?

19. Are teachers who marry allowed to retain their positions? Does the board make requirements as to matters of personal conduct out of school? Are teachers in your community forced to take special oaths of loyalty?

[1] See p. 163.

20. Is there a retirement system, with pay for teachers? A fixed system of sick leave with pay?

21. On what grounds have teachers been dismissed during the past five years? Have they had the right of appeal? With what results in the cases cited?

22. Is there a professional organization of teachers in your community? Are principals members, or only classroom teachers? What are its program and accomplishments claimed?

23. Are teachers encouraged to make suggestions and participate in planning the courses of instruction and choice of textbooks? Are they encouraged to address public meetings, contribute articles to papers and professional journals, and so on, without censorship? To attend local, state, and national educational conferences and institutes?

24. Can you learn of clerical duties which teachers are required to perform (e.g., preparing duplicate copies of reports and grades) which could be done by less highly paid and skilled personnel if it were available?

25. How many hours per week are teachers expected to spend out of school on school work?

26. Have there been major changes in the curriculum during the past five years? Any experiment in democratic education, such as the Springfield Plan,[1] to teach young Americans harmonious relations between the various racial and national groups that make up our population?

27. Is there censorship as to the teaching of civics, economics, and the like?

28. Are books discarded when in poor physical condition? Are textbooks issued free, or must the pupils purchase them?

The Pupils and Their Special Needs. Most school departments can furnish comprehensive and detailed statistics on school attendance. The report of the State Department of Education should contain average daily attendance by school areas.

29. What is the average daily attendance in your school area? How does the daily average attendance compare with other communities in your state?

30. Is there an annual school census? By whom is it taken? How many children of school age were discovered at the latest census not to be in school? How does the number of children shown in the school census compare with the average daily attendance? If there is any marked discrepancy, how do school authorities explain it (epidemics, weather conditions, attitude of parents)? Are children of migratory workers in your vicinity enrolled in the schools?

31. How effective is enforcement of the compulsory school attendance law in your community? How are absences from school followed up? Does a school nurse visit those reported ill? (See page 124.) In other cases, how promptly is the attendance officer able to visit?

32. Has the attendance officer (or officers) had social work training or experience? For how many cases is each attendance officer responsible?

33. How many children were referred to the juvenile court last year for truancy? What disposition of these cases was made by the court?

[1] See p. 233.

Rewards in the form of honor lists for scholarship, attendance, and other meritorious conduct are not uncommon devices in our public schools, although the opinion of educators is divided as to their desirability. Theme-writing contests between high school pupils of a city, a state, or the entire nation are frequently carried on, the prize being in money, scholarships to higher institutions of learning, trips, or simply the joy of seeing one's winning essay published in the newspaper along with one's picture. Some universities currently offer annual scholarships based on combinations of scholastic and athletic ability to secondary school students in their states.

34. Is the honor-list system used in your grade schools, high schools? On what performance is it based?

35. In what theme-writing contests have your high school students participated during the past year?

36. Are scholarships in institutions of higher learning regularly available to students in your high schools? Describe.

Extracurricular activities sponsored and promoted by the schools have increased greatly during the past few decades. The best results from the children's point of view are obtained when these develop as a result of the pupils' own interests and the contagion of interests communicated by the teacher, and are not imposed upon the children merely in order to demonstrate the teacher's enthusiasm and to make a showing for the school.

37. How many of your community's grade schools, high schools, have orchestras, bands, choral societies; dramatic clubs; dancing clubs; debating teams; athletic teams; science, language, art clubs, hobby clubs?

38. How many publish a school paper or magazine? Is there an interschool athletic association? To what degree is there competition in extracurricular activities (a) between the schools of your community, (b) those of other communities?

39. Are excursions arranged by your schools, for nature study or to visit points of interest?

Many school systems have separate departments for helping in the adjustment of individual children.[1] Most frequently found is a school hygiene department, for supervising the health of the individual pupil. For this, see pages 123–126. The vocational guidance department studies the aptitudes of children, advises them about work opportunities, issues working permits, and sometimes also conducts a placement bureau. The attendance department deals with truants, and should not be confused with the department of visiting teachers, which is in reality a social work department, its

[1] For a description of guidance programs see Pupil Personnel Services for All Children, U.S. Office of Education, Leaflet no. 72, Government Printing Office, Washington, 1944.

personnel consisting of trained social workers who make contact between the home and the school in cases where home conditions are thought to be contributing to the pupil's difficulties at school. The child-guidance clinic, where one is attached to the public school system, is a clinic manned by psychiatrists, psychologists, and social workers trained in psychiatric methods, which treats children who develop behavior problems and habits which need to be eradicated, or who show symptoms of mental illness. (See pages 125 and 146.)

40. What efforts are made to keep the interest of parents and children in their remaining in school after they are legally qualified to leave?

41. Is there a vocational guidance department? Does it issue work permits? (See page 73.) Does it actually place students in jobs? How many jobs found last year? How recently has it studied local industrial conditions and needs? Has it a system of regular consultations with public and other employment services?

42. How many students are combining study and work? Are some attempting to carry many hours of work and school to the detriment of health and study?

43. Does it interview all children who leave school, or only those who seek its services? Does it follow up students after placement? Are graduates encouraged to return to use its services?

44. Is there a department of visiting teachers? Is it separate from the attendance department? What types of problems are referred to the visiting teachers? For how many cases is each responsible? How many are members of a professional association?[1]

45. Is there a child-guidance clinic in your public school system? How many psychiatrists, psychologists, psychiatric social workers, employed?

46. From what sources are children referred to it? How close is the co-operation between the visiting teachers, attendance department, vocational guidance department, school hygiene department (see page 125), and the child-guidance clinic? Between it and principals and classroom teachers?

47. Who attend conferences on problems of the individual children? What means are employed to educate the teaching personnel in modern concepts of child behavior and child guidance?

48. How many children were referred to the clinic for treatment last year?

49. Is there a central record of each pupil to which all special departments have access and to the making of which each department contributes its information? Does it follow the pupil through his school career?

Normally, a child who attends school regularly and is regularly promoted should be graduated from the eighth grade at fourteen. Some children better this record.

50. Of the current school population, how many are ahead of grade? How many "skipped a grade"?

51. How many children failed of promotion last year? Of the current school

[1] See footnote 4 on p. 47.

population, how many are two or more years behind grade? Of the children who left school last year, how many were two or more years behind grade?

52. What is the average size of classes, by grades and type of school? How wide deviations in large and small classes? Are any pupils forced to attend part-time on account of lack of buildings or teaching force?

In some school systems, attempt has been made to divide the so-called normal group of children into groups based on their psychological ratings, usually referred to as X-Y-Z groupings. Proponents of this system claim that it permits enrichment of the curriculum and puts more content into it for the abler children, while not discouraging the slower-minded. Those opposed say that any division within the same grade which is based on mental ability makes little snobs of the X group and either afflicts the Z group with conscious inferiority, or causes them to expect better marks than they could secure under free competition. It is undesirable, opponents of the plan claim, to create artificial conditions of competition within the school, different from those which the children will face on graduation.

53. Is the X-Y-Z grouping used for normal children in your schools? What is the basis of classification?

54. Do the marriage laws of your state operate to prevent the marriage of girls under school-leaving age? (See page 195.) Did any girls leave the grammar grades last year because they had been married? At what ages?

55. What special attention is being given in your community's schools to the adjustment of retarded pupils? Are they being given special attention in the school health program (see Chapter 9) to discover and remedy physical defects?

56. If there is no child-guidance clinic (see page 146, question 91), are psychiatrists and psychologists available to give special attention to individual problems?

57. Is manual or trade training given those who cannot profitably pursue academic courses?

58. Are there special classes for backward children? For mentally normal but physically handicapped children? (See pages 141 and 145.)

59. Is special tutoring given outside classrooms? Special classes for foreign children who do not yet speak English?

60. What methods are employed to enforce classroom discipline? For what offenses are pupils reported to the principal for disciplinary action? How many children were suspended or excluded from school last year on account of behavior problems?

61. Are there "central schools" in your community? What provision for transporting children? For supervised boarding care for students unable to live at home on account of lack of transportation facilities?

62. Do your schools provide instruction at home or in institutions and hospitals for children who cannot attend regular schools? What provision is there for the education of children excluded from school by reason of health or behavior difficulties?

The School and the Community.   The work of the schools should be closely co-ordinated with that of other agencies.

63. Is there a publicity department or director in your public school system whose function it is to interpret the schools to the community?   Are there any school-community councils working toward a solution of mutual problems?

64. Are teachers and administrative authorities active in community planning or co-ordinative bodies?   Do they participate in community chest campaigns?

65. Is any nongovernmental and noncommercial agency or group in your community giving children of school age (a) tests of vocational aptitudes, (b) vocational counseling, (c) scholarships to enable students to continue education beyond the legal minimum?

Use of the public school buildings as centers for community activities out of school hours is a generally approved policy.   Many of the older buildings are not well adapted to such use but when new schools are to be constructed provision should be made in the building plans for neighborhood activities.

66. What groups are permitted to meet regularly in school buildings?   What facilities are they permitted to use?   Is a charge made?   Does it cover more than heat, light, and janitor service?

67. What contribution does your school system make toward the recreational program of your community?[1]

The family setting from which children come has been increasingly recognized as of importance to the schools.   Parent-teacher associations form a normal channel of intercourse between the school and the family.

68. Are there parent-teacher associations in each of the schools?   How often do they meet?   How many members?

69. Do parents discuss their individual problems in child training at the meetings?   Are programs with speakers preferred?   Do the parents take responsibility for the conduct of the association or do the teachers take the lead?

70. Are parents encouraged to visit the classrooms?   Are special visiting days a feature?

71. What part have parent-teacher organizations played in bringing about administrative changes, developing publicity favorable to the schools, campaigning for school board elections, securing increased budgets?

Where individual problems arise, many schools have special departments which come into contact with the homes, such as the attendance departments, visiting teachers, child-guidance clinics, and vocational guidance bureaus already mentioned.   Individual conferences between parents and classroom teacher or principal have not, of course, been superseded by the development of special school agencies.   Problems in the family affecting

[1] Suggested reading is The Schools and Recreation Services, U.S. Office of Education, Leaflet no. 73, Government Printing Office, Washington, 1944.

the school child are often discovered which the school has not the resources to remedy.

72. Do the schools in your community attempt themselves to administer relief? In what form: (a) shoes or clothing, (b) glasses or medicines, (c) special nourishment for the child, (d) relief in any form to the family group?

73. How are goods or funds collected: (a) voluntary contributions from teachers or other governmental employes, (b) percentage deductions from salaries, (c) contributions from school children or their families?

74. Under whose direction is the relief given? Are cases cleared through the social service exchange? (See page 234.) Do the other children know what children are receiving help?

The disadvantages of the school's attempting to provide relief have appeared so plainly in many communities that these experiments have been largely abandoned, except for the routine provision of milk to undernourished children or those disposed to tuberculosis. Closer integration with established relief agencies of the community has rather been sought.

75. Is the function of referring families for special care or relief centered in one person or department of the schools? Has this officer had experience or training in social work?

76. How many families of pupils were referred to community agencies for relief or special care during the past year? (Unless records are kept, it may be necessary to secure this information from the agencies to which the referrals were made.) Do the school authorities express satisfaction with the results?

When you have finished this part of your study, ask yourself the questions:

77. Does it seem that the schools of my community are flexible instruments to fit the developing needs of the individual child, or do they form a rigid system to which the individual child must adjust? Do children of all races and nationalities have equal opportunities in the schools?

Further questions to use in making a review of your schools may be found in Our Concern—Every Child: State and Community Planning for Wartime and Post-War Security of Children, issued by the Children's Bureau.[1]

II. PRIVATE SCHOOLS

In most communities the public school system is supplemented by a few or many privately supported educational institutions. Some are managed by sectarian groups, in order that religious instruction may be made an integral part of the educative process. Some are run along experimental lines—the so-called "progressive schools." Some are boarding or day schools, mostly for children of the well-to-do.

---

[1] Publication 303, Government Printing Office, Washington, 1944, pp. 44–50.

78. Are there privately supported educational institutions in your community? List name, date of establishment, auspices, and approximate attendance for each. Where appropriate, list grades covered.

> Kindergartens
> Nursery and other "progressive" schools
> Day schools maintained by church groups
> Other day schools
> Boarding schools maintained by church groups
> Other boarding schools
> Business and trade schools (vocations for which they train)

79. What degree of supervision over curricula and standards in private schools has your State Department of Education under your state law? How frequently are such institutions in your community inspected?

III. INSTITUTIONS OF HIGHER LEARNING

Colleges, universities, and professional schools may be found in your community under either public or private auspices. The federal Office of Education publishes a list[1] of approved colleges, universities, and professional schools, from which you can learn whether or not institutions in your community meet the standards of the chief accrediting agencies for the respective group of schools. It also publishes a list of accredited secondary schools.[2]

80. List any colleges or universities in your community which give a bachelor's degree. Give for each auspices, approximate attendance by sexes, principal departments of instruction, graduate schools.

81. Which are rated A, which B, by Office of Education? Are any in your community not listed? Why not?

82. What professional schools exist in your community? Are they independent, or departments of colleges or universities (above)? Auspices? Approximate attendance by sexes?

> (a) Teacher-training (normal) schools
>   How are they rated?
> (b) Schools of nursing
>   Are any not approved by your state board of nurse examiners?
>   Why not? (See footnote on page 104.)
> (c) Schools of social work
>   Are any not members of the American Association of Schools of
>   Social Work?[3] Why not?
> (d) Theological seminaries[4]

[1] Accredited Higher Institutions, Government Printing Office, Washington.

[2] Accredited Secondary Schools in the United States. (Both of these lists are frequently revised.)

[3] List can be obtained from the Association, 130 East 22d St., New York 10.

[4] The American Association of Theological Schools, 744 Jackson Place, N.W., Washington 6, issues a list of accredited theological schools periodically.

IV. ADULT EDUCATION

Adult education in this country has a history dating back to the old New England town meetings, but it was only within the past two decades that adult education as a movement has become widespread. World War II gave the cause a tremendous impetus by the participation of millions of persons in local civic programs. It is sometimes difficult to discriminate closely between educational and recreational programs for adults, but we shall consider here only groups formally brought together for study and discussion.[1]

83. What agencies in your community offer continuous programs of adult education: (a) public schools, (b) group-work agencies such as "Y's," settlements, and so on, (c) colleges and universities offering extension courses, (d) private educational institutes, (e) museums and libraries, (f) clubs and associations, (g) radio stations?[2]

84. Of the courses offered, what proportion are vocational? What other types of courses are offered?

85. Is there a council on adult education in your community?[3] How organized? Activities? If your community has no such council, how much co-operation in this field is there among agencies such as the council of social agencies, council of churches, central labor union or council, parent-teacher organization, the "Y's," and so forth?

86. What forums exist, meeting regularly for public discussion? On what subjects?

87. Can you learn, either from your State Department of Education, or from agencies interested in adult education or those dealing with the foreign-born, how many persons in your state, your community, are illiterate? How many are functional illiterates (unable to read or write with any facility) in contradistinction to legal illiterates?

88. How does your state compare with other states in this respect? Your community with other communities in the state?

89. What courses are offered and by whom, in English to foreigners, preparation for citizenship, and so on? (See Chapter 17.)

90. What courses are offered, what group meetings arranged for family life education? Is family life education being co-ordinated with the attempt to stem the rise of juvenile delinquency? How? (See Chapter 15.)

91. What provision exists in your community for workers' education in economic, industrial, and labor problems?

92. Are courses available to the public in appreciation of music or art? Under what auspices?

93. Has your state agricultural college placed a county farm demonstration agent in your community to help improve farming methods? A county home demonstration agent to help farmers' wives in the management of farm homes?

[1] Read "Trends in Postwar Adult Education," in Adult Education Journal, January, 1946. The entire issue presents a cross section of various trends in this field.

[2] See also the section on The Radio, p. 243.

[3] The private national agency most active in the field is the American Association for Adult Education. For address see List of Agencies, p. 251.

V. LIBRARIES

The modern public library has developed as a "continuation school for all the people" and also as "the community's intelligence service." It is not only supplementary, but also complementary to the schools and colleges. Good reading references are Public Libraries in the Life of the Nation, by Beatrice S. Rossell,[1] Post-War Standards for Public Libraries, by the American Library Association,[2] and Library Extension: Problems and Solutions, edited by Carleton B. Joeckel.[3]

According to statements of the American Library Association, about 35,000,000 people in the United States, or approximately one-fourth of the population, are without library service, chiefly in the rural and small town districts. Almost 600 counties are without public libraries. Only Massachusetts, Rhode Island, and Vermont provide all inhabitants with library service.

94. Has your community a public library? Private library facilities (e.g., college or university libraries; historical society library; those of commercial, industrial, scientific, or social science bodies, and professional associations) ?

95. Has your state a state library? What services does it offer your community?

96. Is financial assistance from the state available to your community for any part of its library service? What conditions must be met to obtain it?

97. How does the state library commission rate your community's public library service in relation to that of similiar communities in the state?

98. Has your community a library board? Is it elected or appointed? If appointed, by whom? For how long? How many members? What are their qualifications? How is the board divided as to sex? What are its powers and duties?

99. What is the experience and training of the present chief librarian? In what fields may he make independent decisions? In what must he secure the approval of the library board?

100. How is the library personnel selected? What percentage of the public library staff hold library school certificates?

101. How do salaries, vacations, and retirement allowances compare with those in the school system? With the national average for libraries in cities or towns of the same population?

102. From what sources does your public library receive most of its financial support? What other sources of income has it?

103. What was the budget submitted in each of the past five years? Amount appropriated?

According to the American Library Association, good library service costs a community $1.50 per capita a year, minimum service $1.00 per

[1] American Library Association, Chicago, 1943.   [2] Idem.
[3] University of Chicago Press, Chicago, 1946.

capita. Superior service costs $2.00 per capita. This association also recommends that independent public library service should not be attempted without minimum support of $25,000 annually from a population of at least 25,000 people.[1] A well co-ordinated library system reaches each local area and every citizen. There should be constant interchange of books between the central library, its branches, and stations in schools, factories, and stores.

104. How much per capita is your community spending for its public library service? What per cent of total public expenditures? (See page 37.) If your library cannot maintain the minimum revenue standard, is there a neighboring public library with which your library could merge?

105. Are equal library facilities available to Negroes? To minority groups in the community? If there is a separate Negro branch, is its budget comparable to other branches serving the same number of readers? Does it have a trained staff? Does its book collection compare favorably with that in other branches?

106. Does the public library have its headquarters in its own central building? Are there branches? How many? Do any branches specialize, e.g., in foreign language books, commercial books in the business area, and so on?

107. Does the public library maintain a central school library? Branch libraries in school buildings? Permanent or temporary classroom units of reference books?

108. What provision is made to give book-lending service to industrial establishments, settlement houses, and institutions for children or old people?

109. Does the library have a "bookmobile" for circulating books in outlying regions where no branches have been established? If not, what provision is made for making book service convenient for inhabitants of these regions?

110. Do users of the library meet with pleasant, willing, and courteous service from the librarians? Are reading rooms free from overcrowding, well-lighted, and ventilated? Are books generally kept in good condition and rebound when necessary? Do members of the public have access to all shelves? If not, is there an "open-shelf" room with a wide selection of books?

111. How many books are owned—adult fiction, adult nonfiction, children's books?[2] How many new books added last year—adult fiction, adult nonfiction, children's books? How many periodicals are subscribed for?

112. Are there special rooms for children? How do they appear as to lighting, ventilation, adaptation of furniture, general attractiveness? Has the children's librarian had special training? Does she work in close co-operation with grade teachers in the schools? Are story-hours a feature of the work? Does she offer advice to parents on their children's reading? Does she give lessons in the use of the library to school classes or other groups?

113. Are there special collections for young people? What other help does the library offer young people? How much staff time is assigned to this work?

114. Does the public library offer a "reader's guide" service for adult patrons?

[1] Standards and Planning for Public Libraries, Chicago, [1943].
[2] The minimum standard is one book per capita.

115. Are books in Braille and talking books circulated to the blind? (See page 140.) Does the library circulate music records? Music scores? Films?

116. Is photostatic service available? Is there apparatus for projecting photographed pages?

117. What is the per capita circulation of books in your community? What per cent of books circulated are (a) adult fiction, (b) adult nonfiction, (c) children's books? How do these figures compare with national and state circulation figures if you can obtain them?

118. Is the library part of a county or regional system? Does it serve as the central library of such a system? If not, (a) under what terms does it lend books to residents of neighboring communities, (b) what co-operative relationships (such as the maintenance of a union catalog) does it have with other libraries in the county or region? From what other libraries can books be borrowed through your public library?

The modern librarian is no longer a "keeper of books," but makes constant effort to discover what the community is thinking and doing, what educational, social, economic, and political movements are stirring locally and nationally, as well as internationally, and to stimulate the use of the library in these connections.

119. What special services (for example, the help of library specialists, special collections, special lending privileges) does the public library give to local governmental officials, study groups, forums, schools, and other organizations, and in special fields such as parenthood, business and technical occupations, art and music? Is the library departmentalized (i.e., does it have a special department for each subject field)?

120. Does your library take an active part in organizing and carrying on study and discussion groups, radio listening groups, book clubs, poetry and dramatic groups, and similar adult education activities? Are there facilities for such groups to meet in the library buildings?

121. Does your library give free showings of documentary films with special selections for very young children, older children, and adults?

122. Does your library attempt to create a demand for its services where little or no demand exists, or does it serve only those who voluntarily seek it out? Does your library organize book exhibits and exhibits of material relating to its service, such as arts and crafts, photography, hobbies? What means does your library use to bring its services to the attention of the community in general? To groups with special interests? To schools, forums, organizations, clubs, study classes?

VI. MUSEUMS

Museums and other permanent exhibits of educational material are established under municipal, state, or federal management, are incorporated and maintained by nonprofit societies, or are sometimes supported by universities and schools, large industries, or groups of industrial firms. Museums may be mainly storehouses of collections for scholars and specialists, or they may serve as popular educational institutions for the general public.[1]

123. What museum fields are represented or covered by special collections in your community: (a) history, (b) art, (c) science, (d) industry, (e) other?
124. Are the museums members of the American Association of Museums?
125. How adequately financed is your municipal museum? How adequate is its building? Is the museum personnel qualified for its work? Are salaries comparable to those paid in the school system? Is provision made for acquisition of new material? Ample visiting hours to serve the needs of all groups?
126. Are the museums, both public and privately supported, active in educational work and other public service? Does each institution offer lectures, courses, school co-operation through class visits or lending to schools? What program expansion is contemplated in the near future?

VII. OTHER MEDIA OF PUBLIC EDUCATION

Many informal sources of public education and information should also be mentioned. References to the radio will be found on pages 111, 164, and 243; to motion pictures on pages 111, 164, and 244. Use of the newspaper as a medium of public information is discussed on page 242. A feature stressed in rating-scales of homes is invariably the number and kind of books owned, and the number and kind of periodicals subscribed for. Reading may be done, of course, either for recreation or for self-improvement, and an estimate of the reading habits of your community, other than as shown by use of the public library, would be difficult to make. The following suggestions may, however, produce some evidence.

127. How many retail bookstores has your community? What were their total sales (bound volumes) last year? Adult fiction, adult nonfiction, children's books.
128. Make your own list of five or six nonfiction periodicals, informational or educational in character, and ascertain by writing to the publisher the number of subscribers in your community, and how this compares with other communities of similar size.

[1] A standard work on the subject is The Museum in America, by Laurence V. Coleman, American Association of Museums, Washington, 1939. If this three-volume work is not available, send for The Museum as a Social Instrument, by T. L. Low, a small pamphlet (10 cents) published by the Metropolitan Museum of Art, New York, 1942.

12. OPPORTUNITIES FOR RECREATION

KARL DE SCHWEINITZ, as long ago as 1928, wrote interestingly of the impact upon family life of what was already termed "the new leisure."[1] He pointed out that, with the change from the agricultural workday to the industrial workday which occurred about the middle of the last century, and with successive reductions thereafter in the number of hours which must be devoted to earning a living, people in this country have experienced problems in how to adjust their lives. He described graphically the idleness and boredom which really accompanied the long summer evenings and the endless Sundays of a couple of generations ago, in spite of the idealization with which they have been surrounded in literature. He stated that the burden of proof lies with the people who claim that modern adjuncts to recreation such as the automobile, the motion picture, and the radio have destroyed home life in this country, and built a good case for more and better group enjoyment by families under conditions as they are today.

A good book to read before beginning a survey of recreation in your community is Introduction to Community Recreation, by George D. Butler.[2] You may also want to study the laws of your state relating to recreation in local communities. Recent years have seen a rapid increase in the number of legally established town and city recreation departments.[3]

I. UNORGANIZED RECREATION

It is difficult to apply standards to the unorganized recreation which, after all, probably makes up the greater part of a community's relaxation. Family recreation, in the car, around the piano, radio, or phonograph, in the basement game room or around the back-yard picnic fireplace is an important part of the recreation of family groups. The play of children of pre-

---

[1] Chapter 9, "New Tools of Leisure," in Family Life Today, edited by Margaret E. Rich. Houghton Mifflin Co., Boston, 1928.

[2] McGraw-Hill Book Co., New York, 1940. Read also Chapter 5, "A Community Responsibility," in Off the Job Living: A Modern Concept of Recreation and Its Place in the Postwar World, by G. Ott Romney, A. S. Barnes and Co., New York, 1945.

[3] National Recreation Association, Model Ordinance: A Suggested Ordinance for Creating a Public Recreation Commission. The Association, New York, 1943.

school age must usually be in or near the home, where the elders of their families can keep them constantly within sight or call. Saturday evening shopping or window shopping may be an important source of recreation to housewives, a country walk or shirt-sleeved ease over the Sunday paper to their husbands, and the group consumption of sodas at the corner drugstore to their adolescent offspring. Gardening, tinkering in the home carpenter-shop, fishing, or "messing about in boats" are recreations of no mean potency, which are pursued family by family or individual by individual, and of which little account can be made in a community survey.

Not all unorganized recreation lies in the beneficial-to-harmless area. The policeman on the beat looks with a disapproval that is probably entirely justified on the street-corner congregation of aimless young loafers. Arrests for intoxication, drunken driving, and disorderly conduct generally rise to a peak on Saturday night and Sunday, with organized commercial recreation bearing, of course, its full share of blame for this condition. But we are coming to realize that there must be in the new leisure room for self-direction, for grownups and children alike. The earlier condemnation of the activities of those self-organized boys' groups known as "gangs" has given place to an earnest desire to learn how all these youthful energies can be helped to flow into channels of good citizenship, and to find how much tactful guidance gangs and "cellar clubs" can be induced to accept, without losing the independence and self-direction in which lies their chief value and attraction to their young members. As in many other forms of community enterprise, emphasis in the field of recreation is now being laid on helping individuals to develop their own programs, in accordance with their own tastes and desires, rather than on developing patterns into which the individual must fit.

1. How many licenses for pleasure cars were issued to people in your community last year? How many pleasure cars are there per 100 population?

2. If your community is a waterside one, how many pleasure boats are registered from your community? How many sailboats and other craft?

3. Can you secure an estimate of how many families own radios in your community?

4. Has any study been made in your community of the ways in which people choose to spend their leisure time? What amount of preference was shown for (a) "just resting," (b) passive spectatorship, (c) active participation in some form of hobby or recreation?

II. PROVISION FOR RECREATION BY PUBLIC OR NONPROFIT PRIVATE AGENCIES

The close connection between recreation and education has already been suggested.[1] (See Chapter 11.) In studying your community's facilities for recreation, it will be convenient to consider in separate categories those operated for profit and those not so operated. Public and private agencies furnish numerous opportunities for public amusement and recreation where no fee is charged or where fees are fixed so as merely to cover in whole or in part the expense of operation.

Suggested standards for recreation leadership, facilities, and programs in cities and towns have been prepared by the National Recreation Association. It would be well to secure from this agency its Schedule for the Appraisal of Community Recreation.[2] See also the Association's Recreation Leadership Standards,[3] and Know Your Community: Suggestions for Making a Study of Community Recreation Needs.[4]

5. What department of the government in your community is responsible for recreation? Under what form of legislation was it created? If under a board, how are its members chosen? Does it employ a superintendent of recreation? Full-time, year-round? What are the qualifications for this position? What are the qualifications which led to the appointment of its present superintendent?

6. In what kinds of leadership positions are workers employed? How many in each? How selected? Do they have approved qualifications for such positions?

7. To what extent are volunteers used? For what kinds of service? How trained and supervised?

8. What have been your city's annual expenditures for parks or recreation for each of the past five years? Per capita cost? What percentage of total public expenditures? (See page 37.) Is there a separate budget for recreation?

A well-balanced park and recreation system is composed of many types of areas. Some, designed primarily for rest, consist of greensward, trees, and shrubs, with little equipment except benches. Neighborhood playgrounds and playfields, on the other hand, are developed primarily for active and organized use. Larger park properties contain natural features and facilities for many forms of recreation, such as golf, hiking, water sports, or zoos.

9. What is the total acreage of your city's park and recreation areas? Divide your total population by this figure. How many persons per acre? (The National Recreation Association recommends one acre of publicly owned recreation space for each 100 persons.)

[1] For further reference to this connection see Education through Recreation, by Lawrence P. Jacks, Harper and Bros., New York, 1932; and Leisure Time Education: A Handbook of Creative Activities for Teachers and Group Leaders, by Anna May Jones, Harper and Bros., New York, 1946.
[2] The Association, New York, 1944.   [3] Idem, 1944.
[4] Idem, 1943.

10. How many areas listed as parks contain no recreation features? How many of the following features are found in city-owned areas:

Playgrounds for various age groups
Ball fields
Golf courses
Other game facilities
Tennis courts
Athletic fields with running track
Recreation buildings
Swimming pools or beaches
Skating areas and winter sports facilities
Picnic grounds with equipment
Roadside parkways with drinking water, toilet, and picnic facilities
Camping centers
Boating or canoeing centers
Bridle and bicycle paths
Zoo, arboretum, botanical gardens
Open-air theaters
Bandstands or shells
Other special features

Are existing facilities now being reasonably widely utilized? If not, are steps being taken to promote wider use?

11. Are fees charged for any of these facilities? Are such fees reasonable?

12. Are there county, state, or metropolitan parks within 50 miles of your community? List facilities as above. How widely are they utilized?

Opportunities for year-round play within easy reach of all homes in the community are most important and are provided by neighborhood playgrounds and playfields. Playgrounds serve primarily children, but also young people and adults. The neighborhood playfield serves primarily young people and adults, but usually includes a playground for children. The National Recreation Association says "there should be a playground within one-quarter to one-half mile of every home and playground space should total one acre for each 800 of the population."[1] The Association also says that there should be a playfield within one-half mile to a mile of every home and that playfield space should equal one acre for each 800 of the population.

13. How much play space is available in the various sections of your community for (a) detached houses, (b) multiple dwellings? How many housing units lack adequate facilities for outdoor play of preschool children?

14. Locate all neighborhood playgrounds under whatever auspices on a map of your community. How large are they? Are they well-equipped with facilities

[1] See Standards: Playgrounds, Playfields, Recreation Buildings, Indoor Recreation Facilities, National Recreation Association, New York, 1943.

for play? How many provide an acre for each 800 persons in the neighborhood served? Are any homes more than one-half mile from the nearest playground?

15. Similarly, locate the playfields in your community. How large are they? What facilities do they contain? How many provide an acre for each 800 persons in the district served? Are any homes more than one-half mile walking distance from a playfield?

16. If the climate of your community permits skating and coasting, what areas are available for these sports? How is safety assured?

17. Progressive real estate operators hold that it is "good business" to set aside playgrounds in large subdivisions. Is such reservation compulsory in your community? (See pages 88–89.) Have any subdivision playgrounds been developed during the past five years?

18. What public facilities for swimming are provided? Are they adequate? Easily accessible?

19. What recreation facilities are available in special recreation buildings? In schools?[1] In other publicly owned buildings? Are these facilities well distributed throughout the community? Is there a center with diversified facilities within a mile of every home?

20. Have any "teen-age" centers been established for the youth of your community?[2] Auspices? Facilities? Supervision? Program? How supported? Number reached?

21. Are there youth hostels in your vicinity? Auspices? Supervision? How supported? Number using them last season?

Community recreation programs should serve all ages throughout the year, indoors and outdoors, and should include activities that meet a wide range of recreation interests.

22. Is a diversified play program conducted on the playgrounds of your community throughout the year? For how many hours a day? How many different children are regularly served?

23. What types of activities are conducted at the recreation buildings or other indoor centers? For what periods? For what age groups? What restrictions are placed upon participation? How many different persons are served?

24. Has your community a municipal orchestra, band, or chorus? Are any other public concerts available in your community free or at popular prices? Type of programs? How sponsored and supported? Attendance?

25. Are opera or concert series given by performers from outside your community? How many subscribers? Are there any lecture series?

26. Does your community have, or participate in, a music festival? Auspices? How supported? Programs? Attendance?

[1] Recent years have seen increasing use of school buildings for recreation purposes. Two good sources on this subject are: Planning School Buildings for Community Recreation Use, and Community Recreation Center Quiz. Both were issued by the National Recreation Association in 1945. The first concerns itself with the physical layout of the buildings and the other with all phases of recreation and operation in school buildings.

[2] See Youth Centers: An Appraisal and a Look Ahead Based on a Nation-Wide Survey, issued by the U.S. Office of Community War Services, Government Printing Office, Washington, 1945.

27. Has your community a "Little Theater"? How many members? How many performances last year?

28. Are handicraft courses available in your community? Under what auspices? Attendance? Have there been special art or arts-and-crafts exhibits during the past year? Auspices? Attendance?

29. Can you learn of the existence in your community of adult hobby clubs such as garden clubs, radio amateurs' clubs, camera clubs? Membership? Activities? Have any of them put on exhibits or shows during the past year?

30. What private clubs in your community offer facilities for recreation such as swimming, golf, tennis? Fees? Membership? Are any of these facilities open to the public? On what terms?

31. Are there associations to promote interest in the out-of-doors among adults (nature study groups, bicycle clubs, hiking clubs, Adirondack Club)? Membership? Activities?

32. What opportunities for engaging in individual and team sports are there in your community? What types of leagues and tournaments? Auspices? Program? Participation?

33. What supervised noncommercial dances or other social activities are available to the young people of your community? Auspices? Supervision? How frequently held? Admission fees?

34. In what forms is recreation provided for persons confined to institutions in your community (children's homes, homes for the aged, hospitals, prisons)?

35. What programs are provided specially for industrial workers (a) by industry, (b) by labor unions, (c) by the community?

36. What recreation opportunities are available to people over sixty? How adequate are they? Are there facilities for older persons to engage in square dancing, singing, shuffleboard, horseshoe pitching, croquet, card playing, checkers, chess, craftwork, and so forth? (See also sections on Adult Education, Libraries, Museums in Chapter 11.)

In agricultural areas education and recreation are generally inseparable parts of movements fostered by state, county, or community organizations.

37. What is the county extension service of your State Department of Agriculture doing to promote rural recreation?

38. Has your county an agricultural fair? Attendance last year? Is there a grange? A farmers' institute? A county farm bureau? A rural recreation organization? Membership? Program and accomplishments?

39. Are 4-H clubs, Future Farmers of America, or other clubs organized among farm boys and girls in your community? Membership? Program and accomplishments?

Some communities have an annual flower show or a regularly recurring festival or pageant such as the Tulip Festival in Holland, Michigan, the Tournament of Roses in Pasadena, the Mardi Gras in New Orleans. In others, special pageants have been arranged to commemorate special events in the community's history.

40. Has your community an annual festival of the type mentioned? How sponsored, financed, and directed? How many citizens participate? Has there been within the past five years a special celebration or pageant? Does your community conduct an annual old-home week? How many former citizens returned last year?

Churches, settlements, and a wide range of so-called character-building agencies give special care to the recreation needs particularly of children and young people. (For recreation features of the public school system, see Chapter 11. For summer camp care, see Chapter 16.)

41. List the privately supported agencies in your community (such as churches, settlements, community centers, the "Y's," Boy and Girl Scouts) providing recreation opportunities for youth, in the form of space for club meetings, informal dramatics and musicales, playgrounds, other areas for games and sports (indoor and outdoor), supervised hiking, camping and nature study, social and hobby clubs, libraries, supervised dances, music, dramatics, and so forth. Auspices? Membership? How supported? Which agencies also provide appropriate recreation opportunities for children, adults, and aged persons? What activities are provided? Is any agency in your community operating a toy library? Describe.

III. COMMERCIAL RECREATION

Commercial promotion of recreation commonly has to bear the brunt of social disapproval; but many opportunities of excellent social value must be credited to it as well. The sport of horseback riding, for instance, is largely in private or commercial hands (although the bridle paths used are generally part of the public park system). Also, the recent development of skiing, "fold-boating," tobogganing, and bicycling has been stimulated by the fact that the railroads saw and seized an opportunity to employ idle rolling stock as holiday sports trains in off seasons.

42. Are there riding stables in your community? Is the hourly cost (a) for instruction, (b) for use of horses, such as to permit people of moderate incomes to patronize them?

43. Have the railroads of your community organized sports trains? How many passengers carried last season?

44. Is there a roller- or ice-skating rink in your community? Public commercial tennis courts? Opportunity to hire boats and canoes? Commercial picnic grounds, or beaches for bathing, swimming pools, or gymnasiums? Commercial bowling alleys, poolrooms? How many of each?

45. Has your community a professional or semiprofessional baseball, football, or hockey team? How many games on the home grounds per season? Average attendance?

46. Are there commercial public amusement parks in or near your community? Average weekly attendance? Features offered? Are they considered respectable places for young people to visit? How adequately are they policed?

The drama as presented commercially in our communities covers a wide range of social values.

47. How many buildings in your community are devoted to theatrical performances: (a) "legitimate" theaters, (b) motion pictures, (c) vaudeville or burlesque shows?

48. Is there a local stock company? A "summer stock" theater within 50 miles? How many "road companies" visited your theaters last year?

49. Have any attempts been made to censor theatrical performances in your community within the past five years? By whom and with what results?

50. Does any motion picture house in your community confine its program to artistic and nonpopular features?

51. Is there any group in your community concerned with securing presentation of better films? What have been its program and accomplishments?

52. What are the regulations in your community governing attendance of minors at motion pictures?

53. Is there a radio broadcasting station in your community? How much of its program consists of network features rebroadcast? Of original material offered, what proportion is (a) classical music, (b) talks or dramatic features which are informative or educational in character, (c) popular music and entertainment?

54. How many cabarets or night clubs with entertainers has your community? How many roadhouses within 50 miles? What degree of control does the community exercise over the attendance of young girls, nature of the performances, or the behavior of the patrons?

55. How many public commercial dance halls has your community? Below what age are girls excluded? Is liquor allowed to be sold on the premises? Is any supervision attempted by the police department? By other agencies interested in youth?

56. Are there regular excursion boats sailing from your community? Is liquor sold on them? Can staterooms be hired? Are the boats considered to be safe places for unchaperoned young people?

57. How many premises are licensed in your community for the sale of liquor? How does this compare with the number licensed five years ago?

58. Are there race tracks for horse, dog racing, in or near your community? Does your state law permit gambling at race tracks? Can you ascertain how much money changes hands in betting on one of these events? Does your state or local law prohibit lotteries? Slot machines? Are such laws enforced?

59. Are poolrooms in your community licensed? Regulated? By whom? Are there special rules applying to minors? By whom enforced?

60. Is the modified form of gambling exemplified in prizes given away at motion picture theaters legal in your community? How many theaters have this feature? Is the form of gambling known as "playing the numbers" current in your community? What is the police department doing about it? With what success?

61. How frequently is your community visited by traveling circuses? Street carnivals? Tent shows?

Not only are the recreation facilities which the community extends to its own citizens to be considered, but in many communities, the provision of entertainment to citizens of other communities is an important part of its recreational activity. Some facilities are provided chiefly for out-of-towners.

62. Does your community have camps for auto tourists or trailers? What laws or ordinances govern them? What facilities such as water, light, and garbage disposal does your community provide? By whom are they provided? How many cars stopped at local camps last year? Average stay?

63. What does your community do to publicize its recreation facilities to visitors from out of town—hotel guests, users of auto and trailer camps, migrants at nearby work camps? To publicize points of scenic, historic, as well as other interest that both tourists and local residents may wish to visit?

IV. PLANNING THE RECREATION PROGRAM

The recreation program of a community, when looked at as a whole, is likely to show wide gaps. In many communities it has centered about the school child, and been rather oblivious to the needs of the youngsters about to make their entrance into adulthood. In others, many more opportunities for recreation are provided for white children than for those of other races. Frequently communities fail to provide appropriate facilities and services for aged persons who constitute an increasingly important proportion of our population and often have more leisure time than other age groups.

In order to develop a program of recreation for all members of the community, a citywide organization for its promotion is needed.[1] Since the activities are for the benefit of all, there is an increasing tendency to have them supported by taxation and administered by official agencies. However, private initiative is still needed to carry on activities not yet undertaken by the public and to provide stimulus and support for the public administration.

64. Is there a recreation council, including citizens who are interested in the development of wider recreational life? What have been its recent undertakings? What is it doing to train volunteer leadership? What is its relationship to your council of social agencies? (See page 236.)

65. Have any attempts been made to determine the leisure time interests of children, youth, and adults—including aged persons—in your community? What

[1] See Community Recreation Comes of Age: The Story of an American Town, Division of Recreation, Office of Community War Services, Government Printing Office, Washington, 1944; also, Planning for Recreation Areas and Facilities in Small Towns and Cities, issued by the same office in 1945.

action has resulted? To what extent are the people given a share in planning for recreation?

66. Has a long-range plan been developed for a further growth of recreation areas and facilities for your community? What steps are being taken to secure needed land and facilities looking toward future growth of the community?

67. What plans are being promoted to extend recreation services in your community when they are recognized to be inadequate (a) for certain age groups, (b) for certain race groups, (c) for certain income groups?

13. RELIGIOUS AGENCIES

THE CHURCH (including all its subsidiary agencies such as church schools, parish or parochial schools, broader educational, health, and welfare agencies) fills an important place in American life. Most church groups in this country are one of three major types: Protestant, Catholic, or Jewish. However, in certain areas, the most significant of which is Utah, home of the Mormon Church, are found religious bodies not readily classifiable in these categories. Among these groups (as also among different denominations or sects of any one group) will be found important differences in organization, in attitudes toward other religious groups, toward civil government, and toward the church's relation to community health and welfare programs. While these differences are usually amicably reconciled, they frequently create certain tensions in community life and sometimes break out in open conflict.

In many areas the church is the center about which community life revolves and the church or church school buildings the nearest approach to a community building. Churches differ greatly—wide differences being found even among churches of the same general type—in the emphasis laid upon social, educational, and community activities as opposed to the more typical religious ministrations.[1]

I. CHURCHES AND THEIR ACTIVITIES

Health, welfare, and education were all originally functions of the churches. Examples can be found in most urban communities of sectarian agencies still operating in all three of these fields; and nonsectarian agencies, both public and private, look to the churches and their congregations for co-operation, understanding, and sympathetic support.

References to the operation by churches and synagogues of distinct schools, hospitals, and welfare agencies will be found in this book in the

[1] Very detailed suggestions for urban church surveys may be found in How to Study the City Church, by H. Paul Douglass, Doubleday, Doran and Co., Garden City, New York, 1928. This volume is now out of print, but is available in many libraries. A revision is in process.

appropriate chapters. In this division we should consider their parish and community activities. To avoid repetition, it will be understood that the term "church" includes all groups meeting for prayer and worship. General information about the churches in your community (if over 25,000 population) can be secured from the reports of the federal census of religious bodies.[1]

Information about individual church organizations will have to be assembled locally. Where a church federation, council of churches, or ministers' association is in operation, it may be able to supply much of the information here suggested. It may be possible to secure additional information from diocesan or conference offices, chanceries, or other denominational headquarters; or from church year books and directories, and the like. Answers to some of the following questions will probably have to be sought from individual pastors.

1. List and locate on your resources map (see page 16) the churches of your community. How many Protestant? How many Catholic? Jewish? Other? How does their distribution compare with the density of population shown on your density map? (See page 27.) How many members or adherents do the Protestant, Catholic, Jewish, and other groups claim? In each instance how is the term "member" or "adherent" defined? How many churches are regarded as "institutional" churches, conducting broad community social and educational programs; or, like the Salvation Army or Volunteers of America, emphasizing social service activities?

2. How many churches have church buildings of their own? How many have facilities for worship? For church school and religious education? For drama, group meetings, forums, church suppers, indoor athletics and games, social activities? To what extent is use actually made of church facilities for worship? For education? For social activities? If facilities are not widely used, is further use being contemplated? If facilities are overtaxed is expansion contemplated?

3. How many of the churches are served by at least one full-time pastor, priest, rabbi, or other type of trained religious leader? How many churches also have trained directors of religious education, teachers, social workers, or other professional or paid personnel? How many churches are without any full-time trained religious leader? To what extent are voluntary workers used in church educational and social activities?

4. To what extent do churches singly or jointly minister to special groups such as children in church schools, youths, returned veterans, young married couples? Do they serve local institutions such as orphanages, old people's homes, hospitals, jails, prisons? What services are offered?

5. To what extent do churches singly or jointly observe special church days or weeks, such as Children's Day, Family Week, Labor Sunday, Race Relations Sunday?

---

[1] The census of religious bodies is taken during the intervals between general censuses (1916, 1926, 1936, and so on); but its publication has often been delayed for years.

6. Do the churches in your community co-operate in conducting radio devotional services or union services throughout the year? For special periods?

Personal Counseling. In addition to group worship, individual consultation on personal and spiritual problems is part of the service which every church offers its parishioners. In some denominations this service is part of the sacramental system (confession); in others, the pastor has regular hours or makes special appointments for individual consultation. A few churches have experimented with general clinics (family consultation centers, and so forth). Owing to the confidential relationship between pastor and parishioner, it is impracticable and inadvisable to attempt to secure detailed information about these services. However, questions such as the following might properly be raised.

7. In what churches do the pastors, priests, or other leaders have regular consultation periods (or consultation by appointment) for members of their congregations? What consultation service is available to nonmembers?

8. Do any churches in your community offer consultation (not confined to members) on spiritual, personal, and social difficulties? If so, is trained medical, psychiatric, home economics, or social work personnel employed? Available on a voluntary basis? Made available through co-operative arrangements with other agencies? How widely is this consultation service used? Are all cases cleared through a social service exchange? Are there arrangements under which social agencies in your community refer persons to ministers, priests, or rabbis for religious counsel or aid?

Religious Education. Religious education forms an important part of the program of the churches.

9. For each church, list presence or absence of the following features:

Sunday school for children
Young people's groups for religious study
Adult classes
Training classes for group leaders and volunteer workers
Libraries or collections of religious books or pictures for loan to members
Motion picture projectors and equipment for showing religious and social interest pictures

10. Is religious instruction given by any churches, denominations, or other groups on public school time ("released time")? After school hours (e.g., Talmud Torah schools)? How many children enrolled?

11. How many daily vacation church schools operate in your community? Denominations co-operating? Location and attendance of each school?

12. Are there theological seminaries in your community? (See page 160.) Is supervised field work provided for the students? Under what auspices? What training is given to students in social and community service?

Social Activities

13. For each church you have listed, what facilities are offered for recreation for children? Young people? Adults? Are dancing, dramatics, athletic events, permitted or encouraged? What leadership is provided for these activities? How many churches sponsor Boy Scout, Girl Scout, and similar youth organizations?

14. What social and educational features are offered, namely, "sociables," church suppers, lecture courses of general interest, forums?

Various services are offered to members of congregations in their homes by many churches and denominations.

15. What churches employ deaconesses or parish visitors to visit in the homes? What churches use volunteers on an organized basis?

II. SOCIAL-RELIGIOUS AGENCIES

Churches are important to community life not only because of their activities which mean much to participants. Church members, as well as ministers and priests, are frequently found in positions of leadership in other organizations in the community. Also, church members, imbued as they are with religious teachings of man's responsibility to his fellowmen, are frequently among the most active supporters of community welfare and health services.[1] Furthermore, religious groups administer a wide variety of welfare and health services and institutions, including foster placement, adoption or institutional care of children, hospitals, homes for the aged, services to unmarried mothers, and shelters for homeless men.

Services Administered Directly by Church Groups

16. What institutions in your community are operated under church auspices?

17. What welfare or health services (such as family service, child care, provision for the aged or chronically ill) are administered by church groups?[2]

18. How are church-administered institutions and services financed? What proportion of the costs is met from church funds? What proportion from local or state government funds? What proportion from the community chest? What safeguards are there to assure proper standards of care and to avoid use of public funds for purely sectarian purposes? To what extent do church-administered institutions and services actually serve persons who are not members of the church bodies responsible for their operation?

19. What churches have lay groups (sisterhoods, brotherhoods, St. Vincent de Paul Societies, sodalities, and so on) which carry on benevolent activities among

[1] Practical suggestions (equally appropriate for members of churches other than that for which it was prepared) are included in Friends and Community Service—War and Peace, by Arthur Dunham, American Friends Service Committee, Philadelphia, 1942.

[2] See in other sections of this book questions relating to the particular types of institutions or services maintained.

the congregation? What are their activities? Do they register with the social service exchange? (See page 234.)

20. Is any religious order (e.g., Sisters of Charity) operating in your community which gives nursing or other home care to families? How many served?

21. Is there in your community a federation of Protestant, Catholic, or Jewish welfare or health agencies? How is the federation made up? How financed? How staffed? What does it do? What is its relation to your council of social agencies?

Services Administered by Other Agencies. Agencies which, while not themselves churches are nevertheless religious in nature and purpose, are found in most communities. They may be closely connected with a single denomination or faith, or have some implicit relation to a religious faith as have the "Y's" or Knights of Columbus. Or, like the Jewish community centers, they may offer services to a community bound together by ties of religion without themselves being directly integrated with the religious program.

22. Has your community any of the following agencies?

> Young Men's Christian Association
> Young Women's Christian Association
> Young Men's Hebrew Association
> Young Women's Hebrew Association
> Knights of Columbus
> Jewish Community Center

Branches? Membership? Buildings and equipment? Services offered: educational, recreational, vocational? How supported?[1]

23. What churches co-operate with social, health, and welfare agencies by (a) mobilizing volunteer service from the congregation, (b) inviting speakers to present community needs and programs, (c) supporting campaigns for funds or appropriations in these areas, (d) pushing co-operatively for social legislation or in other ways for the improvement of social conditions?

24. What pastors are members of boards or committees of agencies dealing with health, education, and welfare?

III. INTERCHURCH AND INTERFAITH CO-OPERATION

To facilitate co-operation among different churches or church agencies (and in some cases to lessen tension) a wide variety of organizations and mechanisms have been developed. There are, for example, councils of churches which may or may not be restricted to churches of a single type; interfaith councils or committees; or councils of Protestant, Catholic, or

---

[1] See appropriate sections of this book (such as those dealing with recreation, health, adult education) for questions for further study of church-affiliated agencies active in these fields.

Jewish welfare, or other specialized types of church agencies. Or, religious groups having no continuing organizational ties may co-operate on a specific project such as communitywide campaigns to promote racial or religious tolerance, appeals for foreign relief, or the application of religious principles to social problems.

In certain instances church co-operation with various community activities is fostered through designation of church representatives (selected in a wide variety of ways) to such local organizations as councils of social agencies and central trade union bodies.

25. Is there in your community a council of churches? What denominations or faiths are represented? Which ones not represented? What paid staff has the council? How is it financed? What does it do? Does it have a social service department? What is its program?

26. Is there in your community an agency or committee to foster interfaith understanding and co-operation? How is it made up? How financed? What has it done and what is planned for the future?

27. What interfaith projects have been undertaken in your community in recent years? Union services? Forums on interfaith relationships? On the relationship between religion and social or economic problems? Raising of relief funds? Which churches have participated? Which ones not? If objection is raised to interfaith co-operation, have different religious groups agreed to "simultaneous" activities or campaigns? In what fields? What has been the result of interfaith or "simultaneous" activities in your community?

28. Are there in your community any indications of tension or conflict between or among people or groups of different religious affiliations? Have these increased or decreased over the past ten years?

When you have finished this phase of your inquiry, ask yourself the questions:

29. Are the churches of my community alive to the social as well as the spiritual needs of their communicants?

30. Is co-operation between religious and lay agencies such that the lay agencies call readily upon the churches for the spiritual ministries when they seem especially needed; and do the churches understand how and when to call upon social agencies for the services they are equipped to render?

14. PUBLIC ASSISTANCE

"PUBLIC ASSISTANCE" is the modern term for what was formerly called public relief. It means the provision by government of the necessities of life to persons who are temporarily or permanently unable to provide for themselves and their dependents. Its purpose is to alleviate the distress of those who are directly aided and also to safeguard the community against the physical and social effects of leaving needs unmet. Public assistance normally is provided in the form of cash but may also be in wages for work on relief projects and is sometimes granted in kind.

Public assistance, by virtue of providing the necessities of life for a monthly average of between two and three million persons even in times of economic prosperity, fills an important place in American life. In times of serious economic depression the number of persons aided through public assistance represents a sizable proportion and a fair cross section of the American people as a whole.

The term "public assistance" does not apply to a neatly organized and unitary system of financial aid. It refers rather to a complicated combination of "general assistance" and series of "categorical" assistance measures, each affording aid to a particular and well-defined group or category of persons. There are, for example, three special assistance measures, one for needy aged persons, one for needy blind persons, and one for needy parents of young children, which are the only public assistance measures in which the federal government participates. In addition, there are sometimes found further categorical assistance schemes for needy unemployed workers, needy veterans, and perhaps, for other types of needy persons. Also, public assistance may take the form of wages for work provided through work-relief programs. Thus public assistance is a composite of a wide variety of programs.

Sometimes these various measures are all administered by a single local agency, sometimes by two, or perhaps more agencies. Assistance grants paid under the several programs in a given community may be more or less uniform or may vary widely.

The federal and state governments assume different degrees of financial and administrative responsibility for one as opposed to other types of public assistance. The federal government, for example, shares and insists that states also bear part of the cost of old-age assistance, aid to the blind, and aid to dependent children. General assistance, available in most areas to meet residual needs not provided for through the various categorical measures, is not at this writing supported by any federal funds and may or may not be financed from state funds. Similarly, conditions upon which the several assistance programs are administered vary widely. However, because of federal participation and leadership, the three special assistance programs already mentioned are administered in accord with the same broad principles and, in general, are better administered than are assistance measures in which the federal government does not participate.

In this chapter attention is limited to the public assistance functions of the public welfare departments. Up-to-date discussions of public assistance are readily available in the monthly issues of the Social Security Bulletin and in the Social Security Yearbook.[1] In the former are published monthly data such as the numbers of persons aided under various assistance programs in the several states and the average payment in each state. A monumental report on the nation's various public assistance measures was embodied in Security, Work, and Relief Policies, published in 1942 by the National Resources Planning Board.

In relation to practice, easy texts to read are The Public Assistance Worker: His Responsibility to the Applicant, the Community, and Himself, edited by Russell H. Kurtz,[2] and A Guidebook for Beginners in Public Assistance Work, by Ella L. Cowgill.[3] If a more detailed reference is desired, Public Welfare Administration, by Marietta Stevenson[4] is recommended. Your local public assistance agency or perhaps the state agency supervising public assistance in your community has probably issued a manual outlining policies and standards applicable in your community. Such manuals are invaluable aids to the study of public assistance administration.

During a period of economic depression the relief problem is likely to prove one of the most serious difficulties America has to face. In 1936,

[1] Government Printing Office, Washington. The Social Security Administration of the Federal Security Agency publishes at irregular intervals Characteristics of State Plans, presenting state by state the provisions of their several special assistance programs.
[2] Russell Sage Foundation, New York, 1938.
[3] Family Welfare Association of America, New York, 1940. (Renamed in 1946 Family Service Association of America.)
[4] Macmillan Co., New York, 1938.

for example, approximately $2,827,000,000 was paid to recipients of work and direct assistance. However, in 1942 for the first time in American history, social insurance and related payments (including veterans' pensions and compensation, and readjustment allowances to unemployed and self-employed veterans) exceeded public assistance grants. In 1944 social insurance and related payments more than doubled, and in 1945 nearly trebled the assistance totals. It may be hoped, therefore, that even in a new depression assistance measures will never again be called upon to bear so large a proportion of the total burden of maintaining purchasing power as they did in the 1930's, before the social insurances were solidly established.

I. ADMINISTRATIVE ARRANGEMENTS

At its best, public assistance is administered by modern public welfare departments which, in addition to public assistance, may be responsible also for child welfare and family welfare services, institutional care, shelter, and medical care, as well as a variety of other welfare services.[1] These departments may be local units of a state agency or may be units of a county, municipality, or other local government. If the administering body is a local agency, at least the three types of special assistance financed in part by federal funds are subject to supervision by appropriate state agencies.

As presently organized, public assistance measures in a community may be administered not by one but by two or even more separate agencies. This almost inevitably causes confusion, inequity, and duplication which the recent trend toward integration is aimed to eliminate. However, even when the various public assistance programs in a community are administered by a single agency, it is possible that the several types of assistance provided may be administered according to different standards and policies. In studying public assistance administration, therefore, one must be alert both to differences in policies applicable under the various programs and to the justification for observed differences.

Administration of public assistance involves many technical problems requiring trained and competent personnel. Modern public assistance agencies operate under merit systems to assure the highest possible caliber of staff.

Adequate financing is also indispensable to effective public assistance administration. While many public assistance needs can be more or less accurately anticipated, arrangements for financing must be sufficiently flexible to permit the meeting of unexpected needs resulting from sudden unemployment, increases in living costs, or other unpredictable factors.

---

[1] See Chapter 9.

Many public assistance agencies benefit from advisory boards variously appointed to interpret to the agency the opinion of the community and to interpret to the public the needs and program of the agency. When such boards exist, experience has shown the importance of carefully defining the administrative responsibilities of the board.

1. What public assistance programs are now being administered in your community: old-age assistance, aid to the blind, aid to dependent children, general assistance, veteran relief, work relief, aid to farmers, aid to transients, other?

2. What agency administers each type of public assistance available in your community? In all, how many agencies administer public assistance? If more than one agency, how is their work co-ordinated?

3. What state agency (or agencies) supervises or otherwise participates in the administration of each type of public assistance available in your community? Are responsible state agencies equally interested in all your assistance programs? If not, why not?

4. Is the agency administering the several forms of assistance available in your community (a) a town, municipal, county, or other local agency, or (b) a local unit of a state agency? Is the (or each) agency a member of the American Public Welfare Association, the Family Service Association of America, the Child Welfare League of America?

5. Does the (or each) assistance agency have a board of local citizens? What are their functions? What are the qualifications of present incumbents for their responsibilities? How active are they?

6. How is the (or each) public assistance agency organized? How is the head of the (or each) public assistance agency selected? What are the qualifications for this work?

7. What changes in organization, administration, or standards of assistance have supervisory state agencies recently recommended?

8. What proportion of the cost of each program is borne from local funds, state funds, federal funds?

9. Is the personnel of the (or each) public assistance agency selected on a merit basis? Describe operation of the merit system. What are the qualifications for the key jobs?

10. How many employes on the staff of the public assistance agency? How do salaries compare with equally demanding work in your local schools or other comparable public departments? With salaries paid by assistance agencies in other communities comparable with your own?

11. What is the average caseload of the public assistance visitors or investigators? For how many visitors is each supervisor responsible? Do agency officials think present work loads of supervisors and visitors too heavy? Too light?

12. How much did your public assistance agency spend in each of the past five years (a) for assistance, (b) for administration and service? What is its budget for this year? What proportion of last year's expenditures under the various public assistance programs were met from (a) federal, (b) state, and (c) local funds? What provision is made for unanticipated relief needs that might suddenly appear and cannot be met from the fiscal budget?

13. Do the quarters occupied by the public assistance agency afford good light and ventilation, separate desk space for each worker, separate toilet facilities for workers and applicants? Rooms or cubicles providing adequate privacy for interviews with applicants, waiting rooms with seating space and toilet facilities sufficient for applicants awaiting interviews?

14. What administrative function does the agency perform? Does it have a division of reporting and research? A division of public interpretation?

15. How are policies affecting the administration of public assistance established? By the citizen board? Does the agency staff have any voice in policy determination?

16. What is done by your public assistance authorities to interpret to your community the need for and importance of assistance and related services to your local citizens? What organizations in your community are interested in how your public assistance programs are administered? What have they accomplished? Anything in the way of prevention? Are public assistance recipients formally organized? If so, what is the relationship between their organization and the public assistance agency?

II. ELIGIBILITY

The nub of public assistance measures is to select from among applicants those who society has decided shall receive aid and to make available to such eligible persons the assistance they require. The purpose behind this is not only to aid the persons concerned, but also to protect society against the costs—in terms of disrupted family life, sickness, delinquency, more serious later need, loss of respect for government, unrest—of leaving human needs unmet.

The standards of eligibility in force under any particular assistance program in a community may be prescribed by a responsible state agency or by the local agency itself. To be effective, eligibility standards must be simply stated so as to be easily understood both by applicants and the community as a whole. Standards of eligibility should also assure needed assistance without discrimination on the basis of race, creed, political belief, residence, citizenship, national origin, or any other arbitrary factor.

Under the best administered public assistance programs provision is made for appeals or fair hearings by applicants who believe they have not been granted the assistance for which they are eligible.

Instead of being regarded as positive aids to administration, standards of eligibility are sometimes still regarded primarily as devices for denying to particular types of admittedly needy persons (such as newcomers to a community, aliens, or persons unable to meet prescribed age requirements) the necessary assistance.

Economic need which, by definition, is a prerequisite to receipt of public assistance, may be variously measured. The most widely accepted current practice is to appraise need in terms of a person's ability to provide for himself (and, in the case of a family head, for his family also) the food, clothing, shelter, fuel, light, water, medical care, personal care, and other necessities required.

Equally important as the standard by which need is measured is the treatment of a family's resources including insurance policies, equity in a homestead, small savings, earnings of children, earnings of breadwinners, and possible contributions from relatives. Experience in public assistance administration emphasizes the shortsightedness of policies requiring applicants to divest themselves of every possible resource before qualifying for public assistance. Rehabilitation is frequently found to be more rapid if applicants are not required to exhaust all available assets before public aid can be granted.

17. What is the standard used under *each* of the assistance programs to determine an applicant's need for assistance? Is the same standard applied in the case of Negroes or of other minority groups? Do standards vary from one program to another? Why?

18. Are applicants automatically barred from receiving assistance if they have any resources of their own? If they have earnings, even if inadequate? If not, what resources and earnings are allowed under each public assistance program?

19. To what extent are the relatives of applicants required, under your general programs, to contribute to the support of their needy kin? How much support is actually contributed? What is the effect of these policies upon family ties?

20. In addition to being in economic need, what further eligibility requirements must be met to qualify for assistance under *each* program in your community?

21. Are there age requirements to be met? Citizenship requirements? Residence requirements? Must recipients, if employable, register with your local employment office? Other requirements? What differences between requirements for one type of assistance as opposed to another? Why?

22. Are needy persons ineligible for assistance under *any* of your public assistance programs if they are employable? If receiving social insurance benefits however inadequate? If children of school age do not attend school? If workers refuse employment regardless of the rate of pay? If they are on strike? If they fail to meet other requirements?

23. Are applicants required to sign "paupers' oaths"? Promises to repay later any assistance granted? Liens on real or personal property owned?

24. Under each of your assistance programs, who finally decides who shall or shall not be given aid? What machinery is there for hearing grievances or appeals of applicants who feel they have not been justly treated? How frequently is eligibility to continue receipt of benefits rechecked?

25. Are the conditions of eligibility for the various forms of public assistance clearly stated so as to be easily understood by applicants? Is the basis for computing assistance grants understandable so that recipients can be assured they are receiving the amounts for which they are eligible?

26. Is there provision for immediate assistance to persons pending determination of eligibility?

27. What can you find out about the age, race, physical condition, family status, occupation, present employment, length of time on relief, and other significant characteristics of persons receiving assistance? What do these findings suggest with respect to preventive measures; to long-range provisions that would be better than relief?

28. What proportion of assistance recipients are Negroes? How does this ratio compare with the proportion of Negroes among the total population?

29. Are there in your community needy persons who do not qualify for public assistance? Why not? What, in the opinion of your public assistance authorities, should be done for such persons? What is the best estimate you can get as to the number of such persons?

III. NUMBERS ASSISTED

The proportion of the population given public assistance in the various communities of the United States varies widely, depending upon the financial resources available and upon the nature of the programs in operation. Anomalously, these factors often mean that in poorer states and areas where need is most widespread, a smaller proportion of the population is granted public assistance than is the case in wealthier states and localities.

30. How many families are now receiving each type of public assistance available in your community? How many persons are in these families? How many of these are children?

31. How do numbers being aided compare, in proportion to the population of your community, with those aided in neighboring communities? In other communities of comparable size?

32. How do the numbers now receiving assistance compare with those receiving assistance at the same time a year ago? Five years ago? Why the difference?

33. What is the number expected to be a year from now? Are the financial resources in sight adequate for this number?

34. What are the primary reasons for the applications for assistance made during the past several months: (a) loss of employment, (b) underemployment, (c) loss of breadwinner, (d) wage reductions, (e) higher living costs, (f) sickness, (g) labor disputes, (h) other?

35. For what primary reasons have persons left assistance rolls during the past several months: (a) to take employment, (b) recovery from illness, (c) increased earnings, (d) other?

IV. STANDARDS OF ASSISTANCE

Second in importance only to the question as to who shall receive public assistance, is the further question of how much assistance eligible persons shall receive. Although it would appear to be logical to base assistance grants upon the same standard as that used in measuring need, this is not always done. Sometimes the funds available to the administering agency will not permit meeting admitted needs fully; sometimes assistance grants are arbitrarily limited to a specified amount such as that which the recipient might normally be expected to earn; sometimes to a specified percentage of actual needs. Differences in policies and in resources available for the various types of assistance provided frequently result in great disparities not only among assistance programs in different communities but also among the various measures administered in any one community.

By whatever means they may be computed, assistance grants should be sufficient to provide, at locally prevailing prices, the food, clothing, shelter, fuel, light, medical care, personal care, transportation, and other essentials required by assistance recipients.

Particularly since the enactment of the federal Social Security Act which required that special assistance financed in part from federal funds must be paid in cash, public assistance has usually been provided in this form. However, in certain areas assistance is still sometimes provided in kind, or in the form of store orders. These are usually redeemable only by designated vendors and for specified relief goods. The greater freedom allowed recipients under a system of cash assistance[1] is calculated both to bolster morale and to permit more normal living than would otherwise be possible.

Special assistance payments, as well as payments under other well-administered programs, are made unconditionally. They are not used as a lever to compel recipients either to do or to refrain from doing some specified act.

Human needs are so varied and complex that many cannot be met solely through the provision of food, clothing, shelter, and other material necessities. Assistance in meeting child care problems, aid in securing medical care, help in finding employment or in securing vocational retraining, counseling on family problems, and finally, advice on the use of limited resources for household management are typical of the services which public assistance agencies are daily called upon to render.[2] However, unless competent personnel is available, services of these types cannot be successfully provided.

36. What method is used under *each* of your assistance programs to determine the amount of assistance to be granted an applicant? Are maximum or minimum limits set by statute? Otherwise?

---

[1] See Cash Relief, by Joanna C. Colcord, Russell Sage Foundation, New York, 1936.
[2] For further discussion see Common Human Needs: An Interpretation for Staff in Public Assistance Agencies, by Charlotte Towle, Public Assistance Report no. 8, Government Printing Office, Washington, 1945.

37. Under *each* program what allowance is made for food? Shelter? Water? Fuel? Clothing? Medical Care? Education? Transportation? Lunches for employed persons? Recreation? Church or union contributions? Insurance? Household supplies? Supplemental foods for pregnant women, nursing mothers, young children, sick persons? Vocational training? Prosthetic appliances for disabled persons? For other needs? What needs are provided for under one program and not another? Why?

38. What provision is made for adjusting assistance allowances in response to significant changes in price levels?

39. What needs are met through contributions in kind (food, clothing, and so forth) rather than through cash payments? Why?

40. Is medical care directly provided or is provision made through cash grants? Does the chosen method assure the best possible medical care?

41. Are any cash grants made only upon condition that recipients perform some specified act? What? Why? If practices under all public assistance programs are not uniform, what factors are responsible for the differences?

42. Under each assistance program, who finally decides what assistance an applicant shall receive? What provision is there for hearing grievances and appeals?

43. What is the average assistance grant now being given under each of your assistance programs? If there are significant differences under the various programs, how are these explained? Are grants adequate? If not, what action is contemplated?

44. How do average grants compare with those of a year ago? Five years ago? Have grants increased more or less than living costs? How do grants to Negroes or other minority groups compare with the general average? If there are significant differences, how are these explained?

45. How do grants compare with those in neighboring communities? With those in other comparable communities in other areas?

46. How do the various assistance benefits compare with unemployment, old-age and survivors insurance benefits paid in your community? Are noted differences defensible?

47. What home economics, nutrition, social work, medical social work, child welfare, employment, or other services are rendered under your various assistance programs? How many families given these services? What are the qualifications of workers rendering these services?

48. Do the personnel ministering public assistance render counseling or personal service to help relieve feelings of anxiety frequently caused by economic need and the necessity of applying for public assistance? Meet family or personal problems? Meet health, housing, employment, and related needs which may not be the direct responsibility of the public assistance agency? Are the officers in a position to render these services qualified to do so? If not, are they trained to recognize the need for such services and to refer persons to community agencies equipped to deal with them?

49. What is done under each of your assistance programs to protect the confidential nature of case records? Are the names of recipients of any form of assistance ever divulged? Under what circumstances? Why?

V. WORK RELIEF

Notwithstanding widely held beliefs to the contrary, experience has clearly proved that public assistance recipients normally prefer to do what they can to support themselves rather than to remain on assistance rolls. Evidence of this can be found in the eagerness with which employable persons accept proffered employment meeting anything like standard working conditions. Further evidence can also be found in the willingness of assistance recipients, if the opportunity is given, to work on relief projects.[1] Work relief is therefore frequently to be preferred to direct assistance. In addition, it yields tangible returns to a community, and helps to preserve work habits and perhaps imparts new skills. Past experience proves that the closer wages and conditions on work-relief jobs approximate those in private employment, the more successful they are likely to be.

Particularly during the depression of the 1930's, employable needy persons in the United States were aided through employment on work projects rather than through direct aid. In extent, as in the standard of aid provided, these work programs exceeded anything in the history of this or any other country. Experience gained under these programs can be of inestimable help in planning work-relief programs should a future depression throw into need large numbers of employable persons.[2]

50. What is being done to provide work instead of direct assistance for needy persons in your community? For how many workers could jobs be provided in case of necessity? If present plans are inadequate to provide jobs for all likely to need them within the next year what action would be required to provide such employment?

51. How many now employed on what kinds of jobs? Under whose auspices? At what wages? What are the hours and other conditions of work? Who finally decides who shall receive the available jobs? What recourse have workers who feel they have been unjustly deprived of jobs?

Administration of public assistance as a modern public service is beset by many pitfalls. Many of these are attributable to archaic and now disproved misconceptions regarding needy persons and the effect such assistance has upon recipients. It was once thought, for example, that people fell into need only because of some fault in their own character. Now it is known that assistance recipients represent a fairly normal cross section of the American people but are persons whom sickness, disability, unemployment,

[1] Read The Unemployed Worker: A Study of the Task of Making a Living Without a Job, by E. Wight Bakke, Yale University Press, New Haven, 1940.
[2] For detailed analysis of the strength and weaknesses of federal work schemes during the 1930's, see The WPA and Federal Relief Policy, by Donald S. Howard, Russell Sage Foundation, New York, 1943.

death of breadwinner, or some other fortuitous circumstances have temporarily thrown into need.

Similarly, it was once thought that the public interest demanded that such assistance (previously termed relief) as might be given should be as niggardly as possible and its receipt made distasteful and onerous. Now it is recognized that only as human needs are met as fully as possible and without humiliation can unnecessary sickness be prevented, morale sustained, employability preserved, rehabilitation facilitated, and social justice assured.

Unfortunately, public assistance administrators are frequently caught between two fires. On the one hand there are still certain followers of the old school who, today, would like to see assistance administered upon as restrictive a basis as possible. On the other hand there is the growing body of public opinion supporting public assistance as an important function of a modern community and as at least one method of safeguarding family life, of promoting the welfare of children, and of helping—in short—to assure freedom from want.

52. Is public assistance in your community administered as a constructive public service to which needy persons have a rightful claim, or as relief given grudgingly to needy persons for whom application and receipt of aid is purposely made embarrassing and difficult?

53. Are presumptively needy persons assisted in establishing eligibility for assistance or is the burden of proof thrown upon them to prove their own claims without the help of public assistance officers?

54. Is public assistance interpreted to the community as benefiting not only recipients but also the whole community?

15. SPECIAL PROVISIONS FOR FAMILY WELFARE

STABLE families are the best assurance a community can have that its children are getting a fair start in life. Schools, health, and recreation agencies can offer the highest type of services, but unless the children of the community have their basic emotional needs met through the security furnished by good homes, these community agencies are building upon sand. The legal, social, and economic supports which the community offers in the development of sound family life are therefore fitting subjects for study.

In this chapter we shall discuss the family itself in relation to the community, and the agencies, found in many communities, which aim to promote the stability of family life, and to furnish special forms of counsel and assistance to families and adult individuals with varied problems.[1]

Among the numerous texts available on the much-disputed subject of marriage and the family, it is difficult to suggest a single book which will give a modern and yet balanced approach to this subject. The Family: From Institution to Companionship, by Ernest W. Burgess and Harvey J. Locke,[2] and When You Marry, by Evelyn M. Duvall and Reuben Hill,[3] are two which can be recommended as background reading at this point.

I. MARITAL STATUS AND NUMBER OF FAMILIES

In the population series of the census, much detailed information is given about the marital status of inhabitants over fifteen years of age, by sex, color, and nativity.

1. How many persons, and what percentage of the total population in your community were reported as married at the time of the latest census?

---

[1] Other chapters impinge upon other aspects of family life. For instance, family life is affected by cramped and inadequate housing, discussed in Chapter 7. For problems raised by wives working, see section on Protection of Working Women in Chapter 6. See also section on Unorganized Recreation in Chapter 12. Chapter 15 discusses public provision for assistance to financially disadvantaged families.

[2] American Book Co., New York, 1945.

[3] Heath and Co., New York, 1945. A summary of this book, available in pamphlet form, is Building Your Marriage, by Evelyn M. Duvall, Pamphlet no. 113, Public Affairs Committee, Inc., New York, 1946.

2. How many men, women? By sex, how many whites, other races?
3. How many married boys, girls, by race, were under twenty?
4. How many men, women, were reported as widowed? Divorced?

In addition to the population series of the census, you will find an entire volume of the housing reports devoted to further statistical information about family groups.

5. How many families were reported in the latest census in your community, by race and nativity of head?
6. What was the median size of families in your community, by race and nativity of head?
7. How many families in these groups had children under ten?

II. FORMATION OF NEW FAMILIES

That the right of persons to contract marriage is not without legal limitations is clearly indicated by insistence in many state laws that no marriage ceremony may be performed until a public official has issued a license permitting it, and that no marriage may be formally dissolved except through court action.

American Family Laws, by Chester G. Vernier and others,[1] should be consulted in connection with this part of the study.[2] Read the marriage law of your state and consult the legal aid organization, the judge of your family court, or some lawyer experienced in domestic law as to the effect of its provisions.

Some states have not yet taken steps to disallow marriage by private contract ("common-law marriage") under which the two parties, *if both are free to contract marriage,* may agree between themselves to live as man and wife, without securing a license, participating in a marriage ceremony before witnesses, or recording the marriage in any public record.

8. Is common-law marriage prohibited under the laws of your state? If not, how many court actions in your community last year were brought in the attempt to establish the validity of alleged common-law marriages?

In most states, however, securing a marriage license is the first official step toward legal marriage. The object of this formality is to register from the beginning the state's right to control who may and who may not found new families, and to give the licensing official an opportunity to judge by

[1] Stanford University Press, Stanford University, 1938. Law of Marriage and Divorce Simplified, by Richard V. Mackay, Oceana Publications, New York, 1946, is a small reference book in nontechnical language, explaining briefly marriage and divorce laws in all states.
[2] Read also Marriage and the State, by Mary E. Richmond and Fred S. Hall, Russell Sage Foundation, New York. Although published in 1929 it is still one of the best studies of marriage laws and their administration in their broader social aspects.

personal interview whether the facts given in the application are as alleged, or should be further investigated. It depends upon the licensing officers in your community to what extent these purposes are carried out.

9. Does your state law demand that application for a marriage license must be made in person by one of the parties or must both parties appear together?

10. Is your license issuer a salaried official, or does he receive fees in lieu of salary?

11. Visit your license bureau. Is there a "marriage parlor" attached? Is the procedure dignified and seemly? Is there any evidence of collusion with certain officiating officers who thereby profit financially?

12. Do your local newspapers publish lists of licenses issued, marriages performed?

13. What proofs must applicants for a marriage license be prepared to offer on the following points:

> Age of both parties
> Parental consent if either is under age (what age?)
> Residence of bride
> Absence of legal impediment to the marriage
> Freedom from venereal diseases (Are blood tests mandatory? What is the maximum elapsed time permissible between examination and marriage?)
> Freedom from insanity, feeble-mindedness, epilepsy

14. Does your law prohibit marriage between persons of the white race and those of other races? What races? What degree of nonwhite blood is sufficient to make a marriage void or voidable?

15. Within what degrees of consanguinity are marriages illegal in your state?

Obviously, if the law prescribes no interval between the application for a marriage license and its granting, the license clerk has no routine opportunity to ascertain the facts. Some states require such an interval; other states have introduced a delay between the granting of the license and the date on which the ceremony may be performed, but this serves a different purpose— the prevention of hasty marriages.

16. How long a delay is called for in your law between the times of application and issuance of marriage licenses? Between issuance and date when ceremony may legally take place?

17. Under what circumstances may special licenses be issued?

18. Under what conditions may marriages be solemnized without a celebrant (e.g., marriages before a Friends' Meeting)?

19. Who are allowed to celebrate marriage ceremonies? What penalties does your law impose upon celebrants who perform illegal marriages, fail to record marriages?

20. Do any considerable numbers of young people from other communities come to your community for the purpose of getting married? Why?

21. Is there a so-called "Gretna Green" near your community to which your own young people go to be married? Why?

22. How many marriage licenses were issued in your community last year? How many were refused? For what causes?

In addition to the general census reports at ten-year intervals, the Bureau of the Census issues monthly a series on Marriage Licenses Issued in Cities of 100,000 or More. As a result of the war and better economic conditions the marriage rate for 1940–1944 was above normal, but the Bureau forecasts that this wartime increase will be followed by a "subnormal" period.

23. How does the number of licenses issued in your community compare with other communities of similar size? With the number in your community five years ago?[1]

In every community some licenses are issued for which no marriages are subsequently recorded. This may be simply because the parties have postponed or changed their plans; but it also may be because girls, particularly foreign-born girls, have been deluded into believing that the license is a legal certificate of marriage.

24. Is any system in effect in your marriage license bureau of inquiring the cause when no marriage is subsequently registered? Has any study been made of these cases? What did it show?

III. DISSOLUTION OF MARRIAGES

Marriages may be dissolved in several ways. They may be declared by court action to have been void *ab initio*; they may be voidable by legal process; or they may be terminated by divorce.

25. During the past several years how many marriages were annulled in your community? How many terminated by divorce? How does this number compare with that for ten years ago?

26. What was the divorce rate (per 1,000 population) in your community? Your state?[2]

27. For what causes are marriages, if performed, declared to be void in your state? In cases of voided marriage what is done to protect property interests of the principals? The interests of any children of the marriage?

28. For what causes, under what conditions, and by whom may annulment proceedings be brought? In what courts? (See page 197.)

---

[1] Marriage rates are greatly affected by "migratory marriages," either into or out of the community, when these are prevalent.

[2] Divorce rates alone must not be taken as evidence of the instability of family life in a given community because of the frequency with which people go out of their own community to obtain divorces.

29. For what causes may divorces be granted in your state? In what courts are applications for divorce heard in your community?

30. Do people in your community who wish divorces prefer to secure them in other communities? Why?

31. What has your law to say on the subject of collusive divorce actions (when both parties wish the separation)?

32. What efforts must the party bringing the suit make to assure the knowledge of his or her spouse that suit is being brought?

33. If the courts involved are not so-called family courts are there any provisions for (a) social investigations by probation officers or others prior to trial, (b) efforts to bring about reconciliation prior to trial?

34. Is special study given to the problems of children involved in the outcome of divorce trials? Does the court maintain supervision over their welfare for any stated period?

IV. THE FAMILY COURT

Family courts are a recent development in our judicial system, dating back to about 1910. They vary in their organization and jurisdiction. In some instances children's and family courts have been combined, in others the family court is part of a court having wide civil and criminal jurisdiction. Some have very limited jurisdiction, such as nonsupport in relatively minor cases, while others deal with a wide variety of family situations such as nonsupport, separation, divorce, abandonment, paternity. Family courts seek to adjudicate issues and disputes, as they arise out of family discord, in accordance with the law and sound legal practice, thus protecting the rights of all and insuring that justice is done. They recognize that in family disputes the social and personal factors, as well as the legal, must be considered if a constructive approach in the settlement of these disputes is to be made. Therefore, along with less formal court procedures, the social, medical, and psychiatric services are accepted as essential adjuncts in the work of family courts. Special family courts—which, for all their special characteristics, are still courts—are bound by well-defined legal procedures. Their effectiveness is largely conditioned upon whether the dissenting parties bring their rift to court while the case is still open and before the principals have made an irrevocable decision to separate.

35. Has your community a family court or domestic relations court? Is it independent, or part of some other court?

36. How broad is its jurisdiction over family problems? What other courts adjudicate family matters not dealt with by the family court?

37. Which family problems, if any, are defined as crimes in the law? Is nonsupport a crime?

38. What qualifications are required of judges in the family court? Are they appointed or elected? By whom and for what term?

39. Are the physical facilities provided the various units of the court adequate? (Courtrooms, staff rooms, professional services)? Are private interviewing rooms available at the family court for preliminary interviews? To what extent are the court's proceedings informal and designed to give consideration to the social as well as strictly legal issues involved?

40. What social, medical, and psychiatric services are provided in the family court? Are these under court administration or supplied by another resource? What qualifications are required for staff members?

41. How are cases selected for social, medical, or psychiatric study? Where treatment is needed how is it provided?

42. Does the court collect and disburse all payments on orders it makes for nonsupport, or may payments under court order be made directly by one party to the other?

43. Where a husband is committed by the court for defaulting in his payments under a nonsupport order, must the jail sentence be served or may he avoid it by posting a bond or surety guaranteeing future payments for a reasonable period? Can men committed earn money in jail which can go toward the support of their families?

44. Are family desertion and abandonment extraditable offenses? Can extradition, where permitted, be completed in the family court or does some other court have jurisdiction over it?

45. What co-operation exists between the family court and other community social agencies? Is this provided for in the law?

V. FAMILY FINANCES

Costs and Standards of Living. Earnings of the workers of a community must be considered in relation to what those earnings will buy. Read Economic Problems of the Family, by Hazel Kyrk,[1] in which both costs and standards of living are discussed in illuminating fashion. A community's well-being depends in large measure upon the ability of its families to provide for themselves not only the elemental necessities of life but adequate medical care, recreation, education, and other aids to wholesome social life. A family's ability to provide these essentials depends not only upon its resources and income but also upon the costs, locally, of the needed goods and service.[2] That a significant proportion of American families lack incomes sufficient to provide for themselves adequately is evidenced by the fact that even in wartime, when American incomes were higher than normal, at least one-third and perhaps one-half of the families in the country could not afford what might be termed the "American standard of living."

[1] Harper and Bros., New York, 1933. (Out of print, but generally available in libraries.)

[2] Faith M. Williams, chief of the Cost of Living Division of the U.S. Bureau of Labor Statistics, analyzes recent research findings on the national income and the cost of living in the very readable pamphlet The American Standard of Living: Earning and Spending Our Money, National Education Association, Washington, 1944.

For many years and throughout the United States there have been many attempts to estimate the cost of maintaining families at various standards of living. Among the most useful studies in this field is that made by the WPA in 59 cities in 1935–1936.[1] Monthly changes in living costs in most of these 59 cities are published regularly in the Monthly Labor Review, thus making it possible to estimate with reasonable accuracy the current cost in many cities of the "maintenance" standard used as the basis of the WPA study.

46. Was your community one of those included in the WPA report? What was the average cost at the maintenance level, at the emergency level, in 1935, in your community, or in the one nearest to yours in point of size and location? How did these averages compare with the averages of the 59 cities? How have more recent findings compared with those of the WPA study?

47. Has any recent study been made of the cost of living of low-income groups in your community or a comparable community in your region?[2] What does that study show to be the minimum income required by an average family?

48. Do reports in the Monthly Labor Review for recent months show that the cost of living in your area is rising? Decreasing? What percentage of change during the past year? How does it compare with that for the country as a whole? In what items has change been most marked?

49. How do budgets used in determining public assistance or private relief allowances in your community compare with the minimum standards regarded as essential for health and decency?

Family Income. Once it is known approximately how much income an average family requires to assure its well-being it is important to know how many families in a given community have incomes falling below this amount. The most comprehensive study ever made of incomes and expenditures of American families was the Consumer Purchases Study made in 1936 by the Bureau of Home Economics of the United States Department of Agriculture and the Bureau of Labor Statistics, with the co-operation of several other federal agencies. The communities studied in each region fell within five distinct degrees of urbanization: large cities, middle-

---

[1] Stecker, Margaret L., Intercity Differences in Costs of Living in March, 1935, 59 Cities. Works Progress Administration, Division of Social Research, Research Monograph no. 12, Government Printing Office, Washington, 1937. The maintenance standard, for an unskilled worker's family of four, as defined, is not so liberal as a health and decency level but affords more than a minimum subsistence.

As this book goes to press a study designed to measure current dollar cost of a standard of living providing minimum adequacy for an urban family is nearing completion. This will probably be issued under the title "A Standard Budget—1946," and will give figures for an urban family of four at a minimum of adequacy. The March, 1946, cost of the budget will be presented for the 34 large cities where prices are regularly collected by the Bureau of Labor Statistics for the Consumers' Price Index.

[2] State departments of labor or authorities responsible for enforcement of minimum wage laws often make studies of living costs within the state.

sized cities, small cities, villages, and farm counties. Comparisons of consumption patterns of families living in communities of different sizes can thus be made without meeting the problems of regional differences. A sixth degree of urbanization is represented by Chicago and New York City, selected to show income and consumption of metropolitan families. In many previous studies of family consumption families were selected from certain socio-economic population groups and figures presented for the sample as a whole. An earlier series of reports of family incomes and expenditures, though of somewhat narrower scope, shows for the various cities studied, and for white and Negro families, the average size of family and average number of gainful workers per family; occupation and income of chief earner; average family income and expenditure for food, clothing, housing, and other specified items.[1] More limited studies of family incomes, spending, and saving have been made in recent years.[2]

50. What does the Consumer Purchases Study or a more recent survey tell about the amount of incomes received by families in your community or in a comparable community in your region? What can you learn from labor unions, employers, social workers, or other sources about the probable income of families in the lowest income groups in your community?

51. From the data you have been able to gather, what annual income do you think a worker's family of four would need in your community? What should be its average weekly income throughout the year? (Bear in mind that you may have to allow for changes in the cost-of-living index, as reported in the Monthly Labor Review.) How does this figure compare with average weekly earnings reported by your State Department of Labor, by labor unions, or other reliable sources?

52. What measures are being proposed in your community to bridge any considerable gaps there may be between the incomes families actually have and what they really need? Are price controls suggested? Improved minimum wage legislation? Family allowances? More adequate public assistance? Better public services including low-cost housing? What is thought to be the social and physical effect of low incomes?

There are certain items of information, comparatively easy to obtain, which indicate changes in a community's standard of living. For instance, your chamber of commerce or merchants' association may be able to supply you with figures showing changes in the total volume of retail sales during recent years. Changes in the consumption of particular articles—for example, the amount of new furniture purchased, quarts of milk delivered,

---

[1] Bureau of Labor Statistics, U.S. Dept. of Labor, Bulletins nos. 636–649, 1939–1941.
[2] See, for example, "Expenditures and Savings of City Families in 1944," in Monthly Labor Review, January, 1946, pp. 1–5, and "City-Family Composition in Relation to Income, 1941 and 1944," in Monthly Labor Review, February, 1946, pp. 175–180.

residence telephones installed or taken out—may reflect prosperity or a
lowering of the living standards of your community. Other suggestions
can be gathered from the rest of this section. Here is a good place to use
your imagination in devising a list of possible indices of changes in the
community's consumptive habits on which information can be secured with
sufficient readiness to make the effort worth while.

Management of Small Incomes. Unfortunately, community interest in
the problems of management of small incomes has usually been confined to
families below the level of self-support. Some savings banks have undertaken to set up bureaus to advise their depositors on family budget making.
One has only to realize the number of families who normally have difficulty
in making incomes stretch, who get into debt and involve themselves in
ill-advised contracts to purchase goods and property, or who have to revise
their standard of living in consequence of reduced earnings, to realize that
a wide area of potential service is not being touched in our communities
today.

53. Does your public welfare department offer to recipients of public assistance special services in budget making, debt and insurance adjustment, problems
of small business proprietors, and so on? (See page 189.) Is this service available to persons not in receipt of assistance?

54. Do your agencies for family welfare offer these services to their clients?[1]
(See page 211.) Are there any other sources in your community from which
families can obtain disinterested advice on how to manage their income and expenditures? Is this service free, or on a fee basis?

Several of the large life insurance companies became so concerned about
the plight of families which were attempting to carry insurance in excess of
their means that in 1931 they established the Life Insurance Adjustment
Bureau.[2] The Bureau does not extend its services direct to individual
policyholders, but furnishes advice and assistance without charge to social
agencies in all parts of the country in obtaining such modifications in the
policies held by a distressed client as will best protect his investment and
coverage.

55. What social agencies in your community avail themselves of the services
of the Life Insurance Adjustment Bureau for the benefit of their clients?

Home Ownership. You have already ascertained (see page 80) how
many families in your community are living in houses which they own, but

[1] See Family Budget Counseling, by Dorothy L. Book, Family Welfare Association of
America, New York, 1944. (Renamed in 1946 Family Service Association of America.)
[2] For address see List of Agencies, p. 251. The Bureau has published a pamphlet called
Life Insurance: A Handbook for Social Workers Concerning the Examination, Evaluation,
and Adjustment of Life Insurance, New York, 4th ed., 1946.

you do not yet know what equity they possess in those homes. The experience of home owners during the past fifteen years has caused doubt and questioning on a point which this nation had regarded as settled for all time, that is, the superior advantages of home ownership as opposed to renting.[1]

During this time the residential real estate market has experienced both severe deflation and inflation. The wartime expansion of economic activity greatly stimulated the real estate market. Long before V-J Day increased incomes and savings and an intense housing shortage caused home prices to rocket. Discharged military personnel desperately needing homes were compelled by circumstances to bid for accommodations in this market. Current trends in home prices and construction costs in 1946 were expected to give rise to a wave of foreclosures.

56. What are your local housing needs in quantitative terms and in price and rental ranges? What residential construction is under way and what is planned?

57. Can you secure sales prices on representative existing houses in the various price ranges for the past five years? Is there a prevailing tendency for the greatest proportionate price increases to be concentrated in the lower price brackets? Is there evidence of speculative transfers of these properties?

58. Can you secure any estimates of how many homes in your community are owned free from mortgages? Among mortgaged properties, how many loans are less than two years old? Among these "green" loans, what is the average ratio of outstanding balance to the prewar or first selling price?

59. From what sources and upon what conditions may home owners in your community borrow to buy, build, or refinance their homes? What interest rates are charged? What service charges? What are the repayment terms?

60. What proportion of current lending by private institutions is insured through either Title II or Title VI of the National Housing Act? What proportion of this lending is either guaranteed or insured under the Servicemen's Readjustment Act of 1944, as amended? What proportion is nonguaranteed and noninsured?

61. Study the report of your state and local departments of taxation. At what proportion of their value are homes assessed in your community? How are these values determined?

62. What is the tax rate on residence property, including all local, county, state, school, and other taxes? How does it compare with that of other similar communities in your state? How do taxes compare with rentals in your community?

63. How many homes were sold for delinquent taxes in the past fifteen years? Of tax delinquencies in your community in the past fifteen years, what proportion were on homes owned by the occupant?

[1] A full discussion of all angles of the problem is contained in Home Ownership: Is It Sound?, by John P. Dean, Harper and Bros., New York, 1945. See also Tomorrow's Town, issued by the National Housing Committee, Inc., New York, November, 1945. Read also Before You Buy a Home, National Housing Agency, Government Printing Office, Washington, 1946.

64. What is your community doing to facilitate home ownership for veterans? To publicize federal and state aid to this group?[1] How is the federal act, assigning priority in allocation of home building materials to veterans working out in your community?

(For the general subject of taxation, see Chapter 3.)

Facilities for Family Saving and Credit. Most of us are at some time in our lives savers of money, at other times borrowers. You will need to learn where, other than in the teapot on the kitchen shelf, the families of your community put their savings, and to what agencies they turn when they need to borrow money.

The principal depositories for savings are commercial banks, savings banks, building and loan associations, and insurance companies. The purchase of United States government bonds and savings certificates is, of course, another popular form of saving. In some states industrial banking companies are permitted to accept deposits or to sell certificates which are the approximate equivalent of deposits. Still another savings institution is the credit union. Credit unions are co-operative associations in which people, usually those in the low-income group, pool their savings, and from which members can borrow at low interest rates. The most successful are usually organized within homogeneous groups, such as employes of a common employer or residents of a small community.

These institutions are generally supervised by state or federal government departments in the interest of protecting depositors. Other enterprises, which are generally not so supervised, come rather close to being savings institutions. For instance, some investment trusts have sought to attract small periodic savings by selling their shares on the installment plan. Many business and industrial corporations sell their securities to their employes, and some sell their securities to the general public, on small monthly payments. State blue-sky laws and the federal Securities Act provide some protection to those who purchase securities from these sources.

65. Do the commercial banks in your community pay interest on savings accounts? Are there any mutual savings banks in your community? How many building and loan associations and credit unions are there? What are the bases for credit union membership?

66. Are all institutions which accept savings deposits under state or federal supervision? Does the law merely require reports or is periodic examination by the supervising official mandatory?

Building and loan associations and credit unions both receive and lend

[1] Send for Home Loans under the G.I. Bill of Rights: How Your Government Will Help You Finance the Building or Buying of a Home, National Housing Agency, Government Printing Office, Washington, 1946.

money. Other sources from which families obtain cash loans are personal loan departments of banks, life insurance companies which make loans to policyholders, industrial banking companies, personal finance companies, pawnbrokers, and loan sharks.

Protection of Small Borrowers and Credit Purchasers. A very large volume of credit is also extended to families by retail merchants, service industries, and professional people in the form of charge accounts and installment sales contracts. Installment contracts arising out of sales of automobiles, mechanical refrigerators, and some other types of consumers' durable goods are usually sold by dealers to installment finance companies.[1]

Many states have enacted various types of laws to protect small borrowers and credit purchasers. The lending of small sums has been particularly subject to abuse and all but a minority of the states have enacted small loan laws. A large number of states have effective regulatory statutes, based upon the Uniform Small Loan Law sponsored by the Russell Sage Foundation. In most states other types of statutes, such as the usury laws and laws governing the use of wage assignments and chattel mortgages, give some protection against excessive interest charges.

In states which enacted the Uniform Small Loan Law state banking departments are equipped to provide relief from abusive small loan contracts and to mitigate cases of distress. In several states associations of personal finance companies employ qualified social workers to assist in the solution of family financial problems which arise from the making and collecting of small loans.[2]

Read Regulation of the Small Loan Business, by Louis N. Robinson and Rolf Nugent,[3] and Small Loan Laws of the United States, by LeBaron R. Foster.[4]

67. What facilities for small loans does your community offer? What rates of interest are charged and what security is demanded? Which agencies are willing to lend very small sums? To what extent do those who lend money or extend credit take advantage of even slight delays and reclaim or take pledged or mortgaged property or goods upon which only small sums are still due?

68. Are all money-lending agencies in your community subject to state supervision? Are there facilities for co-operation between social agencies and money-lending concerns for the purpose of mitigating cases of distress?

[1] Read Credit for Consumers, by LeBaron R. Foster, Pamphlet no. 5, Public Affairs Committee, Inc., New York, rev. ed., 1945.
[2] The American Association of Personal Finance Companies, 315 Bowen Building, Washington, D.C., can tell you whether such an association exists in your state.
[3] Russell Sage Foundation, New York, 1935. (Out of print, but generally available in libraries.)
[4] Pamphlet no. 37, Pollak Foundation for Economic Research, Newton, Mass., 1939.

69. Do illegal lenders or loan sharks operate in your community?[1] What methods do they use to enforce collections? What are their charges? Have efforts been made to eliminate them? Results?

Recognition of the need for protecting installment purchases against abusive contracts and harsh collection practices appears to be growing. In some states general statutes regulating respectively installment sales of motor cars and all forms of installment financing have been enacted. In several states less comprehensive laws are in force. In many other states laws governing conditional sales contracts and the statutes of fraud provide some protection to installment purchasers.

In most states, the proportion of a debtor's wages that can be attached through garnishment or the amount of wages that can be taken under a wage assignment is limited by law. In all jurisdictions certain types of property are also excluded from attachment.

Legal aid societies are available in many cities to assist persons financially unable to obtain legal representation in the assertion of their legal rights generally. These societies, as well as Better Business Bureaus that exist in many communities, have frequently been exceedingly useful in preventing fraud and abuse in the consumer credit field. Bar associations, attorneys general, local prosecutors, and state labor departments in some areas have taken an active part in the effort to protect small debtors against extortionate interest charges and fraudulent or oppressive credit contracts.

70. What abuses, if any, occur in the field of installment selling in your community? What protections are there against fraud or deception?

71. What is the cost of legal process for the collection of small claims in your community? Are court officers who grant or execute judgments employed on a fee or a salary basis? Do such officers consider that they are agents of creditors or do they interpret their duties to include protection of the interests of debtors?

72. Does your state law (a) exempt from attachment sufficient income to maintain the debtor's family, (b) prevent attachment of assets necessary to earning a livelihood?

73. Does your state law include provisions for protection of installment buyers against loss of equity upon repossession where a large part of the purchase price has been paid?

74. Are assignments of future wages valid in your state? Is there any limitation upon the amount collectible under such an assignment?

75. Can persons be imprisoned for debt in your state? Under what circumstances?

76. Do any agencies in your community interest themselves specifically in the protection of credit purchasers? Have you a legal aid society or a Better Business Bureau?

[1] Read Loan Sharks and Their Victims, by William T. Foster, Pamphlet no. 39, Public Affairs Committee, Inc., New York, 4th ed., 1945.

Opportunity to discharge debts in bankruptcy proceedings is offered through the federal courts. Wage-earners may also obtain adjustments and extensions of debts and arrange for their liquidation under the supervision of the federal court, thereby avoiding suits and wage attachments while the terms of the repayment agreement are complied with. In several states wage-earner receivership laws have been enacted under which the debtor may liquidate his obligations by assigning part of his wages to the court.

77. How many petitions in bankruptcy were filed by residents of your community last year (a) by wage-earners, (b) by others? Has there been an increase, decrease, in bankruptcy during the past five years?

Consumer Protection. Consumer protection, which in past years emphasized primarily safeguards against fraudulent practices of manufacturers and dealers, has in recent years taken a more positive turn: making available to consumers facts by which they can determine which product is the best buy for their money.[1] This new emphasis has been dictated by the fact that consumers in the past have suffered enormous losses through unwarranted prices and because they have not known exactly what they were purchasing. Losses included not only wasted purchasing power but also waste of materials and labor. Recent years have seen tremendous gains in the development of standards for canned fruit or vegetables, drugs, coal, electrical equipment, gas appliances, and textiles, to mention only a few.[2] Significant progress has also been made in the labeling of consumer goods. Wool must be labeled as new, reprocessed, or reused. Rayon must also be labeled, as must mixtures such as rayon and wool. Such terms as "washable" and "preshrunk" have been defined and now help to protect consumers. Labeling frequently goes beyond legal requirements, as in the case of textile manufacturers or dealers who voluntarily report not only the nature of the fabric but indicate also the thread count, breaking strength, weight, color, permanence, and shrinkage, to enable purchasers to make the wisest possible selection for their particular purposes.

While standard setting and labeling have advanced markedly in recent years, there are many important consumer goods on which standards have not yet been established and labeling is mandatory in the case of only a very few items. Further gains in these areas are being urged by various consumer groups, such as the League of Women Voters, the American Associa-

[1] Protection of the buying public in the matter of the quality of food and milk consumed is discussed in Chapter 8.

[2] For a brief account of what standards are, how they are developed, and how put to use, see More for Your Money, by Carol W. Moffett, Pamphlet no. 63, Public Affairs Committee, Inc., New York, 1942. See also Gyps and Swindles, by William T. Foster, Pamphlet no. 109, Public Affairs Committee, Inc., New York, 1945.

tion of University Women, and the General Federation of Women's Clubs. In recent years schools have also stressed nutritional standards, quality and uses of textiles, improvement in home construction and related subjects of interest to consumers, whether these are boys or girls, or college men and women. Better Business Bureaus, where they exist, seek to promote ethical trade practices in labeling and advertising as well as otherwise to eliminate abusive and fraudulent business practices. Consumers' leagues are interested primarily in the working conditions under which goods are produced, but also in the quality and price of goods sold. Cities and counties have usually established some facilities for testing the accuracy of scales and measures used by wholesale and retail dealers.

78. Has your community a Consumers' League, Housewives' League, Better Business Bureau, other similar groups actively educating the consuming public and seeking to improve and enforce legislation to extend standard setting and labeling?

79. To what extent do community groups (such as the League of Women Voters, and so forth) emphasize consumer protection, mandatory and voluntary standard setting and labeling? What consumer education courses are given in schools or colleges in your community?

80. What government agency tests weights and measures used by retail dealers in your community? What penalties accrue for selling short quantity? How many inspectors of weights and measures in your community? How frequently are tests made? How many pieces of defective apparatus confiscated last year? How many court actions brought against dealers?

81. Are prices of any basic commodities subject to control in your community? Are milk prices controlled? Are rents controlled? What agency is responsible for enforcing price controls? How stable have controlled prices been as compared with uncontrolled prices?

82. What legal provisions are in effect with respect to regulating standards of consumer goods sold in your community? Must milk sold in your community meet prescribed standards regarding cream content? Is it required that all flour or bread be enriched?

83. What authority is responsible for local enforcement of laws and regulations regarding the labeling of the most important consumer goods legally required to be labeled in your community? What action has been taken within the past two years?

84. What dealers or groups of dealers in your community voluntarily label important consumer goods or in public advertising describe goods in sufficient detail to permit consumers to make the wisest possible selection?

Co-operatives. To protect their interests consumers often organize co-operatives. Credit unions, already mentioned, are one form of co-operative enterprise. The voluntary organization of producers for joint marketing of their goods is now fairly widespread in this country, especially among farm-

ers.   Consumer co-operatives in the United States are now growing faster
than they have in any other country at any other time.   The Cooperative
League of the United States of America reports that in recent years there
has been a steady increase in merchandising stores in operation, in gas and
oil co-operative associations, farm supply depots, cold storage lockers, co-
operative insurance organizations, hospital and health co-operatives, rural
electric co-operatives, and other forms of co-operative enterprises such as
housing, cafeterias, and nursery schools.

Approximately three million families are members of these types of co-
operatives with business running slightly over a billion dollars a year.[1]
These co-operatives also operate mills, factories, and refineries.   The co-
operatives are now the largest independent oil refiners in the United States,
and are laying plans for international trade in the field of petroleum and
other commodities.

While consumer co-operatives in the United States are young and still
small compared with those in England, Sweden, and other countries, they
are growing rapidly.   A particularly interesting and successful development
of producer and consumer co-operatives among the fishermen, farmers, and
miners of Nova Scotia is described in Masters of Their Own Destiny: The
Story of the Antigonish Movement of Adult Education Through Economic
Cooperation, by M. M. Coady.[2]

85. Are there consumer or consumer-producer co-operatives in your community?   List, and give approximate membership, value of goods traded last year.
86. Are goods sold for cash, bartered, sold for scrip?   Are the stores open to
the public?
87. Are goods priced at the market level, and dividends paid on this basis, or
does the store cut prices?
88. Has the number of co-operatives, number of their members, increased or diminished during the past five years?

VI. FAMILY SERVICE

A group of agencies whose primary interest centers about the family is
represented by the family service movement.   Its members were earlier
known by such names as Associated Charities, Family Welfare Association,
Family Service Association, and so on.   They have always been interested
in preventive and rehabilitative work with families and until the mid-thirties
were the principal communitywide relief-giving agencies, carrying a very
large relief burden.   These agencies are, for the most part, voluntary organizations, yet many public agencies also render family service and may

[1] As of 1946.   [2] Harper and Bros., New York, 1939.

become members of the Family Service Association of America, the national organization of agencies in this field. With the development of public assistance programs (see Chapter 14) by far the greater part of the work of voluntary family service agencies has come to be with self-supporting families. People look to family service agencies for help in their family and social relationships, vocational plans, personal readjustments made necessary by ill health, financial planning, and other personal matters. Marriage counseling is increasingly a part of agency work. Provision for the payment of fees for service by clients financially able and willing to do so is being introduced. Financial grants are sometimes available for carrying out special time-limited plans, as for example, for educational, recreational, or vocational purposes, and for certain kinds of emergencies in marginal income families.

Recent concepts of what the service of a family agency should be can be gained from Theory and Practice of Social Case Work, by Gordon Hamilton,[1] and Social Case Work in Practice: Six Case Studies, by Florence Hollis.[2] See also Organizing a Family Agency, by Francis H. McLean and Ralph Ormsby.[3] Earlier books that might usefully be consulted are The Art of Helping People Out of Trouble, by Karl de Schweinitz[4] and What Is Social Case Work?, by Mary E. Richmond.[5]

89. Is there a family service agency, institute for family service, or similar organization in your community? Under what auspices and when was it organized? Is it a member of the Family Service Association of America?

90. Into what departments is its work divided? How many on its board? Men, women? How elected? Qualifications of present board which led to their appointment?

91. How many caseworkers are on its staff? How many are members of a professional association? Has it a trained home economist? Has it made provision on its staff for psychiatric consultation?

92. If there is an approved school of social work (see page 160) in your community, does it place students for field-work training in the agency?

93. With what types of family difficulty does the agency state that it is willing to help? Has it caseworkers qualified for consultation on marriage problems, or to whom young people contemplating marriage can go for advice? Does it offer service in the adjustment of parent-child relationships? Does it help people who have difficulty in fitting into jobs? Does it help with debt adjustment and the management of small incomes?

94. What is the agency's annual budget? From what sources secured?

95. Has it funds available for financial assistance? What proportion of its

[1] Columbia University Press, New York, 1940.
[2] Family Welfare Association of America, New York, 1939.
[3] Idem, 1944.   [4] Houghton Mifflin Co., Boston, 1924.
[5] Russell Sage Foundation, New York, 1922.

budget? Under what circumstances is financial assistance given? Does the family agency accept for "service only" families obtaining relief from other agencies? To how many families did it give service last year?

96. Does the family agency take leadership in community planning that affects family life? Does it work for better legislation in such matters as public assistance, better housing?

97. Is there a separate family agency serving Jewish families? Catholic families? Protestant families?

98. For each, give name, and secure information as above. With what national agencies is it affiliated?

99. Is there a chapter of the American National Red Cross in your community? Does it specialize in service to families of veterans? Secure information as above.

100. Are there other agencies whose main function is service to families? Give name, and secure information as above. (For agencies dealing with unmarried mothers, see page 214.)

A special form of assistance to disadvantaged families is offered by some family service and other agencies in the form of housekeeper services. When the mother is dead, ill, or otherwise absent from a home, a worker may be sent in to care for the household and the children. When only manual work, such as cooking and cleaning, is involved, these workers are known as "household aides." When home management and child care are also involved, better-trained workers, variously called housekeepers, homemakers, mother-substitutes, or visiting foster mothers, may be supplied. Unless the family is able to pay the wages, the expense is met by the agency.[1]

101. Do any agencies in your community supply housekeeper services? Describe numbers served and nature of services provided. If no such service is available, what is known locally about the extent of need for service of this kind?

The "parent education movement" is a form of adult education, which is alluded to in Chapter 11, but which should be discussed more fully here.

102. Are courses in parent education available in your community? Under what auspices? Are the study groups conducted by professional or lay leaders? What training have the leaders had for the work?

103. How many persons attended study groups last year? Men, women? Do any of the agencies giving parent education offer opportunities for individual counseling on parental problems?

Experiments have been made in recent years toward establishing family consultation centers, marriage advice bureaus, and the like.[2] Usually these

[1] See Supervised Homemaker Service: A Method of Child Care, by the U.S. Children's Bureau, Publication 296, Government Printing Office, Washington, 1946.

[2] Their work is described in Marriage and Family Counselling, a pamphlet issued by the National Council of Parent Education, New York, 1937.

have been staffed by sociologists, psychologists, clergymen, or doctors and, unlike family service agencies, do not offer social casework service. If such consultation agencies are known to be operating in your community, questions already asked concerning the family service societies should guide you in their study.

Birth control clinics also have a definite relation to problems of family welfare, but these have already been mentioned in Chapter 9.

In recent years there has been a sharp increase in the number of agencies which are devoted directly to education for family life. Many colleges, following the early example of the University of North Carolina and Vassar College, now offer courses in this field. In some high schools homemaking courses have been developed. Where examples of these were found in the course of your contact with the schools, they should be referred to in connection with your study which deals with family life.[1]

Service to families upon family problems is by no means confined to the agencies mentioned whose interest in families is implied by their names. Settlements often have a so-called personal service department which undertakes much the same variety of services. Institutional churches are often similarly equipped.

104. What churches, settlements, other agencies, have special departments of family service? Secure information as above about these special services.

Protective agencies which approach the family from the particular angle of the child (see Chapter 16) must inevitably work with family problems as a whole and attempt to bring about adjustments which will make the home a better place for the child. The same may be said of the social work department of the public schools (see page 158), social service departments of hospitals (see Chapter 8), and many other agencies.

[1] The May, 1946, issue of Marriage and Family Living, published monthly by the National Conference on Family Relations, Chicago, presents a symposium on teaching family courses. The book When You Marry, referred to earlier in this chapter, includes a list of agencies in the United States offering marriage consultation service.

16. SPECIAL PROVISIONS FOR CHILD CARE

PRECEDING chapters on health, recreation, education, the family, provision for the physically and mentally handicapped, and public assistance have all borne some relation to care of children who are able to live in normal family homes or with relatives. The principle is now generally accepted that it is better for a child to remain in his own home, or in that of people related to him by blood ties, than to be cared for elsewhere, if such home fits or can be made to fit his special needs. There are many children, however, whose home conditions are abnormal or whose present problems demand other arrangements for their care; and in all communities agencies, either public or private, state or local, exist to serve such children. A most important little publication to read and study in connection with this chapter is Standards of Child Health, Education, and Social Welfare, Based on Recommendations of the White House Conference on Children in a Democracy and Conclusions of Discussion Groups.[1] Read also the section on Child Welfare, in the latest issue of the Social Work Year Book,[2] for a good introduction to the field covered by this chapter. The following books are also recommended for general reading in connection with this section: The Dependent Child, by Henry W. Thurston;[3] One Thousand Juvenile Delinquents, by Sheldon and Eleanor Glueck;[4] New Light on Delinquency and Its Treatment, by William Healy and Augusta F. Bronner;[5] and Delinquency Control, by Lowell J. Carr.[6]

A revolution in provisions for child care took place in this country with the passage of the Social Security Act in 1935. The provisions of the Act

[1] U.S. Children's Bureau, Publication 287, Government Printing Office, Washington, 1942.
[2] Russell Sage Foundation, New York.
[3] Columbia University Press, New York, 1930. (Out of print, but generally available in libraries.)
[4] Harvard University Press, Cambridge, 1934. A later report, by the same authors, shows what had happened to these 1,000 juvenile delinquents after they became of age—Juvenile Delinquents Grown Up, Commonwealth Fund, New York, 1940.
[5] Yale University Press, New Haven, 1936.
[6] Harper and Bros., New York, 1941.

relating to children have been discussed in Chapters 9, 10, and 14. There remains to be discussed in this chapter the federal program under which the United States Children's Bureau is authorized to make grants to states having approved plans "for the protection and care of homeless, dependent, and neglected children, and children in danger of becoming delinquent." These funds are to be expended only for the administration of such services, mainly in rural areas.

1. Has your state an approved plan for child welfare services? By what state agency is it administered? Does your community receive sums from the state for child welfare services? How much? By what agency or agencies are they locally administered?

2. Do these agencies have advisory committees composed of experienced social workers and lay members?

3. Describe fully as to auspices and source of support, appointment and qualifications of board, director and staff, type of services offered.

I. LEGAL PROTECTION OF CHILDREN

The child welfare laws of the several states are not codified in any one publication to which reference can be made. Some aspects of the laws relating to children were brought together by the United States Children's Bureau in its Analysis and Tabular Summary of State Laws Relating to Jurisdiction in Children's Cases and Cases of Domestic Relations in the United States.[1] From this publication you can learn what courts deal with what types of cases in your state, and how your state compares with others in these respects. The Bureau also publishes annually a bulletin of juvenile court statistics, in which some of the data appear for selected cities and counties.

States vary widely in the legal protection they afford childhood. Among provisions sometimes found are requirements that no person unless related by blood or marriage may receive a child unattended by parent or guardian to board without having a license from a state agency; that no person may bring or send into the state any child for the purpose of placing him out or procuring his adoption without first obtaining the consent of and conforming to the rules of the appropriate state agency; that a state agency investigate and make recommendations on adoptions; and that petitions in adoption shall not be granted until after a trial period of six months, which period, however, may be waived by the court for cause when satisfied that home and child are suited to each other.

[1] Chart 17, Government Printing Office, Washington, 1930. Check with your state children's agency as to changes made since this date.

4. Examine your state law in regard to adoption,[1] guardianship, and custody of children outside their own homes, and of children of unmarried parents.

5. Are there official agencies in your community charged with preventing the operation of unlicensed and uninspected children's boarding homes and "baby farms"?

6. Can children be "given away" by their parents without permission of official agencies? May residents of your state procure, or agencies bring in for adoption, children from outside your state without official investigation and approval by your state or local agencies? What agency or official is responsible for reporting to the court on the suitability of adoptions before the adoption is actually granted?

A group of children needing special care and protection from state and community are those born out of wedlock.[2] (For discussion of care for unmarried mothers, see page 122.)

7. What is the legal status of the child of unmarried parents in your state in regard to right to claim paternity, bear father's name, claim support from parents and inheritance from parents' estates?

8. Most states require that birth certificates bear a statement regarding legitimacy. How many illegitimate births were registered in your community last year? How many whose mothers were residents of your community? How many of these per 1,000 total births?

9. Is any state or local body officially charged with the guardianship of children born out of wedlock?

10. Does your state have provision for changing the birth records of children born out of wedlock subsequent to legal adoption, so that the facts of their birth will not have to appear in connection with their school records and other documents?

11. In what court is illegitimate paternity established? Orders for support issued? How enforced?

Comprehensive studies of commercial boarding care for children, adoption, illegitimacy, and so on have been made in many states and communities.

12. Can you learn of such studies in your community? What do they show concerning actual practice? To what extent was it found that children were placed away from their own homes only because relief was not available to maintain the family intact? What recommendations were made for change? What has been done to put these recommendations into effect?

13. What have your child-caring agencies agreed upon as reforms most needed in the child welfare laws?

14. Do approved schools of social work place students for field work training in child-caring agencies and institutions in your community?

[1] Write for a copy of Essentials of Adoption Law and Procedures, U.S. Children's Bureau, Government Printing Office, Washington, 1946. Recent increases in adoptions emphasize the need for adequate legislation and procedures.
[2] Read Services for Unmarried Mothers and Their Children, U.S. Children's Bureau, 1945.

II. THE JUVENILE COURT

Important among institutions existing to serve children in need of special care is the juvenile court.[1] For an understanding of the work of the modern juvenile court read The Child Speaks: The Prevention of Juvenile Delinquency, by Jacob Panken,[2] and Everyone's Children, Nobody's Child: A Judge Looks at Underprivileged Children in the United States, by Justine W. Polier.[3] Read Juvenile Court Standards[4] as a preliminary to studying your own juvenile court.

In its best manifestations, the juvenile court is not an agency for dispensing justice, but is rather a social institution with legal powers to deal with the problems of children. In some communities the judge has an assistant, called a referee, with special experience in social work with children. The juvenile court differs from other institutions for the protection of children only in having the power to order the disposition of a child without the consent of its parents. Read the law under which your juvenile court operates, and compare it with A Standard Juvenile Court Act published by the National Probation Association.[5]

15. Is there a juvenile court in your community? If not, in what courts are children's problems heard?

16. Is the juvenile court administratively independent, or part of some other court or group of courts? (See page 197.)

17. What is the title of the presiding officer? How is he appointed? What are the qualifications which led to his appointment? Does he serve continuously, or is there a rotating panel of judges?

18. What is the maximum age of children who may be brought to the juvenile court? Is it the same maximum as that for compulsory school attendance? If the maximum age does not extend beyond seventeen years, is special provision made for young and first offenders in your regular courts?

In order to emphasize the difference between the juvenile court and ordinary courts of justice, effort is usually made to hold the juvenile court in rooms or buildings separate from other courts. Informal, though dignified, procedure is aimed at.

19. Has the juvenile court its own rooms, its own building? Is it held in rooms used also for other purposes?

[1] The extent to which your community needs the services of the juvenile court depends in part upon your provision for housing, recreation, and family welfare in general. Therefore, see also Chapters 7, 12, and 15.
[2] Henry Holt and Co., New York, 1941.   [3] Charles Scribner's Sons, New York, 1941.
[4] U.S. Children's Bureau, Publication 121, Government Printing Office, Washington, 1937. See also standards outlined in The Juvenile Court Steps In, by Marjorie Bell, National Probation Association, New York, 1943, pp. 11–14.
[5] New York, rev. 1943. See also the Association's publication Juvenile Court Laws of the United States, by Gilbert Cosulich, 1939. A new edition is in preparation.

20. Visit it, and see whether its physical arrangements suggest formal official procedure, or informal conference. Are hearings private, or may other than interested parties attend them? If you were a child in serious trouble, do you think the appearance and arrangements of your juvenile court would tend to put you at ease, or increase your emotional tension?

21. Over what types of cases does the juvenile court have jurisdiction? Does it have jurisdiction over dependent children? May it remove from their homes and make other disposition of neglected children? Persistent truants? Wayward or so-called "delinquent" children? May it issue and enforce support orders for abandoned children? Children of unmarried parents?

22. Has it the power to inflict punishment on adults found guilty of abandoning, neglecting, or impairing the morals of children?

23. What facilities has the juvenile court for physical and mental examinations of children, parents? (If there is a child-guidance clinic attached to the juvenile court, see pages 146 and 156 for questions concerning it.)

24. What arrangements exist for the detention of children pending hearings in the court? Is there a detention home? Under what auspices? Is it designed exclusively for juveniles and observational rather than merely custodial? Are children ever confined in jails with adult offenders?

25. Has your community made any use of foster homes for detention care? (These have been found superior to institutional detention homes in a number of cities.)

26. Is the probation department of the juvenile court independent in status, or part of the adult probation system in the courts? Do other agencies independent of the court furnish it with probation service? Are representatives of other agencies regularly stationed in the court?

27. How is the chief probation officer appointed? Others on the staff? Are they under a civil service merit system? What are the experience and training of the present chief probation officer? How many men, women, serving under him? How many are members of a professional association?[1]

28. What considerations govern assignment of cases to probation officers: age, sex, race, religion, type of difficulty of probationers, or their area of residence?

29. Is the probation department empowered to try to adjust difficulties of children without actually bringing them before the judge? How many children were thus dealt with last year?

30. Where court appearance is necessary, does the probation department render a report to the judge on each child prior to the disposition of his case in court? Does this include results of mental and physical examinations as well as social history?

31. Are all juvenile court cases cleared through and registered with the social service exchange? (See Chapter 18.)

32. How many boys, girls, appeared in juvenile court last year (a) under ten years, (b) ten to fifteen years, (c) over fifteen years? How many separate families did they belong to? How many had been in court before?

33. How many were (a) dismissed without action or with warnings to parents, (b) placed on probation to the court probation officers, (c) placed on pro-

[1] See footnote 4, p. 47.

bation to other agencies, (d) ordered removed from their homes for placement in institutions, (e) ordered removed from their homes for placement in foster homes?

34. How many adoptions were approved by the juvenile court? By other courts?

35. How many children are reported as having successfully completed probation during the year? How many had to be brought back to court for some other disposition?

There are no federal juvenile courts. Children under seventeen who commit offenses against the laws of the United States not punishable by death or life imprisonment, are, however, prosecuted in the United States district courts as juvenile delinquents if the Attorney General so directs and the child consents. A juvenile offender against any federal law may also be transferred to the state juvenile court of his residence.

36. Have any children from your community appeared in federal court during the past year? To what extent did treatment of these child offenders conform to that accorded delinquent children who appeared in your juvenile court? Have any juvenile offenders against federal law been transferred to your juvenile court?

Agencies to whose care children may be committed by the juvenile court fall into three main classifications: (a) protective agencies, (b) agencies for foster home placement, (c) institutions. These will be discussed in the remaining sections of this chapter.

III. PROTECTIVE ORGANIZATIONS

Privately organized agencies for the protection of children or the prevention of cruelty and neglect are found in many communities. The earliest of these grew out of the even earlier organized societies to prevent cruelty to animals, a service now usually under separate auspices.

37. Is there a society for the prevention of cruelty to children, or a protective service under some other name, in your community? Does it also protect animals?

38. Is it statewide or local? Is it a member of the Child Welfare League of America?[1]

39. Does your community delegate police powers to its officers? On what basis of training or experience are its officers selected? What is their relation to the juvenile court?

40. Does it manage a temporary shelter? A permanent custodial home?

41. How many children were in its custody during the past year?

42. Is there a girls' protective agency, other protective agency, operating in your community to prevent cruelty or neglect of children? Questions as above.

---

[1] For address see List of Agencies, p. 251.

IV. PROVISION OF FOSTER FAMILY CARE

The child whose own kin cannot provide a suitable home will require foster care and usually his needs can be met in a foster home better than in an institution. Read the ABC of Foster-Family Care for Children,[1] and In Quest of Foster Parents: A Point of View on Homefinding, by Dorothy Hutchinson.[2] Preferably, a community's equipment for foster home placement should include small institutions or subsidized foster homes in which children can be temporarily placed for careful observation and study, in order to make possible more suitable and permanent placements with full understanding of the peculiar needs of the individual child.

43. Are facilities for temporary observation and study available in your community?

44. What agencies in your community arrange foster family care for children who must be placed elsewhere than in their own homes? Auspices of each agency? How supported? Is the agency a member of the Child Welfare League of America or does it adhere to the League's standards?

45. How many social workers on its staff? How many are members of a professional association?[3]

46. Does the agency maintain separate departments for finding and approving foster homes, and for supervising children after placement? Does it maintain a worker(s) in the juvenile court?

47. How many children did it have in supervised foster homes last year, by sex and age groups? What was the average period that these children had been in foster homes?

48. How many of these were (a) free placements, (b) boarding care paid for by the parents or relatives, (c) boarding care paid from the agency's own funds?

49. How many court commitments did the agency receive for foster family care?

50. How many voluntary applications from relatives?

51. In how many instances were the older children expected to earn some part of their care by work in the foster home or on the farm?

52. How are children cared for who must be removed from their own homes, if no suitable foster home is immediately available to receive them? Or, how are they cared for in the event that none of the resources for foster home care outlined in this section exists in your community?

Often a domestic crisis, such as illness of mother, or necessity of her leav-

[1] U.S. Children's Bureau, Publication 216, Government Printing Office, Washington, 1933. See also Standards for Children's Organizations Providing Foster Family Care, 1941, and Standards of Foster Care for Children in Institutions, 1937, both issued by the Child Welfare League of America, New York.
[2] Columbia University Press, New York, 1943. Read also Reconstructing Behavior in Youth: A Study of Problem Children in Foster Families, by William Healy and others, Alfred A. Knopf, New York, 1929.
[3] See footnote 4, p. 47.

ing the home to work, calls for community provision other than prolonged separation of the children from the home.

53. Is any child-caring agency in your community prepared to offer emergency care, either in boarding homes or institutions to children who need such care only for short periods?

54. Does any agency supply emergency housekeeper service, to avoid the necessity for placement?[1]   (See page 210.)

V. PROVISION OF DAY-NURSERY CARE

The United States Children's Bureau has issued a guide to standard day-nursery practice which should be consulted in studying your local nurseries.[2] Publications of the Child Welfare League of America should be obtained also.[3]

55. Are there day nurseries in your community giving care to children of working mothers? (Not nursery schools, which are mentioned elsewhere.)   For each, give auspices, number of workers, average number of children, of families, served daily last year.

56. Are there social workers on the agency's staff?   How many are members of a professional association?[4]

57. Does the agency make its own investigations of home conditions and ability to pay for care?   Does it accept the investigations of other agencies?   Has it a waiting list?   Is there a nursery school teacher on the staff?

58. Has it outdoor and indoor play space for children?   Provision for children of school age to play or study after school until the mother calls?

59. Is there a separate cot for each child?

60. Does a nutritionist supervise or give consultation on food service?

61. How frequent is medical inspection?   Is there provision for segregating children who show symptoms of illness?

62. Are fees paid by families graduated in accordance with their ability to pay? Minimum and maximum charges?   What proportion of the agency's budget comes from fees?

63. Does any agency in your community provide foster home day care as a substitute for day nursery care?

64. If your community depends upon the work of migrants to pick and can the crops, does it provide day care for the young children sometimes left unattended while adults and older children go to the fields?   If no such facilities exist in your

[1] Read Safeguarding Motherless Children: Problems Involved in Placement of Housekeepers in Motherless Homes, by Thelma Harris, Bulletin 16, Child Welfare Federation of America, New York, 1939.

[2] Standards for Day Care of Children of Working Mothers, Publication 284, Government Printing Office, Washington, 1942.

[3] A Manual for the Beginning Worker in a Day Nursery, by Eleanor M. Hosley, 1946, and The Day Care of Little Children in a Big City, by Leona Baumgartner and others, 1946.

[4] See footnote 4, p. 47.

community and public funds are not available, consult The Home Missions Council of North America[1] as to the possibilities of establishing such centers.

VI. PROVISION OF INSTITUTIONAL AND CAMP CARE

Institutions for Dependent or Neglected Children. Most communities have institutions, many of which were established before this century, where children may be sent for more or less permanent care. More recently the provision of public aid to dependent children has enabled many to remain in their own homes who formerly would have had to go to institutions. For most of those who must be placed elsewhere, foster home placement has come to be preferred as offering more normal surroundings for normal children. For some, however, institutional care is preferred, as for a large group of brothers and sisters, devoted to one another, who would be separated if placed in most of the foster homes available. New institutions usually have small cottages and among the oldest many have been remodeled to allow for smaller groups and more individual attention. Many still are obsolete and should be improved or closed. Some institutions have become child-placing agencies. Others have become homes for temporary shelter, or for the observation and treatment of children with serious problems. Read Institutions Serving Children, by Howard W. Hopkirk.[2]

65. Do your laws make any state body responsible for inspecting and licensing private institutions receiving children for care? How frequently are inspections demanded? What powers are given the supervisory body to effect changes?

66. List the private institutions providing care for dependent or neglected children in your community. Which are members of the Child Welfare League of America?

67. For each agency, where is it located (in urban or rural surroundings)? Date of foundation? Auspices? Support?

68. Is the executive professionally trained as an educator or social worker? Does the agency have social workers on its staff? How many are members of a professional association?[3]

69. Or, are there arrangements by which social work services are supplied by another casework agency? Describe.

70. What is the capacity? How many children at present in custody by age and sex? In how many cases is payment for care being made by parents or relatives?

71. Is the institution congregate, or on the "cottage plan," i.e., are the children housed in small units, each under the direction of a cottage mother or father? How many children in each cottage family? What is the basis of their assignment?

72. What facts must be established as qualification for admission? How are

[1] For address see List of Agencies, p. 251.
[2] Russell Sage Foundation, New York, 1944.   [3] See footnote 4, p. 47.

reinvestigations made as to possibility of returning children to care of parents or relatives? Do the caseloads of social workers permit such rehabilitation?

73. Does the agency give aftercare or follow up children thus dismissed?

74. Has it facilities for placing and supervising children in foster homes? On what basis are children selected for foster home care? How many children thus placed last year?

75. How many returned to their own families? How many discharged as over age?

76. Has the institution facilities for minor illnesses? For quarantining contagious cases? Has it a resident physician? Nurse(s)? How often are medical inspections made? How is needed medical, surgical, dental treatment provided?

77. How often do green vegetables appear on the menu? Fresh fruits, lean meat, fish, poultry, milk or eggs?

78. Do these children attend public school? If privately educated, is there supervision by any public educational body?

79. Is vocational training given? What responsibility does the agency assume for aftercare of children of working age?

80. What part of the work of the institution are the children expected to perform? Does it interfere with their recreation?

81. Are the children given any allowance of spending money? How much? Regulations as to purposes for which it may or must be spent?

82. Do the children use community recreation facilities, or is all recreation supervised by the institution? Has it outdoor play space? Indoor playroom? Gymnasium?

83. Does your state or your county maintain (an) institution(s) (state school) for the care of dependent and neglected children? Where is it located? Capacity? Present total population? Has it a waiting list? How are commitments to it arranged? Does it use foster homes for some?

84. How many children from your community were committed to it last year? How many at present in its custody? How many discharged and under supervision in your community?

85. Read its latest report, and list points in which it seems to meet, fails to meet, standards indicated above.

Summer Camps. Opportunities for city children to spend all or a part of the summer vacation in the country may be offered in expensive to moderately priced summer camps for children whose parents are able to pay for such care. Some agencies, such as settlements, the Boy Scouts, Girl Scouts, and Campfire Girls, furnish summer camping opportunities to their members as part of their year-round program. For less fortunate children, most urban communities provide what used to be called "fresh-air care" in variously sponsored summer camps. Secure from the Children's Welfare Federation of New York City, Inc., copies of The Child Goes to Camp[1] and Aims and Guides for Improving the Practice in Camping.[2]

[1] The Federation, 1941. (435 Ninth Ave.)   [2] *Idem,* 1942.

86. List health camps, vacation camps, to which children from your community go for free care. For each, give location, auspices, source of support, sex and ages taken, capacity, average length of stay, number of different children taken last season.

87. Has the director had training in camping and child care?

88. What training or experience have counselors had? For how many children is each counselor responsible?

89. What medical supervision is given the children?

90. What was the average gain in weight of the children sent there last year?

91. What special provision is there for handicapped children?

92. What is the per diem per person cost of operating the camp?

Institutions for Delinquent Children and Young People. Private institutions to which children and young people are committed for delinquency are frequently found in the form of shelters for girls involved in sex difficulties. A few states have privately managed "Junior Republics" and similar schools for children who present behavior problems. Most public institutions in this field are the state training schools.

93. Are there privately managed custodial institutions for girls, boys, in your community? From what courts are commitments made? Questions as under private agencies for dependent and neglected children above.

94. Are there state or county training schools for juvenile delinquents? Between what ages are children and young people committed?

95. How committed? Capacity? How many from your community are serving sentence? How many were committed last year?

96. How many in your community under parole supervision from the state school? What nongovernmental agencies in your community give special care to the children after they leave these schools?

97. Has any study been made of the percentage of recidivism (i.e., relapse into delinquent behavior) among young people who have been inmates of your state schools for juvenile delinquents? (See page 217.) What does it show?

98. Has any spot map been prepared by agencies in your community interested in studying juvenile delinquency, showing location of homes of children involved in delinquent practices? Compare it with your density map. (See page 27.)

Authorities agree that the prognosis is poor for permanent reform of young people who have been thoroughly initiated into delinquent practices, and who return to the same surroundings and conditions that accompanied their earlier steps in delinquency. Emphasis in all community programs is rightly laid on the *prevention* of delinquency, which is more and more coming to be accepted as the only logical result to be anticipated from neglected or mishandled childhood. A new program has been launched toward the prevention of conditions leading to juvenile delinquency in the so-called co-ordinating councils. (See page 235.)

Most of the preceding and following sections of this handbook have references to prevention of delinquency in childhood and youth; but see especially Chapters 11, 12, and 13.

When you have finished this chapter of your study, ask yourself the questions:

99. Does it appear that any of the serious needs of childhood are not being met in my community? Does this apply especially to any race or nationality groups?

100. Is there an oversupply of certain types of child-caring agencies? What changes in the program of some of these agencies would result in care becoming available in areas where it is now lacking?

17. RACIAL MINORITIES AND THE FOREIGN-BORN

A GOOD preliminary to the study indicated in this chapter would be the reading of One America, by Francis J. Brown and Joseph F. Roucek;[1] Races and Ethnic Groups in American Life, by Thomas J. Wooter, Jr.;[2] and Brothers under the Skin, by Carey McWilliams.[3]

The total nonwhite population of the United States at the time of the 1940 census was approximately 13,500,000. Of these nearly 13,000,000, or approximately one in every ten in the total population, were Negroes. American Indians with a total of some 334,000 ranked second. Japanese and Chinese together came next, with Filipinos, Hindus, and all other races far behind.

Of the nonwhite population only about 168,000 were reported as foreign-born. These, however, represented only a small proportion of the total foreign-born population, inasmuch as there were in 1940 some 11,400,000 foreign-born persons of white stock. This number represented an absolute decrease of about 18 per cent below the number of foreign-born white persons in the United States in 1930, since immigrants are an aging group which, because of immigration restrictions, is not being replaced.

In addition to foreign-born persons of white stock there were in the United States in 1940 some 23,200,000 persons of foreign or mixed parentage but who were born in this country.

1. What is the Negro and foreign-born population of your community by sex and age groups?[4] Has it increased or diminished during the past five years? What are the areas chiefly inhabited by these groups? Locate them on your density map. (See page 27.) How do these areas compare with other areas in your community with respect to housing, streets, sanitation, schools?

[1] Prentice-Hall, New York, 1945.
[2] In the series of monographs called Recent Social Trends in the United States. McGraw-Hill Book Co., New York, 1933. (Out of print, but generally available in libraries.)
[3] Little, Brown and Co., Boston, 1943.
[4] If you secured the information called for in Chapter 2, you already have data on children of foreign and mixed parentage. You also know the number of foreign-born persons and the numbers representing different race groups in the community at the time the latest census was taken; and you have tabulated the relative size of the different foreign-born and racial groups in the community. (See p. 26.)

Two groups of similar backgrounds which are numerically important in certain communities are Puerto Ricans and Mexicans. Though regarded as whites, they are of mixed Spanish, Indian, and sometimes Negro ancestry. They are generally rural in antecedents and conform with difficulty to American urban customs. Their status after arrival is, however, entirely different. Mexicans suffer all the disadvantages of being aliens, while most Puerto Ricans are able to enter the country without restrictions since they are already citizens of the United States.

While Orientals (with the exception of Chinese, Filipinos, and persons of races indigenous to India) can, generally speaking, be neither admitted nor naturalized under our present laws, those earlier admitted form large foreign-born groups in some communities, and their descendants born in this country enjoy full citizenship rights.[1]

Native Amerindians, numbering fewer than 400,000 persons but increasing more rapidly than the rest of the population, are concentrated largely in the states west of the Mississippi, more than half of them living on reservations under the jurisdiction of the Office of Indian Affairs. Because much of their land is poor and unproductive, the Indians are generally in the lowest income group. They are, of course, citizens of the United States.

2. Do native Indians form an appreciable part of your population? Are they on reservations, or living at large in the community?

3. Are there special schools in your community for Indian children? Special agencies (other than the Office of Indian Affairs) promoting their rights or welfare? Are Indians in your community eligible for social security benefits?

I. IMMIGRATION

Because the two Americas were settled by immigrants and very recently settled as nations go, immigration has an importance with us that it has in no other continent of the earth. Before 1917, although immigration from certain countries was prohibited, the only other limitations were those that sought to prevent the entrance of persons physically or mentally diseased, of criminals, and "anarchists," and of persons likely to become public charges. Since that date there have been imposed additional restrictions which control by a quota system the number of people who in a given year can se-

---

[1] If Orientals and their descendants form an important group in your community, a useful book to read at this point would be *Americans in Process: A Study of Our Citizens of Oriental Ancestry*, by William C. Smith, Edwards Bros., Ann Arbor, Mich., 1937. See also *Prejudice: Japanese-Americans, Symbol of Racial Intolerance*, by Carey McWilliams, Little, Brown and Co., Boston, 1944; and *Chinatown, U.S.A.*, by Elizabeth Colman, John Day and Co., New York, 1946.

cure admission from any country, except those of the Western Hemisphere, against which no quota is applied. This means a complete reversal of national policy, which was earlier concerned with recruiting manpower and securing citizens from what were regarded as assimilable stocks. However, when the frontier was gone and unemployment threatened, this country became unwilling to offer unrestricted admittance to persons who might heighten economic competition. Therefore our foreign-born are increasingly a smaller and an older group, longer resident in this country. Early problems of assimilation of large groups with widely diverse backgrounds— which used to be implied by the term "melting pot"—no longer exist in such pressing degree.

Increased racial, nationalistic, and political tensions and hatred, particularly in Europe, are part of the bitter legacy of Nazism and World War II. Countries such as the United States, which can serve as havens of refuge for persons otherwise likely to be persecuted because of race, nationality (or lack of nationality), or political activity face anew the question of opening their doors to immigration.[1]

In the process of immigration local governmental agencies are seldom officially concerned. Our present immigration laws give a "non-quota" or a "preferred quota" classification to relatives of an American citizen or of a foreign-born person legally in this country. (For details consult the immigration law.) The vast majority of our present immigration consists of close relatives of persons who are already here, and who can furnish affidavits of their ability and willingness to support the newcomers and prevent their becoming public charges. Within recent years various social agencies have also been allowed to certify on a group basis that certain immigrants (usually persons who otherwise would suffer persecution) if admitted to the United States would, in case of need, be assisted by the certifying agency and thus not become public charges.[2] The process of securing permission to immigrate usually involves the co-operation of relatives already in this country. However, except in the larger communities, there is no official or unofficial agency especially equipped to give assistance or information to anyone desiring to assist the immigration of relatives.

4. Has your community a social agency specializing in service to the foreign-born? What does it do?
5. Are there sectarian or nationality groups which offer such services?

[1] Read What Shall We Do About Immigration?, by Maurice R. Davie, Pamphlet no. 115, Public Affairs Committee, Inc., New York, 1946.
[2] Among the agencies permitted to file such corporate affidavits are the United Service for New Americans, Inc., the American Christian Committee for Refugees, and the War Services Section of the National Catholic Welfare Conference.

6. Does the local chapter of the American Red Cross or other agency offer counsel on immigration problems to veterans? To persons other than veterans? Is there in your community an agency or a local unit of a national agency that supplies affidavits guaranteeing that certain emigrants if admitted to this country will not become public charges?

7. Is help in preparing immigration forms given by offices of steamship companies? Foreign banks? Foreign departments of local banks?

8. What agencies or groups in your community welcome or otherwise show special interest in recent arrivals such as the wives of servicemen married abroad, political refugees, or others?

It is often desirable to make inquiries concerning the situation of the prospective immigrant in his own country before seeking to further his admission. Then, too, the foreign-born resident here often faces difficulties requiring social action abroad. The International Migration Service[1] has branches with special correspondents in many of the principal countries from which immigrants come, and is prepared to secure for social agencies pertinent information from abroad regarding prospective immigrants or those already in this country. The Hebrew Sheltering and Immigrant Aid Society, the National Council of Jewish Women, the National Catholic Welfare Conference, the American Federation of International Institutes,[2] and a few other organizations maintain workers at the principal points of entry, and notify local agencies with which they maintain relations of the expected arrival of immigrants. At the port of New York the New York Travelers Aid Society renders a similar service.

Still another important agency serving people in this and other countries is the Central Location Index[1] whose purpose is to register and clear applications for location of persons abroad who have been displaced as a result of prewar and war conditions, and to seek people in the Western Hemisphere whose present addresses are unknown to their relatives abroad.

9. How many of these agencies are known to, or used by, organizations offering services to the foreign-born in your community?

II. DEPORTATION

Aliens who have outstayed their permission to remain, who have entered the country illegally since July 1, 1924, or who have after arrival violated some of the numerous conditions presented by our immigration laws are liable to arrest, trial, and deportation.

On the other hand, repatriation or return to one's native country is

[1] For address see List of Agencies, p. 251.
[2] For addresses see List of Agencies, p. 251.

purely voluntary.   Furthermore, a law-abiding alien without resources can apply voluntarily to the United States government for financial aid to pay his transportation to his homeland.   It should be noted, however, that any person thus "removed by consent," as governmental regulations phrase it, "shall forever be ineligible for re-admission except upon approval of the Secretary of State and the Attorney General."   Fuller discussion of these problems will be found in Deportation of Aliens from the United States to Europe, by Jane P. Clark.[1]

10. Where is the district immigration station serving your community? Can you learn from it how many aliens from your community during the past five years were (a) removed by consent, (b) deported? What were the reasons for the deportations?

III. NATURALIZATION

Social agencies in the community which assist in problems of immigration may also carry on other programs to help in the adjustment of foreign-born persons after arrival.   Naturalization for those who intend to remain and throw in their lot with the country is naturally to be desired; but the process of naturalization introduces new hurdles which many of the foreign-born are unable to leap unaided.   Ability to read as well as to speak English is a heavy demand for people to meet who were beyond school age on arrival.[2]   Our law of September 22, 1922, which demands that a wife make a separate application for citizenship contrasts sharply with provisions in other countries where a wife automatically shares her husband's citizenship status.

11. What agencies, public and private, offer assistance to the foreign-born in the process of acquiring citizenship?
12. Are classes in English for foreigners conducted in your community? (See page 161.) Under what auspices? Where and when held? (Have in mind that working people can attend more readily in the evening, while the afternoon is more convenient for housewives.)
13. How many sessions does the course comprise? How many attended last year? How many men? Women?
14. Are citizenship courses offered for the foreign-born? Information as

---

[1] Columbia University Press, New York, 1931.
[2] The naturalization law does not state in so many words that the applicant must prove ability to read English. It does, however, demand that he prove that he is "attached to the principles of the Constitution of the United States and well disposed to the good order and happiness of the United States." A number of naturalization courts have held that a reading knowledge of English is necessary to an informed point of view about our institutions, and citizenship has frequently been denied on this basis. See Educational Requirements for Naturalization, by Marian Schibsby, National Council on Naturalization and Citizenship, New York, 1936, p. 4.

above. Is any agency offering individual instruction in either of these subjects in the homes?

15. How many applications for (a) first papers, (b) full citizenship, were (a) granted, (b) denied, by the courts in your community last year? How do these numbers compare with those of five years ago? For what reasons were applications denied? Are applicants denied citizenship on account of language or other difficulties encouraged to try again?

16. What agencies in your community serve foreign-born persons? For example, are there settlements or community centers located in foreign neighborhoods; churches which conduct special foreign-language services, maintain special dormitories for foreign-born students, international institutes, and so on?

17. Are "naturalization parties" arranged in honor of new citizens? Does your community honor new citizens through special ceremonies on "I Am an American Day," which, by Presidential proclamation, is celebrated on the third Sunday in May?

IV. ASSIMILATION

Problems of immigration and naturalization by no means exhaust the points at which the foreign-born need the sympathetic help of the community. Much broader questions of assimilation should also be considered. How can the foreign-born be helped to become an integral part of the community? We now recognize that this consists not in attempting to make them over to the dominant pattern, but in enabling them to find their own adjustments and to contribute their own qualities to molding the future of America.[1]

The term "Americanization" which was long applied to educational work with the foreign-born is no longer widely used. It connoted considerable pressure upon the alien to accept American customs and ideals, and implied that what immigrants brought with them and contributed to the common life was of little value. It also fostered, even though unintentionally, a cleavage between foreign-born parents and their American-born children which often brought disastrous results in family life. Of recent years the emphasis of social and educational agencies has been laid rather upon teaching children to respect and enjoy the old-country customs, language, literature, handicrafts, folk dances, music and other arts, and by so doing to dignify the position of foreign-born parents.[2] A national agency active in this field is the American Federation of International Institutes.[3]

[1] A scholarly and helpful discussion of assimilation of the foreign-born is to be found in Americans in the Making: The Natural History of the Assimilation of Immigrants, by William C. Smith, D. Appleton-Century Co., New York, 1939.

[2] A good book to read in this connection is Immigrant Gifts to American Life, by Allen H. Eaton, Russell Sage Foundation, New York, 1932. (Out of print, but generally available in libraries.)

[3] For address see List of Agencies, p. 251.

18. What social and benevolent groups exist among the foreign-born, based upon race or former nationality? (See page 248.)

19. Do the programs of these agencies (whether organized *for* the foreign-born or *by* the foreign-born) offer opportunities for descendants of earlier immigrants (which includes of course everybody we call American), to mingle with foreign-born persons and learn their customs and enjoy their contributions to American life?

20. Have there been recently in your community exhibitions of foreign handicrafts? Folk dancing or musical events featuring the foreign-born? Pageants to which they have contributed scenes out of their historical backgrounds?[1]

21. Are typical foreign handicrafts included in manual training courses in the schools? Foreign dishes featured in cooking classes?

22. Are restaurants offering foreign cuisines patronized by Americans in your community? Are there foreign-language theaters? Do Americans attend them? Are foreign educational or propaganda films shown in your motion picture houses?

23. To what extent are representatives of foreign-born groups active in community enterprises? Are they found on boards of directors of social agencies? Are they made welcome at meetings of civic and commercial bodies? Are they prominent in the organizations of political parties?

24. What foreign-language newspapers appear on your newsstands? Are any published in your community? Get someone familiar with the language to read them occasionally over a period of a few weeks and report on what they tell their readers on questions of national and local interest.[2]

Refugee movements of persons seeking escape from persecution have been common in our history. These enforced waves of emigration have brought to these shores persons of outstanding intellectual achievement, and families whose descendants have greatly enriched American life. The past decade has seen a small, but dramatic immigration wave, consisting of refugees from Nazi and Fascist dominated countries. A comprehensive, nationwide study of recent refugees, their number, their characteristics, how they adjust themselves to American communities, how they earn their living, whether they have proved to be assets, and so forth, is being made by the Committee for the Study of Recent Immigration from Europe.[3]

25. Can you learn of the presence in your community of refugees who fol-

[1] See Around the World in St. Paul, by Alice L. Sickels, University of Minnesota Press, Minneapolis, 1945.

[2] The Common Council for American Unity, a national agency which seeks to promote better understanding of America by foreign groups through the foreign news services, will be glad to furnish you information about newspapers and periodicals of national circulation, and would be very glad to receive from you a report of any such brief local study as that suggested above.

[3] A preview of the findings is available in The Refugees Are Now Americans, by Maurice R. Davie and Samuel Koenig, Pamphlet no. 111, Public Affairs Committee, Inc., New York, 1945.

lowed professional or intellectual pursuits in their own countries? What are they doing in this country?

26. Have your institutions of higher learning appointed on their faculties displaced scholars from abroad?

27. Are any groups in your community undertaking to aid in the adjustment here of refugee intellectuals, professional persons, businessmen, or others from foreign countries?

28. What professions in your community are not open to persons who have received all their professional education in foreign schools or universities?

29. What public assistance, work relief, or social security benefits are not available to noncitizens on the same basis as to citizens? (See pages 186, 187.)

V. DISCRIMINATION ON GROUNDS OF RACE OR NATIONALITY

Discrimination and prejudice against racial minorities and the foreign-born are unfortunately rife in many communities (see page 41 for popular beliefs about crime and the foreign-born) and have been intensified, here as well as elsewhere, in times of economic depression by prejudice engendered by chauvinistic propaganda.[1]

Social prejudice and discrimination embrace whole groups, some of them citizens by birth, who differ racially from the dominant pattern. In connection with this part of your study, read Race Attitudes in Children, by Bruno Lasker,[2] and The Races of Mankind, by Ruth Benedict and Gene Weltfish.[3]

Since World War II more and more Americans are becoming aware of the discrepancy between our affirmations of democracy and the actual treatment of many of our citizens. A change can be brought about only by work at the grass roots of prejudice, or in local communities. For particular discussion of the problems faced by Negroes, read The Negro in America, by Maxwell S. Stewart,[4] and Brown Americans: The Story of a Tenth of the Nation, by Edwin R. Embree.[5] If there are branches in your community of the National Urban League or the National Association for the Advancement of Colored People they should be able to help you secure the information asked for in this section of your study. If your community is in one of

---

[1] A comprehensive discussion of race and culture conflicts in the United States is to be found in American Minority Peoples, by Donald R. Young, Harper and Bros., New York, 1932.

[2] Henry Holt and Co., New York, 1929. (Out of print, but generally available in libraries.)

[3] Pamphlet no. 85, Public Affairs Committee, Inc., New York, 1943. Read also "Controlling Group Prejudice," edited by Gordon W. Allport, in The Annals of the American Academy of Political and Social Science, March, 1946.

[4] Pamphlet no. 95, Public Affairs Committee, Inc., 1944. This is a summary of a very comprehensive study of the Negro problem in this country, entitled An American Dilemma, by Gunnar Myrdal, published in 1944 by Harper and Bros., New York.

[5] The Viking Press, New York, 1943.

the southern states, you should also get in touch with the Southern Regional Council.[1]

30. What occupations are chiefly followed by Negro men and women? How do the wages compare with those of white persons for the same work? Do your local trade unions discriminate against Negro membership?

31. Is there in your community a fair employment practices committee to carry on the types of work initiated by the National Fair Employment Practices Committee to overcome job discrimination against Negroes? In times of unemployment how does the percentage of Negroes unemployed compare with that of white workers? During slack industrial periods are they first to be laid off and last to be rehired?[2]

32. Are any Negroes members of elected bodies in the government of your state? Your community? Are they called to serve on juries?

33. Are any Negroes serving as appointed public officials of your state and local governments? Can they teach in your public schools?

34. Are Negroes admitted to take civil service examinations in your community? Have there been recent instances in which, while appearing high on the qualified list, they failed to obtain appointment?

35. Are Negroes obliged to occupy special seats on local street cars and buses? On railroad trains in your state? Have there been changes in practice in your community since the United States Supreme Court in June, 1946, ruled against segregation in interstate buses, trollies, or trains? Are they allowed to visit theaters, moving picture houses patronized by white persons? Are they seated in segregated sections of the house?

36. What do (a) your state laws, (b) custom and actual practice decree in regard to serving Negroes in hotels and restaurants patronized by white persons?

37. Do Negro children attend the same schools and classes as white children, or are they segregated? Do Negroes have library facilities equal to those for the white population? (See Chapter 11.)

38. Have there been in your community within the past ten years any outbreaks or violence affecting Negroes? Read (a) files of local newspapers, (b) national journals of opinion, (c) the Negro journals Opportunity and The Crisis for the period covering the incident and list what seemed to be the alleged and the actual facts which initiated it, and the aftereffects on interracial relations.

39. Is there in your community a local unit of the Urban League? Of the National Association for the Advancement of Colored People? Of any other organizations to promote the well-being of Negroes, of other racial groups? What have been their primary activities?

Although there are in some communities certain organizations fostering racial antagonisms there are increasing numbers of groups interested in developing more constructive relations among different racial groups.[3]

---

[1] For addresses see List of Agencies, p. 251.
[2] Read Will Negroes Get Jobs *Now?*, by Herbert R. Northrup, Pamphlet no. 110, Public Affairs Committee, Inc., New York, 1945.
[3] The American Council on Race Relations is a national agency working in this field. The National Conference of Christians and Jews sponsors interfaith seminars and local Round Tables for group discussion of better race relations. The Federal Council of the Churches of

40. Do you know of the existence in your community of organized groups whose program includes the promotion of racial antagonism, such as anti-Semitism, opposition to Negroes, Mexicans, various Oriental groups? Do reputable citizens belong to them?

41. Are certain racial groups selected by your community for public disapproval? What shortcomings are alleged concerning them?

42. Is there any agency whose program includes the promotion of better interracial relations? What does it do?

43. What are the public schools, churches, and other organizations of your community doing to combat race prejudice?[1]

For questions relating to health, education, recreation, and general welfare of Negroes, see Chapters 8, 9, 10, 11, and 12.

Theoretically and actually, foreign-born workers have greater opportunities to earn a living here than in many other countries where foreigners are prevented by law from taking positions for which there is a demand on the part of the country's own nationals. In the United States there is, theoretically, free competition between native citizens and aliens for private employment. However, the "contract labor" provision in our immigration law prohibits manual workers from being brought into the country by employers in order to fill particular jobs.

In periods of unemployment there seems to be a breakdown of normal public tolerance toward foreigners who have come here to earn a livelihood. Large employers of labor then sometimes restrict new hiring to those who can show proof at least of application for citizenship. The law in certain states, and actual procedure in many others, prevent employment of noncitizens by state and local governmental units. Rulings by relief agencies, if not actually excluding the noncitizen, sometimes place him in a deferred category as regards eligibility for direct assistance or work relief.

44. Does your public employment service report occupations (other than the public service) in which lack of citizenship alone acts as a barrier to employment?

45. Have any large private employers recently been known to refuse to employ, to dismiss, workers on grounds that they were noncitizens?

46. What labor unions in your community exclude noncitizens?

47. Does the press play up every unfavorable incident involving certain nationalities or races so as to create an impression that they are less law-abiding than others?

48. What is being done in your community by agencies constructively engaged in overcoming prejudice and discrimination against foreign and other national groups?

Christ in America also sponsors community interracial clinics. For addresses see List of Agencies, p. 251.

[1] For the story of the methods used by one community to root out racial and religious bias, read The Story of the Springfield Plan, by Clarence I. Chatto and Alice L. Halligan, Barnes and Noble, New York, 1945.

18. AGENCIES FOR COMMUNITY PLANNING AND CO-ORDINATION

THE MULTIPLICITY of agencies to promote health, education, and welfare in modern communities has made necessary the establishment in most of them of means for the interchange of information and of co-operative planning. The steady progress of joint financing of private health and welfare agencies during the past twenty-five years has encouraged this development. World War II gave the movement further impetus.

I. THE SOCIAL SERVICE EXCHANGE

Agencies dealing with individual problems would be constantly conflicting in the advice they offer or the services they render unless some central index were available from which they could learn what other agencies had had contact, in the present or in the past, with the same families or individuals. This is furnished through the social service exchange, sometimes known as the social service index. See the latest volume of the Social Work Year Book[1] for a description of this device. You can also obtain from Community Chests and Councils, Inc.,[2] for a few cents each the following pamphlets which explain the purpose and function of a social service exchange: Handbook on Social Service Exchange, by Committee on Social Service Exchange; The Social Service Exchange in the Community Program of the Future, by Kenneth L. M. Pray; and Organizing a Social Service Exchange, by Committee on Social Service Exchange.

The best exchange practice demands that no information be registered on its cards except identifying information—names, ages, and addresses—and names of agencies interested and dates of their registrations. These cards should be as impersonal as is a library catalog. In other words, the exchange should be *unable to tell* even an authorized inquirer what problems exist in a given family, what services have been rendered it by the agencies registered, or what further information may be in those agencies' possession. The exchange reports only the bibliography of records cata-

[1] Russell Sage Foundation, New York.
[2] For address see List of Agencies, p. 251.

loged in its files. It is the responsibility of the inquiring agency thus to get in touch with agencies already registered, and secure additional information directly from them.

Most exchanges, however, permit member agencies to make inquiries for information only to help them decide whether to accept a given application. In these instances the inquiry is not recorded in the index files.

The index is a co-operative service for recognized social and health agencies; it should refuse any information to inquirers who seek only to satisfy curiosity or to serve their own interests.

1. Has your community a social service exchange? When was it established? Is it an independent agency? If not, of what agency is it a department?

2. How many agencies register cases with the exchange? Are there any important agencies, public or private, which do not register?

3. How is the exchange supported?

4. Who may inquire and receive information from the exchange? Is any information given out other than the identifying details spoken of above?

5. How many inquiries were received last year? How many agency registrations made? What percentage of total inquiries was identified as already being known to registering agencies?

II. COUNCILS AND FEDERATIONS OF SOCIAL AGENCIES

A community welfare council (often called council of social agencies, social planning council, or community council) is a voluntary association of organizations and individuals for planning and co-ordination in the field of social welfare. Membership ordinarily includes citizens who finance health and welfare services, those who act in a policy-forming capacity, professional people who administer the services and those who receive the services. Representatives of both public and voluntary agencies are included. The purpose of the council is to develop the best possible program of community services for all groups—the young, the aged, the sick, the well, families, homeless persons, veterans, minority groups, and member agencies. This is done by co-ordinating the work of existing agencies; studying community needs; joint action to eliminate gaps and duplications; improving the quality of individual services and promoting public understanding of community needs and services. To help labor and other general community groups to participate in health and welfare planning a variety of devices including "labor participation" committees is being promoted.

Community welfare councils and community chests are closely related since both foster the orderly development of an adequate program for the health and welfare of the community. Sometimes the chest and council are departments of a single organization. More often they are separate organizations with provision for interlocking devices. Community Chests and Councils, Inc., is the national organization for both types of agencies. Pamphlets covering most aspects of chest and council work may be secured from this organization.

A useful, more general discussion is included in Community Organization for Social Welfare, by A. Wayne McMillen,[1] and another helpful reference is Health and Welfare Planning in the Smaller Community.[2]

Occasionally, there may be found several fund-raising groups—for instance, a Jewish, a Catholic, and a nonsectarian group—in the same community, with but one central welfare council. Special mention should be made of the Jewish community councils, whose membership includes social and health agencies, but goes beyond this to include any religious, fraternal, or industrial groups whose program relates to the Jewish community. Jewish councils[3] and also federations for fund-raising are represented by a national agency—the Council of Jewish Federations and Welfare Funds.[4]

Public agencies, and private agencies which do not wish or are not allowed to participate in joint fund-raising, may nevertheless be active and valuable members of planning councils. In a few communities there are health, recreation, or other functional councils separate from the general welfare council, with some agencies carrying duplicate membership.

6. What agency or agencies bring social, educational, and health agencies together in your community for purposes of joint planning?

7. What is the relationship between the joint planning and the joint fund-raising organizations? If independent agencies, do they share the services of the same executive or staff?

8. When was the community welfare council in your community organized? How many agency members? How many public agencies? Are any prominent agencies not members of the council? Why?

9. How are delegates to the council selected? What proportion of delegates are paid executives, lay board members, members-at-large? Are labor unions or other nonagency community groups represented?

10. Has the council a full-time or part-time paid executive? How many other paid professional staff members? Is it a member of Community Chests and Councils, Inc.? How many volunteer staff members?

11. What active divisions, departments, or committees has it?

12. What joint services does it maintain—for example:
Social service exchange (see page 234)

[1] University of Chicago Press, Chicago, 1945.
[2] Community Chests and Councils, Inc., New York, 1945.
[3] See Jewish Community Organization in the United States, by Maurice J. Karpf, Bloch Publishing Co., New York, 1938.
[4] For address see List of Agencies, p. 251.

Charities endorsement bureau (service of reporting to donors on the merits
   of agencies which solicit contributions)
Information and referral service
Publicity service
Research bureau
Information or training courses, study groups
Volunteer service bureau
Holiday bureau (to "clear" and facilitate agency provision for summer
   camp care or for Thanksgiving and Christmas cheer)
Central purchase of supplies

13. Has the council a research department? What reports of agency activities
are regularly received? What regular statistical or descriptive reports does it make
available? To whom are reports distributed?

14. Does it publish a directory of social agencies? What is the date of the
latest edition? Any periodical publication?

15. What special reports on local conditions has your council published in the
past five years?

16. During that period, what new community facilities have been established
as a result of studies and action by the council? What services have been improved or modified? What services have been discontinued?

17. What does the council point to as its most outstanding accomplishments?
What evidence is there that it has improved co-ordination in the social work of
your community?

18. Aside from the joint services mentioned above, what are the current projects and activities of the council?

An important function of a council is to promote co-operative understanding and agreements between public and private agencies.

19. In each of the major functional fields represented in the council, what
agreements are in effect between public and private agencies in regard to (a) the
respective functions of each, (b) types of problems which each will accept on
transfer from the other, (c) types of problems on which they will work jointly?

The neighborhood approach to community organization is receiving increased attention in many cities. Neighborhood councils are organized in
order to mobilize local energy and goodwill and to give scope for activity to
all who are interested.[1] They are also a means for co-ordinating services in
local areas of the city. Ordinarily, the neighborhood council is an autono-
mous body composed primarily of people living or working in the neighborhood. It is important, however, for the neighborhood council to have a relationship to the central council so as to provide channels for bringing local
needs to the attention of the central planning body and for informing neighborhood groups about needs and services which must be considered on a
citywide basis.

[1] See Reveille for Radicals, by Saul D. Alinsky, University of Chicago Press, Chicago,
1946.

20. What neighborhood councils are dealing with community problems in your community? Are they connected with the council of social agencies or independent? How many? Membership? Program? Accomplishments?

III. COMMUNITY CHESTS

During the past twenty-five years community chests have been formed in virtually all large and medium-sized cities. The chest not only conducts a joint campaign for the support of voluntary agencies but is also the trustee for contributed funds. It must, therefore, assume responsibility for seeing that the funds are budgeted and spent wisely and fairly in the greatest public interest. To do this requires a thorough knowledge of the health and welfare needs of the community and of methods by which these may be most effectively met. For this reason community chests promote and finance the previously discussed community welfare councils for joint study and planning.

If there are separate fund-raising federations for Protestant, Jewish, or Catholic agencies in your community, the following questions apply to them also.

21. What agency or agencies discharge the function of joint fund raising?

22. When was the community chest or other fund-raising agency established in your community? If it has been discontinued, what date? What caused the discontinuance?

23. Is the program of the chest confined to joint financing, or does it also carry the function of joint planning? Is it a member of Community Chests and Councils, Inc.?

24. How is its governing board appointed? What proportion are men, women? What proportion are members of agency boards, what proportion are contributors without agency connection? What proportion represent general community groups such as labor unions? What proportion represent the large number of small donors as opposed to the fewer large contributors?

25. Is there a full-time or part-time paid executive? What has been his training and experience? How many others on staff (exclusive of clerical workers)?

26. What departments, divisions, committees carrying on a year-round program?

27. When is the annual campaign? Have there been supplementary campaigns during the past five years?

28. Are contributors to the annual campaign promised immunity from further appeals from chest agencies?

29. Under what conditions may member agencies conduct independent appeals for funds?

30. Are contributors allowed to designate the agencies to receive their contributions?

31. Is the staff service for the campaign provided by a year-round chest executive or by a commercial money-raising firm?

32. What methods are employed: (a) solicitation at place of employment, (b) house-to-house solicitation, (c) others?

33. During the past ten years, what changes have there been with respect to the number of agencies participating in the chest, total allocations received by local agencies, goal set for campaign, number of contributors secured, number of "small gifts" (under $10) secured, amount pledged, amount pledged per capita of the population, percentage of pledges collected?

34. Compare these changes with figures for other communities of similar size and resources, as published annually in Community, the news bulletin of Community Chests and Councils, Inc. What differences do you note?

35. How many agencies in the chest from the several functional fields—that is, family service, child welfare, health, recreation, and so forth?

36. What new agencies have been admitted to the chest during the past five years?

37. Have any agencies withdrawn from the chest within the past five years? Why? Have any been dropped? Why?

38. Have any services or agencies been combined or discontinued? Describe.

39. Has the chest a budget committee to review agency budgets? How does it work? Are budgets decided upon before or after campaigns?

40. Is each agency given opportunity to explain its budget?

41. Does the community welfare council participate in selection of budget committee members? Does it participate in the budgeting process?

42. What centralized services does the chest perform for the agencies? (See question 12.)

43. Does it carry on a year-round program of interpretation of the agencies to the community? Does it publish a periodical?

44. What income do chest agencies have in addition to what they receive from the chest?

45. What is done (a) to assure the best possible distribution of the smaller total and (b) to secure needed incomes from other sources?

IV. CONFERENCES OF SOCIAL WORK

Conferences of social work are usually simply forums for discussion and exchange of views, and not agencies for social action. The National Conference of Social Work meets annually in different parts of the country; and most of the states have state conferences of social work. A few large cities also hold citywide conferences regularly.

Three important national conferences represent the major religious and racial interests in social work. These are the Church Conference of Social Work (largely Protestant), the National Catholic Welfare Conference, and the National Conference of Jewish Social Welfare.

46. Does your community regularly hold a conference on social work? How frequently? How many members last year? What program divisions has it set up? Does it publish its proceedings?

47. Is there a state conference of social work in your state? Does it employ a full-time, part-time executive? Does it carry on educational work (institutes or short study courses) in connection with its annual session? At other times? Does it hold regional conferences in different parts of the state between the annual sessions?

48. What program divisions has it set up? Does it publish proceedings?

49. How many from your community attended its last five annual sessions? The regional conference last held in your vicinity?

50. How many names from your community appear in each of the last few membership lists published in the Bulletin of the National Conference of Social Work?

51. Have the social agencies in your community adopted any joint policy about granting leaves of absence, paying expenses, for staff members to attend conferences? What is it?

Conferences are frequently and sometimes regularly arranged in different regions or areas by national functional agencies, in order to bring together their own members and others interested. Such are the Great Lakes Institute and Blue Ridge Institute held annually by Community Chests and Councils, Inc., the regional round tables and institutes conducted each year by the Family Service Association of America and the Child Welfare League of America, and the Silver Bay conferences of the YMCA and the YWCA.

52. Are regional conferences arranged by national welfare or health agencies held regularly in or near your community? What was the attendance from your community at such conferences last year?

V. FACT-FINDING BODIES

In addition to the research and statistical departments which are part of many social organizations, and of community welfare councils and community chests, we frequently find other agencies that temporarily or permanently devote themselves to study and fact gathering in the area of community welfare.

53. Has any group of citizens organized a temporary fact-finding campaign within the past five years? Area of interest? Are results available in report form?

54. Within the past five years has any state or local legislative body, official committee, or other governmental authority conducted any study of welfare or health services or needs in your community?

55. Is there a foundation (set up with funds bequeathed for the purpose) devoted to research and demonstrations in social or economic fields, in your community? Date of founding? Area of interest? What reports has it published during the past five years?

56. Is there a bureau of municipal research in your community? Date of founding? What regular reports or statistical series does it make available? What special reports has it published within the past five years?

57. Have local colleges or universities made studies in your community in social or economic fields during the past five years? What published reports, manuscript theses, are available?

58. If any fact-finding surveys have been made in your community during the past five years under whose auspices were they undertaken? What state, national agencies participated? What recommendations resulted? What steps were taken to call needed action to the attention of responsible agencies or persons? To interpret findings widely to the community? To organize the community for action? What state, national agencies, have helped put recommendations into effect?

VI. PUBLIC INFORMATION ABOUT HEALTH, EDUCATION, SAFETY, AND WELFARE[1]

Community planning and co-ordination cannot be successfully accomplished if knowledge about a community's needs in health, education, safety, and welfare is confined to a small group of insiders, however devoted. The ordinary citizen as well must be made aware of these needs. From what sources outside and within the community does he become familiar with local affairs and learn to relate them to standards such as have been suggested in the reading references throughout this volume?

We have already considered a number of channels of public information —the school, the library, and the educational activities of religious, civic, and social clubs and associations. We have seen also that there is a constant flow of information and ideas into a community from outside sources, such as national magazines, programs of the radio networks, educational motion pictures, outside speakers taking part in lecture courses, special magazines, bulletins, and letters sent to members of special groups from their national offices. In community as in personal affairs, the parochial stage has passed, so that it is difficult to separate the outside sources of information which influence local opinion from those within the community.[2]

The two main sources of local information which have most to do with keeping citizens currently informed about their own problems and resources are the newspapers and local radio stations. These two cross all lines of special interests, and touch all aspects of community life. In an effort to understand your community, therefore, it is important to examine these channels of communication to see what they tell the public about the topics considered in this study.[3]

[1] See also pages listed in Index under public information.

[2] Read Print, Radio and Film in a Democracy, edited by Douglas Waples, University of Chicago Press, Chicago, 1942.

[3] Citizen groups wanting to make their communities aware of health, education, and welfare needs, and to arouse them to action, will find helpful suggestions in two pamphlets:

The Newspaper.　An analysis of the content of your local newspaper over a period of a few months should provide a fairly good sample of its reporting and interpretation of these topics.[1]　The questions below relate to news, and to comment of local origin found in the newspapers.　Most newspapers also give much space to news features and syndicated columns from outside sources.　Questions about general policies of a newspaper are also included.

The questions should be answered for each daily newspaper if there is more than one.

59.　Is the newspaper owned locally?　If not, is it one of a chain of papers, whose policies are, in the main, determined by the owner or management?　What, in general, are the policies of the management?　How might these be expected to affect the selection and treatment of news stories?

60.　What was its last reported circulation?

61.　Does it publish a Sunday paper?　What is its circulation?

62.　Does political or other bias affect reporting or editorial policy in regard to matters of community health, welfare, and so forth?

63.　What are its chief characteristics in handling local news and information? A preference for human interest material?　Many short items in preference to fewer and longer articles?　Or the reverse?

64.　Is it a "crusading newspaper," sponsoring certain causes or issues in which it takes a vigorous stand editorially and in its selection of news?

65.　Are there on its staff special writers who prepare signed articles on such topics as relief, housing, the courts, and so on?　Does it use signed articles on these subjects by local authorities?

66.　What percentage of its space, exclusive of advertising, is devoted to local affairs, on each of six days in *one week?*

67.　How many *informative* articles or editorials on local aspects of health, education, safety, and welfare were printed during the period selected for newspaper study?[2]

68.　Do your local health, welfare, and education agencies supply the press with interesting and informative items concerning activities and plans?　Ask your local editors whether material supplied is suitable and well-timed or whether much of it goes unused into wastebaskets?[3]

69.　How many of the articles counted appeared in an important position,

How to Interpret Social Welfare, by Helen C. Baker and Mary S. Routzahn, Russell Sage Foundation, New York, 1947; and Here's How It's Done: A Popular Education Guide, by Florence B. Widutis, Postwar Information Exchange, New York, 1945.

[1] Suggested reading is The Newspaper: Its Making and Its Meaning, by members of the staff of The New York Times, Charles Scribner's Sons, New York, 1945.

[2] We do not suggest a measurement of the space given to these articles.　This would be misleading because a given article may occupy, say, 20 column-inches of space, whereas only one or two inches contain information on one of the subjects under consideration, the rest being devoted to lists of names, facts about holding a meeting, and so on.

[3] Read Working with Newspapers, by Gertrude W. Simpson, National Publicity Council for Health and Welfare Services, New York, 1945.

that is, on the front page, or front of second section? How many were inconspicuous in position and headlines?

70. Has any attempt been made to run in your local paper in recent years a series of articles on "know your community" answering the types of questions raised in this book?

71. Does your local press emphasize race or nationality in reporting items concerning crime, disturbances?

72. Do you find any articles in which names or pictures, or both, identify local people in need of relief? Children in need of foster care? Persons accused of delinquency or crime? Persons involved in cases of family discord? If so, how many of these persons were minors? Has the newspaper an established policy about the use of names and pictures of children in need or in trouble?

The Radio. If there are one or more local radio stations, their programs may be analyzed for the same period as for the newspaper. Questions about the length of the program are omitted, because, as in the matter of space in newspapers, a broadcast of, say fifteen minutes, may devote only five minutes to discussion of the main topic, the remainder of the time going to station announcements, advertising, music, and so on.

Records of radio programs may not be so readily available as newspaper files, but it should be possible to secure the co-operation of your broadcasting stations in checking the topics and general nature of local programs given during the period selected for study.

73. How many programs on health, education, safety, and welfare were given during the period covered? Has any attempt been made in recent years to present over the radio a series of programs on "know your community"? Under what sponsorship was each program given? With what success?[1]

74. Can you note for each program whether it was given in the morning, afternoon, or evening? In other words, did it reach chiefly housewives or the whole family, including the men?

75. What method of presentation was used in each program—talk, interview, discussion, forum, or sketch?

76. Were electrical transcriptions of educational programs used?

77. Do local study groups listen to locally or nationally sponsored programs? On what topics?

78. Do programs ever exploit or give undue publicity to persons who are in need of (a) financial assistance, (b) foster home care, (c) court service, (d) personal counsel?

Other Media of Public Information. Mass production and outside control prevent the motion picture as commercially presented from being generally of use in enlightening citizens about local affairs and local needs. Oc-

---

[1] A manual on radio for noncommercial broadcasters is being prepared by the National Publicity Council for Health and Welfare Services.

casionally, and with increasing frequency of late years, special-interest
groups have, however, succeeded in producing films of a quality permitting
their use before audiences in commercial motion picture houses, to call attention to the work of particular agencies or social and health needs which
are widespread.   Such showings usually take place in connection with some
special campaign for health and safety, or with a community fund campaign.

79. How many special informative films such as those described have been
shown at commercial motion picture houses in your community during the past
year?

One of the best ways for a citizen to become informed and interested
about local programs is through his voluntary participation in community
affairs.   Particularly in time of war, large numbers of lay persons volunteer
for work with local welfare and health agencies.

80. What opportunities for such participation are provided by the community
fund, by any of its member agencies, by private organizations working with public
departments?
81. What is done in peacetime to capitalize upon the interest shown by volunteers in wartime in working with local health and welfare organizations?

The average citizen who does not take an active part in organized movements usually learns about local affairs as he reads his newspaper or sits be-
side his radio.   However, the citizen who is alert and makes an effort to
learn more than comes to him casually through such general channels has
opportunities which many people overlook.   In some cities occasional tours
are arranged by public departments or by community fund agencies in which
small groups visit parks, institutions, and offices of social agencies.   Some
institutions have regular visiting days on which the public is invited.   During the annual "American Education Week" many schools invite parents
and citizens to visit classes throughout the week.

Some meetings of government boards are open to the public and the
subjects to be presented are publicly announced.   In some cities classes in
civics in the high schools work out "projects" in which phases of the community's activities are made the subject of study and observation.

82. What health, social, or educational agencies have arranged "come-and-see"
tours during the past year?   What departments of local government?
83. On what local problems have elementary or high school classes in civics
carried on study projects?
84. To what extent do local officials or organizations urge citizens to attend
budget hearings or meetings of governmental bodies, public or private agencies,
when welfare or health questions are discussed?

Finally, there is the oldest and still perhaps the most general method of disseminating information and understanding—the public meeting. This ranges from the decorous lecture or course of lectures where the audience takes notes and asks a few polite questions, to the free-for-all of the old-fashioned town meeting, whose presiding officer bears the significant title of "moderator." Experimentation with the meeting as a device for public information has recently developed new variations, such as the "panel discussion," in which speakers discuss a subject informally among themselves with the audience joining in later.

We are learning that while basic information can be conveyed through pictures and graphs, through the written and spoken word, to passive readers and listeners, it is mainly through active participation—through discussion, volunteer service, and self-study such as we have here been trying to outline—that the people of a community can be brought actively to care about its development, and personally to engage in efforts for its improvement.

19. CLUBS AND ASSOCIATIONS

AN IMPORTANT force in community betterment is the multiplicity of membership organizations which flourish within its borders. The impulse of people to associate for the prosecution of common aims or the enjoyment of similar tastes is nowhere more fully exemplified than in the United States.

Many communitywide associations frequently referred to in earlier chapters are primarily interested in the improvement of community health and welfare services. These organizations depend upon the presence in the community of persons with the concept of citizenship so well set forth by L. P. Jacks:

. . . To be a citizen is to be an actively responsible person, a person, that is, who ought to do things, a person with duties. The citizen is, no doubt, a recipient of services from his fellow-citizens, enjoying benefits which the State or the social system confers upon him, the fortunate heir of the social inheritance, a person protected by the law, sitting in security under his own vine and fig-tree, none daring to make him afraid. But this good fortune of his, as the recipient of benefits conferred upon him by his fellows, or as the heir of former ages, measures the service his age demands of him. The greater the benefits conferred upon him, the more extensive become his responsibilities. His security is guaranteed him not that he may enjoy it in selfish isolation, but that he may have an assured basis for serving the community. His rights are nothing without his duties. At no point do his rights relieve him of his responsibilities; they create them at every point.[1]

But there also exists a variety of other associations whose direct purpose is not primarily to participate in general community movements, but to further in some way the interests of their own members.

Some organizations are small neighborhood groups, which nevertheless function in the formation of public opinion. In addition they often furnish the setting in which the future civic leader and the young politician first "learn the ropes."

1. List the neighborhood associations in your community which are actively

[1] Constructive Citizenship. Doubleday, Doran and Co., Garden City, New York, 1928, pp. 189–190.

interested in local improvements. In what improvements have they been active during the past year?

Communitywide clubs and associations which are not limited to a specific neighborhood may be purely recreational and social, such as bridge clubs, athletic clubs, dramatic clubs, and so on. Or, they may exist to further the professional and occupational interests of members, to serve some civic or political purpose, to keep alive some cultural, religious or historical interest, hold together persons whose tie is with some educational organization or some region of common origin. Organizations of these types generally have a more or less direct interest in the social and civic affairs of the community.

In your study of these groups the first thing is to list all such organizations as completely as possible. Sources that may be helpful to you are the council of social agencies (see Chapter 18), which may publish a directory of social agencies or have special lists of associations. The chamber of commerce may have lists as may the classified telephone directory.

Factors to be studied are not necessarily size of membership, so much as program, purposes, and activities of these associations as they relate to the field of your study.

Local organizations might be grouped as follows:

1. Professional Associations; e.g.,
   Bar associations
   Medical associations
   Ministerial associations
   Nursing associations
   Social workers' associations
   Teachers' associations
In larger communities, there may also be under this heading:
   Architects' associations
   Engineers' associations
   Interprofessional associations
   Librarians' associations
   Personnel managers' associations
2. Civic and Political Associations; e.g.,
   Associations allied with particular political parties
   City clubs for men
   City clubs for women
   Consumers' leagues
   Good government leagues, improvement societies
   Leagues of women voters
   Taxpayers' leagues

3. Religious Associations (see Chapter 13)
4. Cultural Associations; e.g.,
   Garden clubs
   Literary, art, music, drama clubs (see Chapter 12)
   Parental education groups (see Chapters 11 and 15)
   Other study clubs and forums
5. Social Clubs with Some Civic Purposes; e.g.,
   Service clubs, men's (such as Kiwanis, Lions, Rotary, and so forth)
   Service clubs, women's (such as Business and Professional Women, Zonta, and so forth)
   Junior league
   Young people's associations
6. Veteran and Patriotic Societies; e.g.,
   American Legion, American Veterans Committee, Veterans of Foreign Wars
   Disabled American Veterans Association
   Sons, Daughters of the Revolution, Confederacy
   Colonial Dames, and so forth
7. Fraternal Organizations; e.g.,
   Eagles, Elks, Masons, Moose, Odd Fellows, Woodmen, and so forth
8. Business Associations; e.g.,
   Better Business Bureau
   Chamber of Commerce
   Employers', manufacturers' associations
   Labor unions (see Chapter 6)
   Merchants' associations
9. Miscellaneous Associations; e.g.,
   American Association of University Women
   Associations of the Negro and Foreign-Born
   College alumni and alumnae associations
   Historical societies
   Pioneer associations
   State societies

    2. Which of the clubs and associations in your community are affiliated with corresponding state or national associations?
    3. Which issue regularly a periodical or news bulletin to their members? Which of these carry notices or comments on topics of community interest?

The interest of a membership organization in community affairs may be fairly extensive, or it may be expressed by little more than providing an occasional audience for speakers on community affairs, and responding to a request or two for co-operation.

In general, participation may be classified roughly as follows:

(1) Passive, through listening to speakers, passing resolutions on request, or occasionally sending a representative to an outside meeting to consider some community matter.

(2) Active through

>(a) Maintaining or contributing to the support of some philanthropic enterprise, or contributing volunteer service.
>(b) Promoting intelligent and informed opinion through courses of lectures and planned discussion.
>(c) Engaging actively in civic campaigns, making surveys, issuing statements, and supporting or opposing legislation.

4. Which of the above-mentioned functions are carried on by the various clubs and associations in your community?

5. For associations designated (a), describe the activities carried on.

6. For associations designated (b), analyze the programs for the past year, and learn how much attention they have given to broad questions of national and international import, and how much to problems of your community. (Analyses such as these have usually shown a tendency on the part of such organizations to concentrate on the broad areas and neglect the home community.)

7. For associations designated (c), describe the programs. What accomplishments do they claim? What committees have been appointed to work in the areas of their interests? What co-operative relations are maintained by organizations having similar interests? What social legislation did the associations support, oppose, during the past year?

LIST OF NATIONAL AGENCIES

GOVERNMENTAL—Washington 25, D.C., with two exceptions

Agriculture, U.S. Department of
Bureau of the Census, U.S. Department of Commerce
Bureau of Human Nutrition and Home Economics, U.S. Department of Agriculture
Bureau of Labor Statistics, U.S. Department of Labor
Children's Bureau, Federal Security Agency
Farmers Home Administration, U.S. Department of Agriculture
Federal Home Loan Bank Administration, National Housing Agency
Federal Housing Administration, National Housing Agency
Federal Security Agency
Geological Survey, U.S. Department of the Interior
Home Owners' Loan Corporation, Federal Home Loan Bank Administration, National Housing Agency
Immigration and Naturalization Service, U.S. Department of Justice (Franklin Trust Bldg., Philadelphia 2)
Labor, U.S. Department of
National Housing Agency
National Labor Relations Board
Office of Education, U.S., Federal Security Agency
Office of Indian Affairs, U.S. Department of the Interior (222 North Bank Drive, Chicago 54)
Office of Vocational Rehabilitation, Federal Security Agency
Public Health Service, U.S., Federal Security Agency
Social Security Administration, Federal Security Agency
United States Employment Service, Federal Security Agency
U.S. *See under* bureau or department
Veterans Administration
Women's Bureau, U.S. Department of Labor

VOLUNTARY

American Association for Adult Education, 525 West 120th St., New York 27
American Association of Medical Social Workers, 1129 Vermont Ave., N.W., Washington 5
American Association of Personal Finance Companies, 315 Bowen Bldg., Washington 5

American Association of Psychiatric Social Workers, 1790 Broadway, New York 19

American Association of School Social Workers (address varies, but may be obtained from the Public Education Association, 20 West 40th St., New York 18)

American Association of Social Workers, 130 East 22d St., New York 10

American Association to Promote the Teaching of Speech to the Deaf, 1537 35th St., N.W., Washington 7

American Bar Association, 1140 North Dearborn St., Chicago 10

American Cancer Society, Inc., 350 5th Ave., New York 1

American College of Surgeons, 40 East Erie St., Chicago 11

American Committee on Maternal Welfare, 24 West Ohio St., Chicago 10

American Committee for Protection of Foreign Born, 23 West 26th St., New York 10

American Council on Race Relations, 32 West Randolph St., Chicago 1

American Dental Association, 212 East Superior St., Chicago 11

American Epilepsy League, 50 State St., Boston 9

American Federation of International Institutes, 11 West 42d St., New York 18

American Federation of Labor, American Federation of Labor Bldg., Washington 1

American Foundation for the Blind, Inc., 15 West 16th St., New York 11

American Friends Service Committee, 20 South 12th St., Philadelphia 7

American Hearing Society, 1537 35th St., N.W., Washington 7

American Heart Association, Inc., 1790 Broadway, New York 19

American Hospital Association, 18 East Division St., Chicago 10

American Humane Association, 50 Madison Ave., New York 10

American Library Association, 520 North Michigan Ave., Chicago 11

American Medical Association, 535 North Dearborn St., Chicago 10

American Municipal Association, 1313 East 60th St., Chicago 37

American National Red Cross, 17th and D Sts., Washington 13

American Nurses' Association, Inc., 1790 Broadway, New York 19

American Planning and Civic Association, 901 Union Trust Bldg., Washington 5

American Psychiatric Association, 9 Rockefeller Plaza, New York 20

American Public Health Association, 1790 Broadway, New York 19

American Public Welfare Association, 1313 East 60th St., Chicago 37

American Social Hygiene Association, 1790 Broadway, New York 19

American Society of Planning Officials, 1313 East 60th St., Chicago 37

Associated Youth Serving Organizations, Inc., 134 East 56th St., New York 22

Association of Junior Leagues of America, Inc., Waldorf-Astoria Hotel, New York 22

Boy Scouts of America, National Council, 2 Park Ave., New York 16

Boys Clubs of America, Inc., 381 4th Ave., New York 16

Braille Institute of America, 741 North Vermont Ave., Los Angeles 27

Central Location Index, Inc., 165 West 46th St., New York 19
Chamber of Commerce of the United States of America, Washington 6
Child Welfare League of America, 130 East 22d St., New York 10
Church Conference of Social Work, 297 4th Ave., New York 10
Common Council for American Unity, Inc., 20 West 40th St., New York 18
Commonwealth Fund, 41 East 57th St., New York 22
Community Chests and Councils, Inc., 155 East 44th St., New York 17
Congress of Industrial Organizations, 718 Jackson Place, N.W., Washington 5
Cooperative League of the USA, 343 South Dearborn St., Chicago 4
Council of Jewish Federations and Welfare Funds, Inc., 165 West 46th St., New
    York 19

Family Service Association of America, 122 East 22d St., New York 10
Federal Council of the Churches of Christ in America, 297 4th Ave., New York 10

Girl Scouts of America, 155 East 44th St., New York 17

Hebrew Sheltering and Immigrant Aid Society, 425 Lafayette St., New York 3
Home Missions Council of North America, 297 4th Ave., New York 10

Institute of Public Administration, 684 Park Ave., New York 21
International City Managers Association, 1313 East 60th St., Chicago 37
International Migration Service, American Branch, 122 East 22d St., New York 10

Knights of Columbus, 45 Wall St., New Haven 7, Conn.

Life Insurance Adjustment Bureau, 450 7th Ave., New York 1

Medical Administration Service, Inc., 1790 Broadway, New York 19

National Association for the Advancement of Colored People, 20 West 40th St.,
    New York 18
National Association of Housing Officials, 1313 East 60th St., Chicago 37
National Association to Control Epilepsy, 22 East 67th St., New York 21
National Catholic Welfare Conference, 1312 Massachusetts Ave., N.W., Wash-
    ington 5
National Child Labor Committee, 419 4th Ave., New York 16
National Committee for Mental Hygiene, 1790 Broadway, New York 19
National Committee on Housing, 1 Madison Ave., New York 10
National Conference of Christians and Jews, 381 4th Ave., New York 16
National Conference of Jewish Social Welfare, 1841 Broadway, New York 23

National Conference of Juvenile Agencies, State Colony, Woodbine, N.J.
National Conference of Social Work, 82 North High St., Columbus 15, Ohio
National Conference on Family Relations, 1126 East 59th St., Chicago 37
National Congress of Parents and Teachers, 600 South Michigan Blvd., Chicago 5
National Consumers League, 348 Engineers Bldg., Cleveland 14
National Council of Community Churches, 1320 Cambridge Blvd., Columbus 8, Ohio
National Council of Jewish Women, 1819 Broadway, New York 23
National Council of Parent Education, 221 West 57th St., New York 19
National Foundation for Infantile Paralysis, Inc., 120 Broadway, New York 5
National Health Council, 1790 Broadway, New York 19
National Industrial Conference Board, 247 Park Ave., New York 17
National Jewish Welfare Board, 145 East 32d St., New York 16
National League of Nursing Education, 1790 Broadway, New York 19
National League of Women Voters, 726 Jackson Place, N.W., Washington 6
National Municipal League, 299 Broadway, New York 7
National Organization for Public Health Nursing, 1790 Broadway, New York 19
National Probation Association, Inc., 1790 Broadway, New York 19
National Public Housing Conference, 1015 15th St., N.W., Washington 5
National Publicity Council for Health and Welfare Services, 130 East 22d St., New York 10
National Recreation Association, 315 4th Ave., New York 16
National Rehabilitation Association, State Capitol, Frankfort, Ky.
National Safety Council, 20 North Wacker Drive, Chicago 6
National Social Welfare Assembly, 1790 Broadway, New York 19
National Society for Crippled Children and Adults, 11 South La Salle St., Chicago 3
National Society for the Prevention of Blindness, 1790 Broadway, New York 19
National Travelers Aid Association, 425 4th Ave., New York 16
National Tuberculosis Association, 1790 Broadway, New York 19
National Urban League, 1133 Broadway, New York 10
National Women's Trade Union League of America, 317 Machinists Bldg., Washington 1

Pictograph Corporation, 220 5th Ave., New York 10
Planned Parenthood Federation of America, Inc., 501 Madison Ave., New York 22
Public Administration Service, 1313 East 60th St., Chicago 37
Public Education Association, 20 West 40th St., New York 18

Red Cross. *See* American National Red Cross
Regional Plan Association, Inc., 205 East 42d St., New York 17
Russell Sage Foundation, 130 East 22d St., New York 10

Salvation Army, 120 West 14th St., New York 11
Social Legislation Information Service, Inc., 930 F St., N.W., Washington 4
Social Science Research Council, 230 Park Ave., New York 17
Southern Regional Council, Inc., 63 Auburn Ave., N.E., Atlanta 3, Ga.

United Service for New Americans, Inc., 105 Nassau St., New York 7
United States Conference of Mayors, 730 Jackson Place, N.W., Washington 6

Volunteers of America, 34 West 28th St., New York 1

Young Men's Christian Association, National Council, 347 Madison Ave., New York 17
Young Women's Christian Association, National Board, 600 Lexington Ave., New York 22
Young Men's Hebrew Association, National Office, 145 East 32d St., New York 16
Young Women's Hebrew Association, National Office, 145 East 32d St., New York 16

INDEX